Louis C Tiffany, Rebel in Glass

Group of vases by Louis C. Tiffany in the collection of The Metropolitan Museum of Art. *Courtesy of the Metropolitan Museum of Art.*

Iridescent bowl by Louis C. Tiffany in the collection of The Museum of Modern Art, New York. Gift of Joseph Heil. *Courtesy of the Museum of Contemporary Crafts. Joseph Heil photo.*

Louis C Tiffany, Rebel in Glass

by Robert Koch

Second Edition

CROWN PUBLISHERS, INC. NEW YORK

Permission to quote copyrighted material is gratefully acknowledged to the following publishers, authors and their authorized representatives:

From *Critic's Eye*, copyright 1962 by Maurice Grosser, reprinted by permission of The Bobbs-Merrill Company, Inc., Indianapolis and New York.

From *The Old Masters* by C. Lorgues Lapouge, Crown Publishers, Inc., New York, 1963.

From *Stained Glass in America* by John Gilbert Lloyd, Foundation Books, Jenkintown, Pa., 1963.

From *And The Bridge Is Love*, copyright 1958 by Alma Mahler Werfel, reprinted by permission of Harcourt, Brace & World, Inc., New York.

From *Glass and Man* by Anne Huether, copyright 1963. Reprinted by permission of J. B. Lippincott., Philadelphia and New York.

From *Once Upon A City: New York from 1890 to 1910* by Grace M. Mayer, 1958. Reprinted by permission of The Macmillan Company, New York.

From *Nineteenth Century Glass: Its Genesis and Development*, by Albert Christian Revi, Thomas Nelson & Sons, 1959.

From *Interesting People: Eighty Years with the Great and the Near Great* by Corinna Lindon Smith. Reprinted by permission of the University of Oklahoma Press, Norman, Oklahoma, 1962.

From *American Painting in the Nineteenth Century: Main Trends and Movements* by John I. H. Baur, Frederick A. Praeger, Inc., New York, 1953.

Condensed from *The Proud Possessors* by Aline Saarinen. Reprinted by permission of Random House, Inc.

From *The Americanization of Edward Bok* by Edward Bok, reprinted by permission of Charles Scribner's Sons, New York.

From *The Works of Oscar Wilde*, Spring Books, London, 1963.

From *The White House* by Jane and Burt McConnell, Studio, 1954. Reprinted by permission of Random House, Inc.

Library of Congress Catalog Card Number: 63-21121
ISBN: 0-517-097346
Printed in the United States of America
Eighth Printing, Second Edition, May, 1978

Contents

Color Plates

Illustrations

To Gladys

"Styles are merely the copying of what others have done, perhaps done better than we. God has given us our talents, not to copy the talents of others, but rather to use our brains and our imagination in order to obtain the revelation of True Beauty."

Louis C. Tiffany

MEMORIES OF LOUIS C. TIFFANY

by

Comfort Tiffany Gilder and Dorothy Tiffany Burlingham

Daffodils

I

His joy captured beauty
  in the curve of the lotus,
    the design of a cluster of grapes,
    the butterfly weed ablaze.
Music from the trumpets of the daffodils
  drew him and the children to the field.
From a tiny oven in a corner of the attic
  he pulled out bits of glowing glass—
    those were the miracles of the early years.
Then came the rush of wealth.
Still nothing mattered but beauty—
  beauty in immense creations:
    masses of yellow lilies,
    the largest anemone,
    the highest tower.
Iridescent glass poured from flaming furnace,
  and the world talked only of the great mosaic curtain.

II

His kingdom a castle
  full of color and treasures of the Orient,
    yellow moon hanging over clear pool,
    green-stencilled velvets for the throne,
    bell chiming in the tower—
    a Treasury, not a home.
Garden with gravel path hedged by boxwood,
  children walk up and down sedately, talk in whispers,
  admire from a distance but do not touch—
    red peonies splash in one section,
    blue iris stand stiffly in another,
    fragrant roses in restricted places.
Blooms, blooms everywhere;
  was one single flower loved?
Far away from the castle,
  daffodils grow wild in a field,
  thousands and thousands of them.
In early spring the children leap from the palace,
  and run to the daffodils.
Stop first to gaze with rapture,
  then darting here and there with soaring voices,

slowly pick one by one,
sun lighting the flowers and their hearts.

III

When the King died,
fire destroyed the castle with its precious world of art,
bells clashed dully as they tumbled to the ground,
burned flowers scattered like dead leaves in the garden.
But in the field,
music came from the trumpets of the daffodils,
loved by him and the children long ago.

Comfort T. Gilder, 1962

In 1965, Louis C. Tiffany's youngest daughter, Dorothy Tiffany Burlingham, wrote to Robert Koch from her home in England:

It is interesting how a character can look from different points of view. As I read your book most carefully, I appreciated the great trouble you had taken to weigh all the sources at your disposal and realized how unavoidable it was that the picture of his personal life could not be better understood. My father had a very complex character with many eccentricities but with loving and humane traits. He was driven to create what filled his imagination, but he also cared greatly for his family and what they did with their lives. We all felt this and appreciated how much he cared for us.

Except when abroad with my mother for summer holidays he was always at home. He left punctually for work, walking us to school and returning at five o'clock. We rushed to meet him when we heard the front door opening, and our mother was ready to welcome him with tea in the library. Our family life was divided between the city and the country. Immediately on reaching our summer home my father would set out to inspect the garden. He knew every plant and flower and spent much time directing the planting. To watch the flowers grow from bud to full bloom was his greatest pleasure. Wild flowers were as much of a delight to him as the ones he cultivated with such care. Some springs he would drive us to a wild spot blue with bird's-eye violets, where we dug them up, replanting them to run riot in a lovely secluded woodland.

In New York on Christmas morning we children, and later the grandchildren too, gathered around the big circular chimney in the studio. A chair piled with presents for each member of the household stood in front of the fire. My father sat among us, receiving his presents and enjoying the festive scene.

On moving to Laurelton as adolescents there were many house parties. My father had seen to building tennis courts and a squash court which he liked to see in use, and there was a great deal of liveliness at such times. But woe betide anyone who stepped on a plant. The greatest crime was unpunctuality, but even after such an occasion he could soon enjoy conversing with the young offenders and they with him, which amazed us greatly.

Another thing that angered my father was when he found the young men smoking in their rooms, which was strictly forbidden. For one wall of the smoking-room my father bought a painting of an opium-smoker, lying on the floor, his head on a cushion and a pipe at his side, dreaming of dreadful creatures in grotesque positions. These were sadistically mutilated, dripping blood and variously colored. Visitors, while admiring the painter's skill, were revolted by Father's readiness to display this object. Consequently, one day my father took paint and brushes and covered the ghastly dream with a cloud of smoke which emanated from the pipe and dimmed the horrors. The result was generally admired.

Sarah Hanley, the young Irish girl who came to nurse my father when he was ill, stayed with him until his death, doing everything for his comfort and delighting him with her simple, vivacious and engaging ways. He wished to marry her, but she refused, thinking that his children would resent it.

Louis C Tiffany,
Rebel in Glass

INTRODUCTION

There exists a strange parallel between the life of Louis Comfort Tiffany, a New Yorker born and bred, and his work (falling between the last decade of the nineteenth century and the first two of the twentieth), and the lives and artistic output of certain fifteenth-century Florentines. The American's vast energy, vitality and versatility, his constant restlessness and abounding curiosity, his creative ability and scientific concern, his experiments and technical discoveries, and his mastery of many media are the all-embracing qualities that we associate with the *quattrocento*. Even the organization of his workshop, the Tiffany Studios, had the quality of a Florentine *bottega*.

Whereas it was not unusual for a Tuscan artist to be a goldsmith, sculptor, painter, designer of wedding chests, ecclesiastical embroideries and princely pageants, Tiffany was a painter in oil and watercolor, a decorator, an architect and landscapist, a designer of memorials in mosaic and granite—and a master of pageantry. He is best remembered, however, as a highly skillful and original maker of entrancingly beautiful opalescent glass and a daring designer and inventor of new processes for making and using stained glass. For instance, to observe the symphonic succession of light and, with it, form, on the stupendous colored glass screen Tiffany produced (in 1911) for the Mexican National Theatre is a singularly powerful and unforgettable aesthetic experience. His delight in the unusual and unconventional, in fêtes, his love of beauty, and even his unabashed showmanship all have an Italianate ring.

It is dangerous, however, to press this pleasing parallel too far; to carry similarity to absurdity. It is not unfair to say his charming and sophisticated work lacked the virility and robust quality of that of the earlier men. The cultural climate of his day lacked the strong driving force of philosophic and theological conviction. Tiffany possessed a passionate love of beauty, but sheer beauty is insufficient; excellence is made of sterner stuff.

Although some of the aforementioned complimentary comparison may be superficial, sufficient time has now elapsed since his death, in 1933, to revalue his contributions dispassionately. His work was admired extravagantly a half-century ago. With drastic changes of taste, the craze for "Tiffany glass," purchasable badges of culture, diminished and this ware fell into the limbo of neglect. It is only recently that we have begun to appreciate the contributions made by the originators and practitioners of *Art Nouveau*. Among the few American masters of this engaging and highly imaginative style, Louis Comfort Tiffany holds a high, enviable and undisputed place.

This book by my friend and former student is a just and timely reappraisal.

Theodore Sizer, *Professor Emeritus, Yale University*

[*1*]

PREFACE TO THE FIRST EDITION

Ten years ago I stumbled on my first reference to the work of Louis Comfort Tiffany. I was studying American architecture at Yale University and preparing a paper for Professor Carroll L. V. Meeks on armory buildings in New York City. Tiffany, I found, had decorated the Veterans' Room and Library for one of these.

The following semester, during a course with Professor William Jordy, I presented a seminar report on Tiffany as the leading American exponent of Art Nouveau and, just for fun, I purchased a Favrile glass bowl made by Tiffany as a demonstration of the quality of his work. It cost four dollars, and I thought it was expensive. Today it is worth a great deal more. When I brought it home my wife asked, "How long do we have to keep it?" We still have it—and many more. My two children, Elaine and Mitchell, have also learned to enjoy it.

The subject of Tiffany and his place in art intrigued me. It was a challenge in aesthetic evaluation. In a dissertation, "The Stained Glass Decades," which I presented to the Yale history of art faculty in 1957, Mr. Tiffany played a leading role. The research for that thesis and for this book led me into some interesting adventures.

In 1955, for instance, I felt it was most important for me to see Mr. Tiffany's showplace, Laurelton Hall, for myself. The owners of the property at that time would not allow me to inspect the interior of the main building, but I managed to photograph the exterior from all angles. Later I met the family who lived in what had been the art gallery of Laurelton Hall and was cordially received by them. Three of Tiffany's grandchildren came to my rescue and supplied me with photographs, old newspaper clippings, mementoes and recollections. Since then the heritage of Tiffany's art has assumed a permanent place as a part of my own family history. As a

[2]

third-generation New Yorker I have found my family linked to the Tiffanys in a variety of unexpected connections. At times I have even been made to feel a member of the family circle. When a fire broke out at Laurelton Hall, Louise Platt, Tiffany's grand-daughter, who still resides in Oyster Bay, Long Island, called me at 11:00 P.M. to tell me the news. I was examining the ruins before they had stopped smoldering. Her brother, William T. Lusk, president of Tiffany & Company, has been extremely cordial, and Louis Tiffany Lusk, another brother, is now a friend and neighbor in Norwalk, Connecticut.

Many others have assisted with advice and encouragement. These include art historians, clergymen, collectors, dealers and friends too numerous to mention. I wish to acknowledge my gratitude for the help of the following persons, who have assisted me in assembling both information and illustrative material for this book: David Aronow, Michael Arpad, E. Maurice Bloch, Walter P. Chrysler, Jr., Leland A. Cook, Helen Eisenberg, Maude Feld, William J. Fielding, Martin Grossman, Jonathan Joseph, Robert Laurer, George Love, Louis T. Lusk, William T. Lusk, Hugh F. McKean, Lillian Nassau, Louise Platt, Ogden Pleissner, Herwin Schaefer, Marvin Schwartz, Julia Sherman, Emanuel Shulman, my editor Helen E. Sterling, Thomas S. Tibbs and F. Van Brink. For typing the manuscript, my thanks to Gloria Mansfield. To Professor Sizer, my gratitude for his kindness in providing the introduction, and to President Hilton C. Buley and my colleagues at Southern Connecticut State College, my appreciation for granting me the time necessary for putting together a work of this type.

Perhaps the most important contribution to an appreciation of Tiffany's real importance was made by Thomas S. Tibbs, who prepared a superb exhibition of his work and a handsomely illustrated catalogue for the Museum of Contemporary Crafts in the spring of 1958. My only hope is that this volume may arouse, in those who are seeing Tiffany's art for the first time in the reproductions included here, a measure of the response evoked in those who were privileged to see it in its own time, or at the 1958 exhibition.

Robert Koch

South Norwalk, Connecticut
June, 1964

[3]

PREFACE TO THE REVISED EDITION

In the few years since *Louis C. Tiffany, Rebel in Glass* was published, Tiffany glass has more than doubled in value; the vogue for it has not lessened, and Art Nouveau as a whole has received greater attention. Notable items produced under Tiffany's direction have suddenly appeared on the market such as a window designed by Frank Brangwyn and made by Tiffany for S. Bing's exhibition of Art Nouveau at the Grafton Galleries in London in 1899 and an elaborate punch bowl made by Tiffany for exhibition in Paris in 1900. Hardly a week goes by without some mention of the amazing variety of wares produced by Tiffany's versatile and prolific designers.

In this revised edition some changes have been made in the text and illustrations on the basis of new information about Tiffany's life and work. I now have reason to believe, after discussions with one of the few surviving glassworkers from the Tiffany Furnaces in Corona, that Arthur J. Nash was not a master glassblower and that credit for the unique quality of Tiffany's Favrile glass should be given to Thomas Manderson, Tiffany's first gaffer.

Robert Koch

September, 1966

[4]

part one

Artistic Interiors

THE LIFE OF AN ARTIST

The Tiffanys of New York City could trace their New England physical and moral fortitude to their New England ancestors. Squire Humphrey Tiffany settled in the Massachusetts Bay Colony about 1660. Some generations later, in 1812, a son, Charles, was born to the Comfort Tiffanys of Killingly, Windham County, Connecticut, who would found a famous silver and jewelry company. He was the father of Louis Comfort Tiffany, who would leave the bold imprint of his style on the decorative arts of the late nineteenth and early twentieth century.

Educated in Connecticut at the Plainfield Academy, young Charles L. Tiffany gained his business experience in his father's mill and mercantile experience by managing his general store in Brooklyn, Connecticut. He made occasional buying trips to New York City, and in 1837, having borrowed $1,000 from his father, he invested in a small stationery and dry-goods store with his friend John B. Young. The gross sales of this establishment, at 259 Broadway opposite City Hall, amounted to $4.98 for the first three days of operation. Within a few decades, however, this modest venture became the world-famous firm of Tiffany & Company and its name a hallmark for elegance.

[5]

In 1841 Charles L. Tiffany married his partner's sister Harriet, and J. L. Ellis became a third member of the expanding firm. In 1847 the store was moved to larger quarters, and in the following year, that of Louis Comfort Tiffany's birth, the young merchants established a jewelry department, taking advantage of political unrest in Europe to acquire a stock of diamonds. The son born to the Tiffanys on February 18, 1848 was destined to become as famous in his own right as his father's firm.

Louis C. Tiffany was raised as the eldest son. The youngest was Burnett, or Bernie, and the boys had two sisters, Annie and Louise. The family regularly attended Sunday services at the Congregational church, and the Tiffany household was run along strict, no-nonsense principles. The ladylike Annie conformed readily, but Louis baffled his father, and there were continual conflicts. A talented, creative child, he was hard on his toys and mercurial in his interests. He was small and wiry, with reddish-brown hair. Fond of animals, he was a leader among his peers and always in trouble with his elders. His moods were unpredictable, and his ingenuity led him to devise all kinds of practical jokes. Apparently he repeatedly harassed his younger brother, but he could be tender, loving and demanding of affection from his parents. The Tiffanys assumed that young Louis would someday succeed his father as the head of the rapidly growing concern, which was known, after 1853, as Tiffany & Company. Recognizing their limitations in their handling of this headstrong boy, his parents sent him to boarding school, first to the Flushing Academy on Long Island and then to a military academy.

Like his father, Louis C. Tiffany had a vast store of energy and a tremendous capacity for work. But his ambitions did not lie in a mercantile direction. He had little or no interest in business matters. His primary concern was with the arts and he often left to others the handling of financial details. His father found it difficult to understand the boy who hated schoolwork but liked to collect and play with the colored pebbles or bits of broken glass he picked up on the beach during the summers at Montauk on Long Island.

After the Civil War, in 1866, when young Louis was eighteen, he announced to his startled father that he wished to study art rather than go to college. He was a romantic with a great love for nature, and found he had quite a flair for painting landscapes. He often sat for hours in the studio of the painter George Inness, watching him at work, and, at gatherings in the studio, conversing with other young men of similar interests.

By the middle of the nineteenth century the opening of the American West had inspired a notable landscape school, including Asher Durand, Frederick E. Church and Albert Bierstadt. A later, more subjective school was represented by such artists as Inness, Winslow Homer and J. Alden Weir. Inness was known for his skill in adapting the atmospheric style of the Barbizon school to American landscape painting.

John I. H. Baur, in his *American Painting in the Nineteenth Century: Main Trends and Movements*, noted a post-Civil War trend toward visual realism which "rendered objects as the eye alone perceived them, greatly modified by light, shadow and atmosphere. With it came a freer handling of paint, a livelier surface, often a delight in brushwork for its own spontaneous effects. Contours were deliberately broken, form suggested rather than analyzed, detail blurred by strong sunlight or lost in shade. Tone rather than design became the prevalent means of unifying a picture."

In Inness' studio he met the playwright James Steele MacKaye, a frequent visitor, who introduced him to Oscar Wilde, whose aesthetic views would greatly influence Tiffany's own career. In the evenings MacKaye, who had gone to Paris to study painting but became interested instead in Delsarte and dramatic expression, would often hold the floor for hours with his monologues, and Louis Tiffany soon declared the life of an artist to be the "only" one for him. Inness, impressed by the restless, intense, well-dressed young man, gave him some small canvases and some paints, to see what he could do, and Tiffany became his first and only pupil. Inness is reputed to have remarked of his young follower, "The more I teach him the less he knows, and the older he grows the farther he is from what he ought to be." Tiffany could never, however, be merely a follower but had to inject himself fully into whatever he did. His obvious intensity and seriousness of purpose soon gained for him both the respect and the envy of his contemporaries, who marveled at his prodigious output. He said very little, immersing himself in his work, but he could not abide criticism. While his artist friends attended classes in drawing and took courses in anatomy to perfect their draftsmanship he took long walks alone and sketched rural scenes in upper Manhattan. In 1867 the nineteen-year-old artist exhibited a painting entitled "Afternoon" at the National Academy of Design.

During the winter of 1868/69 Tiffany worked in Paris with the French artist Leon Bailly in very much the same way he had worked in Inness' studio, mostly on his own. Bailly, who had traveled in North Africa and Palestine, had exhibited Islamic genre scenes and landscapes, and it was he who opened the young American artist's eyes to a new world of pattern and color. In the spring of 1869 in Spain Tiffany met Samuel Colman, a pupil of Asher B. Durand and the founder and first president of the American Water Color Society. Since he also was in search of exotic subjects they decided to go together to North Africa, landing at Oran. Colman taught Tiffany the value of watercolors for sketching and interested him in Islamic textiles. When they returned home, Louis did not go back to the Tiffany home at 212 Fifth Avenue but rented instead a studio in the Y.M.C.A. on 23rd Street, across from the National Academy of Design. Among other young painters then living at the Y.M.C.A. with whom he exchanged views were the illustrators Edwin Austin Abbey, who was to paint murals for the Boston Public Library, Swain Gifford and William Sartain.

[7]

In 1870 Tiffany became the youngest member ever to be elected to the Century Club. Made an associate member of the National Academy of Design in 1871, he became a full-fledged Academician in 1880. Extremely popular among his fellow artists, he was active in several organizations, including the American Water Color Society, and he became one of the founders of the Society of American Artists, whose members included Inness, Colman and John La Farge. He was elected treasurer of this society in 1878. Tiffany soon gained the reputation of being a "live wire" who could carry out any kind of task quickly and efficiently. At social gatherings he was never still and "never missed a trick." He contributed little to the general conversation. His impatience and, to some, overbearing ways, were, perhaps, a cover for his excessive shyness. He was, however, usually sensitive to the feelings of his fellows, putting them at ease. His bright eyes, set in the shadow of heavy brows, his sensuous mouth and strong, determined chin gave him a look of sincerity and determination that disarmed even those who disagreed with him.

It disarmed immediately the young woman who was to become Mrs. Louis C. Tiffany in 1872. In 1871 Louis had gone to New Haven with his sister Annie to meet her fiancé, Alfred Mitchell, to whom she was married on April 27, 1871. In the house of Alfred's brother, Donald G. Mitchell of Westville, Connecticut, Louis met Mary Woodbridge Goddard. During his year-long courtship Tiffany was a frequent visitor to the lively Donald G. Mitchell household. Mitchell, a popular essayist, used the pen name of "Ik Marvel." He was interested in the arts as well as in literature and admired Tiffany's boundless energy and ambition. Although frail, Mary Goddard was energetic and shared Tiffany's deep love of nature. She loved to take long walks through the fields, gathering flowers, and responded quickly to the ever changing moods of her companion. She was always agreeable to whatever Louis might suggest and was confident that he was a genius.

They were married in Norwich, Connecticut, on May 15, 1872, and their first daughter was born in New York on April 3, 1873. A year later the three Tiffanys were on their way to Europe, where they spent the summer in Brittany. On December 9, 1874, she bore a son in Menton who lived only three weeks, a sorrow from which Mary never fully recovered. Her health was also impaired, for she had contracted tuberculosis. On January 7, 1878, they became the parents of a son, Charles, and they moved into an apartment at 48 East 26th Street in New York. A second daughter, Hilda, was born on August 24, 1879. Tiffany spent the summer with his family at his father's estate in Irvington-on-Hudson, where he experimented with photography and painted his family in the fields during the leisurely holiday months.

Between 1875 and 1880 Louis C. Tiffany painted a number of canvases, some of which were scenes based on his travels in Europe and North Africa. He showed three oils and six watercolors at the Philadelphia Centennial of 1876, an oil and two watercolors at the Paris Exposition of 1878, sixteen paintings at the National Academy of Design in New York and twenty paintings at the Century Club. They had a generally favorable reception and many were sold for about $500 apiece. "Duane Street," painted in New York in 1875, was exhibited at the National Academy of Design and at the Paris fair of 1878. It remained in his personal possession until his death. Clearly anticipating the work of the painters who were characterized some thirty years later as members of the "Ashcan School," it utilized as its subject the drab quality of the city slums. Thinly yet surely painted, it is one of the most penetrating pictures of the spirit of a city street. The predominantly brown tonality helps to focus attention on the occasional spots of brighter color in the two figures and the plant boxes. The critic and historian John I. H. Baur, in his *Revolution and Tradition in Modern American Art*, said it marked "the beginning of a new approach to the urban landscape."

THE APPLIED ARTS:
DECORATOR TO THE CARRIAGE TRADE

Although Tiffany continued to paint until the end of his career—landscapes, flowers, scenes of his travels—and although he made sketches and cartoons for stained-glass windows, he was all too aware of his shortcomings as a painter. He was not satisfied with painting landscapes and found the pace set by such artists as John LaFarge and Edwin Austin Abbey in their large-scale works one which he could not match. Then, too, Tiffany yearned to reach a larger audience than that which was possible by means of traditional painting techniques. At this juncture two associates were particularly influential in directing Tiffany to the applied arts. One was Charles L. Tiffany's chief designer, Edward C. Moore, who had learned silversmithing from his father and had worked exclusively for Tiffany from 1851 on. In 1868 he became director of the silver-manufacturing department of Tiffany & Company and by his efforts won for American silverware the first award by a foreign jury at a Paris exhibition. In 1878 he won a special gold medal at the Paris Exhibition, at which Tiffany's paintings, along with some by artists of the Hudson River school, were displayed. The Parisian critic and dealer in Oriental art, Samuel Bing, was of the opinion that Moore's designs in silver, although derived from the art of Japan, could be considered original designs in a new style. Moore, who was a collector of Oriental art, was interested in ancient and Oriental glass and encouraged young Louis C. Tiffany to acquire objects of interest and to study the values of non-European cultures. Samuel Bing, who imported Oriental items, supplied them both with many unique articles. Once interested, Tiffany assembled the first major collection of decorative

Japanese sword guards in America, which he later incorporated in his interiors.

The other strong influence in diverting Louis C. Tiffany from a career in the fine arts was Donald G. Mitchell. He was active in encouraging the development of the Yale art gallery and designed the Connecticut Building for the 1876 Centennial held in Philadelphia, described as "a tasteful two-storey cottage . . . intended to represent a colonial homestead of a century ago." In his capacity as chairman of the judges for the decorative arts sections, he cited in his report three individuals, the French architect and writer Viollet-le-Duc, the architect who had designed the Japanese exhibit and the English illustrator Walter Crane. All of these were to provide basic sources for the style of decoration Tiffany was to make well known in America. Commenting also on the use of painted and stained glass, Mitchell found this style of glazing "full of suggestion to those living in cities whose rear windows look upon neglected or dingy areas or courts, where the equipment of a window with rich designs would be a perpetual delight." Before many years had passed, Louis C. Tiffany, who had several of his Algerian scenes in the Philadelphia Exposition, would be providing the first of his "rich designs" in stained glass.

The Centennial Exhibition provided a timely impetus for a new interest in decoration. Tiffany was to be drawn still further into the applied arts by Candace Wheeler, a friend of many prominent artists and personally very much interested in textiles and needlework, and another friend, Samuel Colman, who had a collection of rare textiles. As Candace Wheeler recalled in her memoirs, she had been much interested in the Centennial exhibit of English needlework from the newly founded "Kensington School of Art Needlework," which had been established in order to help indigent gentlewomen eke out an existence by embroidery and handwork. Out of her desire to establish an American "Kensington School" that would include all articles of feminine manufacture came the beginnings of the Society of Decorative Art in New York. Its purposes were "to encourage profitable industries among women; to accumulate and distribute information; to establish rooms for exhibitions and sales; to form auxiliary committees in other cities and towns; to make connections with various potteries, manufacturers and importers; to endeavor to obtain orders from dealers; to induce each worker to master thoroughly the details of one variety of decoration and endeavor to make for her work a reputation of commercial value." To William Morris, who championed fine craftsmanship and felt cheap art was impossible, since art demanded "time, trouble and thought," the "mainspring of decorative design" was "beauty, mingled with invention, founded on observation of nature." He declared that "if it was not beautiful it had no right to exist; if it was not invention it became wearisome; if not founded on nature it could hardly be beautiful or inventive." Mrs. Wheeler recalled that the "designs of artists like Morris, Burne-Jones and, above all, the direct and graceful work of Walter Crane, founded always upon forms of growth skillfully chosen and carefully adapted to needlework, gave great value to the new revival of embroidery."

Groups similar to the New York Society of Decorative Art were soon formed in Philadelphia and Boston, and in 1878 Samuel Colman persuaded Louis C. Tiffany to devote some time to the society. Mrs. Oliver Wendell Holmes, Jr., had sent to Mrs. Wheeler some embroidered and woven landscapes and these may have piqued his interest. Mrs. Holmes, Jr., who rendered in her embroidered landscapes vivid "natural effects," was termed by *Scribner's Monthly* "one of the most sensitive colorists among American artists," being especially successful with opaline, pearly tints. Classes were organized for women in art needlework, medieval embroidery, china and tile painting. Under the direction of Mr. Tiffany and Mr. Lockwood de Forest, who was interested in the art of India, a class was offered in unbaked pottery. Mrs. Wheeler often enlisted the aid of her artist friends to judge the quality of articles submitted for sale by the Society.

One day in the spring of 1879 Tiffany told Mrs. Wheeler that he wished to resign. "It is all nonsense, this work," he said. "There is no real bottom to it. You can't educate people without educational machinery, and there is so much discussion about things of which there is really no question. My wife says she cannot afford to have me stirred up every Wednesday, but I have been thinking a great deal about decorative work, and I am going into it as a profession. I believe there is more in it than in painting pictures."

In an article on the "younger painters of America" in *Scribner's Monthly*, July, 1881, Louis C. Tiffany was described as having been for some years "a very clever painter" of Oriental phenomena, cathedrals and "naturally unromantic, not to say hideous localities" [an uptown green-grocer's shanty and garden] . . . "Of his new sphere of professional decoration," the article continued, his work showed "the same freedom from conventionality in intention and generally in accomplishment to which he first gave rein in his street studies."

The 31-year-old Tiffany was so convinced of the rightness of his decision to enter the field of decorative work that he promptly took Samuel Colman and Candace Wheeler into a partnership, which operated as Louis C. Tiffany and Associated Artists. The Board of Managers of the Society of Decorative Art entered into an arrangement with Tiffany and Mrs. Wheeler, making them "the sole agent for the sale of beautiful embroideries, executed from their designs and under their supervision." The painter Lockwood de Forest contributed his knowledge of East Indian carvings and fabrics.

Their efforts were commended by Constance Cary Harrison in her book *Woman's Handiwork in Modern Homes*, published in 1881. "Perhaps the broadest, most original and richest development yet seen in America," she remarked, "is from a little band of associated artists, who, headed by Mr. Louis C. Tiffany, have only recently established an atelier in New York. Their work is as yet little known to the general public, and has been executed chiefly for luxurious interiors intended to show every detail harmonized according to the highest standard of decorative art." She included a design for a drapery by Tiffany, golden fawn plush with a "frieze of cloth of gold, crossed by trellis-work of plushes so disposed that light, striking upon the curtains, gives them the effect of being suspended by an illuminated network from their rods." The play between pattern and light on a flat surface was the essence of the unique quality of Tiffany's style of 1880. The drapery, like his early windows and wallpaper designs, was based on a clear pattern contradicted by the reflective surface of the material. Both Tiffany and Colman had made a set of wallpaper designs for the New York firm of Warren, Fuller and Company, some of which were reproduced in *What Shall We Do with Our Walls?* by Clarence Cook, published in 1880. Cook, a founder of the American Pre-Raphaelite movement, felt the purpose of such designs was "to make a breach in the wall of old ideas and fashions of the past, that hedge us in, and to create something that shall have an unborrowed, individual look." One Tiffany paper was a snowflake pattern, printed in black on a gold ground. Thin, complex and overly refined, it resembles an Islamic interlace. The other, a design of clover and spider-webs of black on a buff ground, depends on the character of the web for a similar effect. Both have the flat, linear quality associated with the Japanese papers then coming into vogue.

Tiffany duly called upon Candace Wheeler's embroidery department to make a drop curtain for the Madison Square Theater, which was to present as its first play *Hazel Kirke* by his old friend Steele MacKaye. The theater opened on February 4, 1880, with an interior designed by Hughson Hawley, the first moving elevator stage and overhead electric lighting, installed under the personal supervision of Thomas A. Edison. The decoration, according to *Appleton's Journal*, was a tribute to Tiffany, "one of the foremost of our young painters and a noted colorist." The article continued. "The Madison Square is decorated with that sense of color and harmony that go into a great painting."

The curtain, according to Candace Wheeler, "enlisted us all—Mr. Tiffany for design and all sorts of ingenious expedients as to method; Mr. Colman casting the deciding vote upon the question of color; Mr. De Forest looking up materials, and I directing the actual execution." The curtain was a landscape effect rendered in textiles, including oak and birch trees, wisteria and yucca. "All sorts of materials came into use, velvet and plushes for trees and great-leaved plants in the foreground, shadowy silks for perspective and bits of misty blue distance in iridescent stuffs of any material which would produce illusion or give the required effect . . . Unfortunately, it took fire and went up in smoke before the season was over, but we replaced it with an improved copy."

[*12*]

Candace Wheeler's studio was a lively gathering place. As she related, "Everybody came to the studio in those days. Who but Oscar Wilde [who had been discussing with Steele MacKaye the possibility of producing the play *Vera*] should wander in one afternoon just before nightfall, introducing himself with great self-possession and self-content, looking around the studio with approval, taking an offered cup of tea with alacrity, and bestowing an hour of twilight upon us, filled with speculative conversation." Wilde had lectured widely on "House Decoration" during an American lecture tour in 1882/83 and was accused by James McNeill Whistler of "picking from our platters the plums for the puddings he peddles in the provinces." The keen interest in interior decoration may well have stemmed from a new synthesis of various decorative arts. Peter Selz, in an introduction to *Art Nouveau*, commented on the unity of the arts, "most evident in the comprehensive design of the house." Wallpaper designs were "related to light fixtures and cutlery. The design of the book carefully echoed that of the cabinet. For their predominantly decorative qualities, murals, tapestries and stained glass were preferred to paintings and sculpture, which, when introduced, were intended to be seen as a part of a larger whole."

To the people living in this new industrial age elegance and status were patently indicated by a miscellany of ornamental objects in rooms full of clutter. A voracious "taste for antiquity" was evident also. Styles of the past were enthusiastically reproduced—in luxurious versions if money were no object or in pretentious cheaper models if pennies were counted. As Cecelia Waern, an English visitor interested in the arts of America, commented after an American tour in the 1890's, "It would be almost absurd to expect a serious 'return to simplicity' in the land of mushroom fortunes." Bright colors and rich textures Louis C. Tiffany believed were ideally suited to the "sumptuous" American climate, but undoubtedly some of the peacock blues and greens he often favored were too rich for English non-theatrical tastes. She compared Tiffany the decorator to "a clever milliner adapting adroitly to any problem presented," and characterized his style as eclectic, in which old objects were, without hesitation, incorporated into a scheme of decoration. Maurice Grosser, in *Critic's Eye*, called him, in retrospect, "the most important and successful American decorator of the turn of the century working in the Medieval style . . . derived from the Gothic revival of the early nineteenth century and distinguished by its insistence on handicraft and its modernization of the traditional grammar of ornament into contemporary and semi-realistic decorative forms."

The style of interior decoration popularized in New York by Tiffany had its genesis in London in the work of James McNeill Whistler. Tiffany was probably familiar with the Peacock Room, which had been completed in 1877, and had certainly seen the Primrose Room, which Whistler had decorated for his own home and which he had exhibited in Paris in 1878.

Tiffany's first complete interior was executed for the home of George Kemp on Fifth Avenue. The salon had a distinctly East Indian flavor, stemming from the wood carvings supplied by Lockwood de Forest. The room was covered with a variety of flat patterns, each framed in a rectangular space. Exotic lamps hung from the Islamic interlace of the ceiling. The fireplace was lined with tiles made by Tiffany, who had been experimenting with glass for several years, and bric-a-brac from Samuel Colman's collection lined the mantel. The frieze, painted by Tiffany, was the most successful bit of ornament. The patterns were rather strong in spite of their small scale, the forms did not harmonize too well and the effect was restless and complex.

Nevertheless, George Kemp was pleased. Samuel Colman had inquired from Easthampton as to Tiffany's progress in late August of 1879. "How are you getting along with your work on 'Kemps' drawing rooms?" He also inquired as to Mrs. Tiffany's health, complained that some wallpaper designs he had submitted had been changed, "put into smooth curves and insipidity," and asked how Tiffany was getting on with his. He added that he had written him a month or more ago. Tiffany rarely found time for letter-writing, and words came slowly from his pen. He was impatient with the limitations of language and found it impossible to explain or express himself without gestures or effects. Even in simple conversation he had considerable difficulty. He was a lover and collector of art and technical books. He did, however, dash off letters in his own hand to members of his immediate family or friends.

As a result of the Kemp commission Tiffany and the Associated Artists were asked to decorate "one of the noble public rooms" of the Knickerbocker Greys' new Seventh Regiment Armory on Park Avenue at 67th Street. The building was designed by Charles W. Clinton to serve as a military club, storehouse and drill shed, the first of its kind. By November, 1879, the shell was completed. The Associated Artists received a fee of $20,000 and worked from April to September of 1880 in order to complete their job before the building was opened to the public. By the time of the grand ball on December 15, 1880, their work had been admired by more than 38,000 visitors.

Candace Wheeler, who was responsible for the hangings, recalled that in the capable hands of the Associated Artists the Veterans' Room and Library embodied the idea of the veteran, since they all understood "the significance of decorative media . . . the power in colors and in lines to make an atmosphere." Tiffany, who was responsible for the over-all scheme, planned the work and selected the materials. He retained Stanford White, then a pupil of H. H. Richardson, as architectural consultant. It was White who designed the balcony. Tiffany also employed two artists, George Yewell and Frank D. Millet, to paint the frieze. Millet had worked with John La Farge on the decoration of Richardson's Trinity Church in Boston in 1877.

[*14*]

In the Veterans' Room of this Seventh Regiment Armory a large fireplace framed by Tiffany glass tiles is the focus. Over the mantel, framed in hammered iron, is a plaque of stucco and glass representing a struggle between a dragon and an eagle. The undulating curves suggest the style of the American painter and illustrator Elihu Vedder, like Tiffany a leading exponent of the Art Nouveau style. A high oaken wainscoting surmounted by a band of carving similar to the Japanese *kamoi*, or molding, is carried around the walls at the height of the mantel and decorated with rectangular bolted panels treated to develop flecks of rust. The carved band is an elaborate scroll of Celtic interlace, probably one of the earliest examples of this kind of ornament in America. The frieze is also an elaborate network of interlace patterns, providing a symbolic narrative.

In the opinion of Herbert Oppenheimer, who as a young architectural student was one of the first to re-evaluate, some decades later, Tiffany's interiors, "One can see familiar motifs, but they are done with such freedom that they are only suggestive of their source. The design can best be described as Art Nouveau. It might be compared to the work of the Scotch architect Charles R. Mackintosh or of Frank Lloyd Wright." Of the effect as a whole, Oppenheimer felt that the "first reaction is not pleasant. It is overdecorated . . . the chandeliers are too heavy . . . but the details are a surprise and often pleasant and the final effect is quite positive." Only the fireplace cranes and wrought-iron chandeliers can be associated with European tradition, but even here it is the decorative quality of the Gothic which is emphasized, in clear contrast to the other rooms of the Armory, decorated by Thomas Hastings for the Herter Brothers in an essentially classic treatment of organization and detail.

A booklet privately printed by the veterans' organization in 1881 praised the military effect: "What most impresses, and what is most worthy to impress, in the artistic treatment of this Veterans' Room is the positive, practical and yet poetic adaptation of decorative material to the purposes in hand . . . by the very noticeable accordant chime of all side decorations; the clamp and clang of iron, the metallic lustres, the ponderous soffit beams (with axe-cuts showing on them) are all clearly and undeniably assimilable and matchable with the huge, hard, clanging ponderosities of wars and tramping regiments and armories."

Translucent glass mosaics were suspended in front of the larger windows of the Veterans' Room. Chartreuse and mother-of-pearl opalescent glass, arranged in rectangles and semicircles, combined with the dominant yellows and greens of the painted ornament and set off the rich, dark browns of iron, leather and oak. In the Library the irregularly-shaped pieces of glass of various colors and thicknesses gave the appearance of the inside of a kaleidoscope.

The original hangings, described by Constance Cary Harrison in 1881, enhanced the over-all effect with their metallic colors and varied textures. "Of the four plush window-curtains for the Veterans' Room at the Armory, two are made of Damascus red, two of antique blue. A network of gilded leather is embroidered upon the plush, leaving flame-shaped interstices like the slashing of an ancient doublet. The portière is of Japanese brocade, bordered with plush representing leopard skin. Upon the main body of the portière are plaid appliqués of velvet in small squares, each exhibiting a design taken from the days of knighthood and romantic warfare. Over the intermediate spaces of brocade are sewn tiny rings of steel representing the surface of a coat of mail."

In a critical analysis of the newly decorated Veterans' Room and Library, in *Scribner's Monthly* of July, 1881, William C. Brownell summed it up as not quite a success. "Until Mr. Tiffany is convinced that the planning of a work of monumental dignity demands more of him—or of some single mind, whoever it may be—than the preparation of a general sketch and the selection of specialists to advise as to the details, as well as to execute them, and the confining of his further effort to a mere harmonizing of possible discords, we may be sure that the work of the 'Associated Artists' will not differ substantially from this decoration."

During the early eighties Louis C. Tiffany and the Associated Artists were well on their way to becoming one of New York's top decorating concerns. Only the New York firms of Marcotte and Co. and the Herter Brothers were considered more fashionable, but the Tiffany firm was known as the most "artistic." The Associated Artists not only decorated dozens of interiors but produced many of the decorative accessories to go with them. Much of their work came to them from the rapidly growing architectural firm of McKim, Mead and White, although Stanford White favored La Farge for his interiors until they disagreed in 1888. The former Villard House, now the administrative offices of the Roman Catholic Archdiocese of New York, is a good example of a White-La Farge collaboration. Here the ornament is controlled with a classic balanced harmony, a rococo lightness and an extreme refinement, reflecting the thinking of a precise draftsman restrained by architectural discipline. Unlike interiors by Tiffany, the ornament is subordinated to the definitions of the space.

Tiffany and La Farge both worked on the new building erected at Fifth Avenue and 39th Street for the Union League Club. The architects were Peabody and Stearns; the builders, the Norcross Brothers, who had built Trinity Church in Boston. Ground was broken in the spring of 1880 and by the fall of the year the shell was up. The decoration took most of the winter, so as to have it ready for club members to move in on March 5, 1881. Charles L. Tiffany was one of the founders of the club and probably had some influence with its president, Hamilton Fish, who had been Secretary of State under Grant. Fish's niece's husband, D. Maitland Armstrong, a painter and illustrator, was associated with Tiffany in the preparation of paintings for the Paris Exhibition of 1878 and illustrated articles by Donald G. Mitchell on Tiffany's decoration of his own apartment.

La Farge, assisted by the sculptor Augustus Saint-Gaudens and the painter Will H. Low, was responsible for the decoration of the club's main dining-room and most of the other smaller rooms. Tiffany and Candace Wheeler planned the decorations for the main staircase, with its colored windows, the hallways and the hangings. A writer for *The Century* described the green and silver halls as leaving the strongest impression on the visitor "on account of their size and their quasi-splendor . . . The windows of the main hall are the best portion of Mr. Tiffany's work . . . the little window on the third-floor landing of the main staircase . . . is very pretty, simple and unconventional." The main window was evidently composed of a series of small-scale, complex geometric patterns and interlaces similar to those for the Armory. The dominant feature of the whole scheme is the round arch, which is characteristic of Richardsonian buildings. According to the club's librarian, "most of the members think it was one of the handsomest buildings they have ever seen." The building was used until February 2, 1931, after which it was demolished.

Tiffany could, of course, indulge himself to his heart's content in his own apart-ment, and he stamped these rooms with his own far-ranging tastes. The top floor of the Bella Apartment House at 48 East 26th Street was photographed in 1882. Donald G. Mitchell discussed Tiffany's style of decoration in a series of ten articles in *Our Continent*, declaring that in these rooms Tiffany had "welded the decorative art of the west and the east into one harmonious whole." In the course of planning these articles, Mitchell had asked Tiffany to let him see a book by Leopold Eidlitz, one of the more imaginative architects of the day. Tiffany supplied him with both books and sketches of details for the first of the articles; Maitland Armstrong and Frederick S. Church supplied the remainder.

In the lobby of the Bella there was a flavor of the East in the rugs, wallpaper and collection of arms and armor. The exposed beams, the opalescent glass window, with its pattern of leads in a series of flowing curves, a hanging lamp with a simple cone shade, the simple moldings and straight-lined furniture all contributed to a sense of great originality and virility. It was bold without being showy. The elements were not integrated, but neither did they conflict.

Tiffany some years later recalled for a collaborator the details of the lobby—in *The Art Work of Louis C. Tiffany.* "As you entered from the lift you found yourself in a lobby, lighted with stained glass, which reached high up into the peak of the gable where the beams themselves showed in a rich dull color scheme, lighted here and there with plates and studs of bronze, the broad surfaces of the beams showing the knots and grain of the wood. The roof-slopes were set with thick glass tiles to aid the light from windows, and the windows themselves were made up of rounds of glass of uneven thickness. What with staining and carving and inlays of metal and glass, the dark, brown-beamed ceiling made a foil to the warm India-red walls and trim.

"A novel effect in the treatment of window sashes was to be seen in the gable. The stained-glass sash was heavy, and to raise it there was need of a strong pulley. Mr. Tiffany used a large wooden wheel and chain and exposed these to view, turning them in fact into decorative objects by simply providing a handsome wheel and chain. It would have been a pity indeed to box in such objects after the ordinary fashion. The counterweight, a shallow box playing up and down a groove to one side of the window, was turned likewise into a thing of beauty.

"Not far off a standing torch-bearer with a hood suspended above it gave at night the pleasant effect of a moving flame. The hall adjacent, with its tall clock and metal-bound *cassone*, its carved settle and shelves set with spoils from Algiers, its hanging lamps and quaint Oriental keramics stamped the entrance to this apartment with the seal of the artist."

In the library, or sitting room, was a fireplace surrounded by a symmetrical arrangement of bookshelves. Vincent J. Scully, professor of art at Yale University and author of *The Shingle Style*, commented that "the light bookcase over the mantel in the library recalls considerably later Art Nouveau work in England, such as that by Voysey, Mackintosh and Baillie Scott as well as such Viennese Art Nouveau interiors as those by Hoffman." As described in *The Art Work of Louis C. Tiffany:* "In the library he treated the fireplace in a novel manner, using the whole width of the chimney breast for shelving for books and bric-a-brac and forming out of iron plates an advanced hearth for wood fires without disturbing the hearth behind. The combination of books and open fireplace was an idea which commends itself to book-lovers, for on those shelves are places for favorite authors and, high above easy reach, shelves for particularly admired bric-a-brac."

On the wall facing the bookcase, the wall-matting was divided into rectangular areas by plain strips of wood molding. A Colman seascape was framed within one of the rectangles. A floor lamp in the style of the English decorator Eastlake demonstrated the heaviness of the accessories of this type which were then available. The description as given in *The Art Work of Louis C. Tiffany* pointed up the art of simulation: "Wherever not covered by the books, the walls were clad with Chinese matting, touched up here and there with suggestions of flower and leaf. The iron plates of the hearth and the metal doors of an adjoining wood-closet were decorated with discreet figures in rust color and black, not painted so much as suggested, like the decorations on old metal pieces which have been toned down and almost obliterated by age."

The drawing room, or parlor, was a tribute to Lockwood de Forest's devotion to the arts of India. Fabrics "used as scarves by native dancing-girls" were then popular for sash-window curtains. Indian wood-carvings framed the windows, and an Indian lamp table and chair occupied the center of the room, lending an Oriental flavor. The fireplace, with its spiderweb pattern of colored glass, was a typical Tiffany touch of light and color. On the mantel was a collection of vases. On the far wall was an oil painting of Tiffany's family, "In the Fields at Irvington," which was done in 1879. The use of a large unframed mirror at right angles to the windows on the left side of the room effectively emphasized the treatment of walls and textures.

The dining room, with its over-mantel painting of a turkey and pumpkins, marked Tiffany as one of the first appreciators of early American decorative styles. As described in *The Art Work of Louis C. Tiffany*, "The dining room gave a chance for many ingenious arrangements for the display of platters, plates and cups, which were nicely calculated as to their effect upon the general color-scheme of the walls. About three feet from the floor ran a rack about the room to carry the larger plates, and on both sides of the tiled fireplace, as well as above it, were shelves and nooks and wall-closets for the more delicate ware, the silver, etc. The upper walls were hung with blue Japanese textile work embroidered with birds and cloud symbols. The tiled fireplace with its dogs and blazing logs was framed by a wooden hearth-front and mantel of the eighteenth century, carved in low relief with fan-shaped patterns. Above, against the wall, was a painting of pumpkins and half-stripped corn and a turkey-cock 'making his wheel,' but this painting was not set in a projecting frame, merely held in place by strips of brown wood. The brilliant yellow of the pumpkins and the red and iridescent blues of the turkey made this painting a focus of color for the manifold and varied notes which sprang from every part of the room, lined as it was with Oriental keramics and textiles, brass and bronze, silver and dull gold."

On the whole, these rooms, which provided a highly personal background for Tiffany, were treated by a surface decoration of small and delicate scale. Although there was throughout a sense of newness and freshness which were the results of experimentation, a sense of architectural integration was lacking.

In the summer of 1881 Louis Tiffany and Candace Wheeler redecorated Samuel Clemens' (Mark Twain's) home in Hartford, Connecticut, by adding stenciled decorations designed after Indian motifs to walls and ceilings. As Mark Twain wrote early that spring, the Farmington Avenue house, not yet ten years old, would be given a more up-to-date look: "In June we shall tear out the reception room to make our front hall bigger . . . and at the same time the decorator will decorate the walls and ceilings of our whole lower floor." The original stencil-work may still be seen on the panels of walls and doors; some of the tiles used for the fireplaces are duplicates of those used in the Armory and other interiors decorated about this time by Tiffany. For the dining-room fireplace, above which a window was placed at the author's suggestion, where he "could watch the flames leap to reach the falling snowflakes,"

[*19*]

Tiffany supplied tiles in three different colors—turquoise, amber and brown—in a combination of transparent and opaque glass. When the work had been completed Tiffany's famous client sent him a check and a note: "I have been down the Mississippi River or I would have answered sooner. I am happy to say that the work is not merely and coldly satisfactory, but intensely so."

The most elaborate—and also the most troublesome—interiors at this stage of Tiffany's career were those executed for the Goelets and the Vanderbilts. The Associated Artists received commissions to decorate the homes of Ogden Goelet, at 59th Street and Fifth Avenue, and Cornelius Vanderbilt II, at 58th Street and Fifth Avenue, at almost the same time. The Goelet work was completed first for a fee of more than $50,000. Lockwood de Forest kept Tiffany informed as to the rugs and fabrics his clients were likely to take. A letter to Tiffany dated December 23, 1882 mentioned that he had been "trying to get more rugs off on Mr. Goelet and have done fairly well but Mr. G. has decided views. The Vanderbilts did not take the kincobs for furniture covering after all—it was too expensive."

The Vanderbilt house was being built by George B. Post, a pupil of Richard Morris Hunt, who had built the William K. Vanderbilt mansion in New York in 1881 and later designed "The Breakers" at Newport and "Biltmore" at Asheville, North Carolina. Hunt never employed Tiffany but preferred other decorators, such as the Herter Brothers, over whom he could exert greater control. Tiffany was already developing a reputation for independence and for unorthodox methods. The New York mansion was built in the style of a Henry IV château, and evidently Tiffany's suggestions for decoration suited Mr. Vanderbilt, who wrote to him on June 2, 1881, "I like the plan very much indeed. Please show it to Mr. Post as soon as possible so that all building plans will work in together." More than a year and a half later, when Tiffany was in Washington, D. C., busy redecorating the White House, Candace Wheeler wrote him of her difficulties with the job: "I have been put to so much expense in completing this [Vanderbilt] contract that I think an allowance of cost should be made me on certain things which I will state—In the first place, when the tapestries were ready to place, borders completed and all, I found the constant handling of the last two years had made a toning of color in them which would not allow the new canvas to come in contact with them."

She went on, "After calling a consultation of Mr. Dufais, Mr. Armstrong and Mr. Mitchell, we decided to use plush to fill out the wall spaces and this I furnished. . . . After the curtains were hung—the front window and wide portière—Mrs. Vanderbilt came to see me and absolutely refused to have the green plush. This time Mr. Colman was called in and we decided to change it, using the same pale tint which was on the wall. . . We have been greatly hurried by having the Vanderbilt work to complete so immediately following the Goelet work and yet not lose other orders. I have still work enough to occupy my regular force for two months or perhaps more, but am letting the extra ones go."

Louis C. Tiffany's pre-eminence as America's leading decorator was virtually acknowledged by an invitation to redecorate the White House. This was accomplished by the Associated Artists in seven weeks during the winter of 1882/83, at a cost of more than $15,000, and included furnishings and alterations to the corridor, East Room, the State Dining Room and the Red and Blue parlors. Candace Wheeler supplied hangings in keeping with Tiffany's motifs of eagles and flags. President Chester Alan Arthur, whose wife had died ten months before Mr. Arthur's election as vice-president, refused to move to the White House until it was cleaned and renovated, declaring that if the government would not approve the expense, he would pay for it himself. Congress later paid the bill.

According to the account in *The White House* by Jane and Burt McConnell, Arthur, who had lived in New York City on Lexington Avenue near 28th Street, "set up temporary headquarters at the home of a friend and promptly engaged the services of Louis Comfort Tiffany of New York to do over the Executive Mansion. Each evening he inspected the progress and made suggestions. At his direction, twenty-four loads of furniture were removed and sold at public auction. The East Room ceiling was resplendent in silver and ivory, but the crowning achievement was the opalescent glass screen. Reaching from floor to ceiling, it was placed in the first-floor hall to provide more privacy for the President's family." (About 1904 President Theodore Roosevelt apparently ordered architect Charles F. McKim, in charge of remodeling the White House in the neo-classical style of the Monroe era, to "break in small pieces that Tiffany screen." Its current replacement value was estimated, in an article on the redecoration of the White House in the *Saturday Evening Post*, at $50,000.)

While the glass screen was the major attraction, Tiffany's glass-mosaic sconces in the Blue Room also received attention in contemporary accounts. "The magnificent screen of mosaic glass which shuts off the inner corridor from the public . . . fills the space between the columns . . . is the most elaborate of the exquisite decorations in glass designed by Mr. Louis C. Tiffany and added during President Arthur's administration. Glowing and rich in subdued colors, it is a thoroughly artistic piece of work, exceptional in taste and in perfect harmony with its surroundings . . . Four circular sconces, each having seven gas-jets, are each provided with a background, or rosette, 3 feet in diameter, composed of fantastic shapes of colored glass interspersed with little mirrors, to produce a scintillating effect of great variety and brilliancy, which is enhanced by the pendant drops of iridescent glass affixed to the arms that hold the jets." Evidently "all Washington was impressed and delighted that winter with the transformation . . . and agreed that the charming and handsome President Arthur had excellent taste."

Among other clients of the Associated Artists were Hamilton Fish, Henry de Forest, the brother of Lockwood de Forest, J. Taylor Johnston, founder of the Metropolitan Museum of Art, and Dr. William T. Lusk, who became the Tiffany family's physician. Photographs of some of the interiors decorated by the Associated Artists were featured in a series of portfolios entitled *Artistic Houses* assembled by George W. Sheldon. These were published in two large-size volumes by Appleton from 1882 to 1884. The first apartment to be described in the portfolios was that of Louis C. Tiffany. Many of the clients of the Associated Artists had decided views of their own, still in the "High Victorian" tradition. But the Associated Artists successfully created a new style which, although not yet Art Nouveau, was based largely on the blending of exotic elements with Tiffany glass tiles, Islamic carvings, embroidered hangings and painted friezes. The mélange, more often than not, incorporated colored glass, which was becoming Louis C. Tiffany's own personal province.

part one
ILLUSTRATIONS

Louis C. Tiffany
AS A PAINTER AND DECORATOR

The firm of Tiffany & Company became New York's leading jewelers, headed until 1902 by Charles L. Tiffany, photographed (*above*) in 1893. From 1870 to 1905 they were located on Union Square, in the city's first fireproof building. They exhibited the 30-carat Brunswick Yellow Diamond (*below*) at The Philadelphia Centennial of 1876.

CHRONOLOGY

1837 TIFFANY & YOUNG

259 Broadway, New York

1841 TIFFANY, YOUNG & ELLIS

259–260 Broadway, New York

1847 TIFFANY, YOUNG & ELLIS

271 Broadway, New York

1850 TIFFANY, REED & CO.

Paris, France

1853 TIFFANY & CO.

550 Broadway, New York

1861 TIFFANY & CO.

550–552 Broadway, New York

1868 TIFFANY & CO.

Paris, France

1868 TIFFANY & CO.

London, England

1870 TIFFANY & CO.

Union Square and 15th St., New York

1905 TIFFANY & CO.

Fifth Ave. and 37th St., New York

1910 TIFFANY & CO.   Paris, France

25 Rue de la Paix and Place de l'Opéra

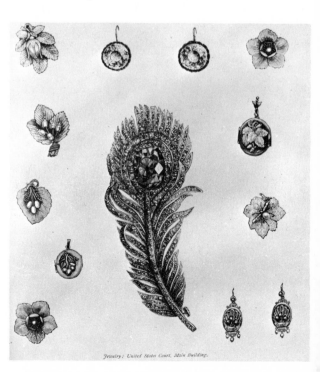

Jewelry: United States Court, Main Building.

Louis Comfort Tiffany, photographed in 1878 (*top left*), painted his self-portrait in 1880 (*top right*). He photographed his wife and daughter gathering apple-blossoms (*left*) and painted a watercolor of his family "In the Fields at Irvington" in 1879 (*above*).

George Inness's Brittany landscape, "Etretat," (*above*) was painted in 1874. Tiffany's watercolor "Fuller's Country Store, Norwich," a Connecticut scene, was painted in 1872. His "Snake Charmer at Tangier," (*below*) was exhibited at the Centennial in 1876.

Tiffany's oil, "Duane Street, New York," (*top left*) was painted in 1875, his "View of the Palisades" (*top right*) in 1876, "Market at Nuremberg," (*left*) in 1889, and "Trees," a watercolor, (*below*) about 1900.

Schinkel's exotic "palm-house" diverted Berliners and was painted by Karl Blechen in 1834 (*top right*). The glass-roofed Saracen-style Horticultural Hall (*bottom right*) was a feature of the Philadelphia Centennial of 1876. Donald G. Mitchell designed and furnished the Connecticut pavilion (*below*).

The Royal School of Art Needlework sent over an embroidered fire screen (*top left*), and Minton, Hollis & Co., also of London, sent a tile mantel (*bottom left*). Samuel West of Boston exhibited a window entitled "St. Paul," "after Raphael," (*top right*). A wallpaper design, "La Margarete," by Walter Crane, received a Centennial award (*bottom right*).

Aug 27th

S. Colman

I am glad to say that I have been very well all summer, and I hope to continue so; but I say, hope, with a sigh, as malarial troubles seem so very uncertain, or very certain I should say.

I hope you have continued to improve, as you wrote me, you had been doing at New London. Do write now as soon as you can, and let me know all about your doings &c.

The weather here has been cool all summer and very pleasant until about the 5th or 6th of Aug - since then it has been variable and not picturesque.

I heard from Smillie yesterday. James and George are at Magnolia near Boston.

Very sincerely yours
Saml Colman -

P.S.
I wrote you about a month or more ago

East Hampton L.I. Aug 24th 1879.

My dear Louis,

I congratulate you, and your wife, for the accession to your happiness, by the arrival of another little girl: I hope she will be as sweet, and charming, as little May. I hope your wife still continues to improve, and that she will soon be quite strong again. Let us know as soon as possible how it is going.

I finished my wall paper designs, and sent them to Warren last week: but I am very doubtful about the result: they sent me a specimen drawing from one of my other things, and it made me feel like tearing my hair, as they had changed my work so much; put it all into smooth curves, and insipidity!. I have written them that I would prefer they should trace my new drawings, and not change a line. How do you get on with yours? I hope they are all finished -

Samuel Colman, a colleague, wrote Tiffany in 1879 to congratulate him on the birth of a daughter and to discuss their designs for wallpaper (*above*). The first venture of the Associated Artists—Tiffany, Colman, Candace Wheeler and Lockwood de Forest—was a landscape curtain (*below*).

Inaugurated February 4th 1880. Madison Square Theatre. View of Interior and Embroidered Curtain.

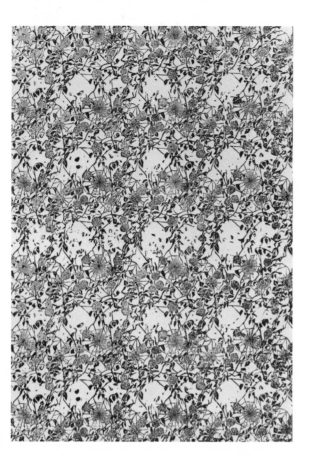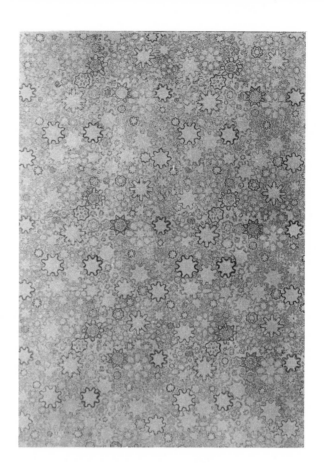

Tiffany designed two wallpapers in 1880, one black on a buff ground, utilizing a spider-web and clover motif, (*left*), the other a snowflake design in black on a gold ground, resembling an Islamic interlace (*right*). Tiffany also designed in 1880 a drapery of golden fawn plush, crossed by trellis-work of plush, with a frieze of cloth-of-gold (*bottom left*). An advertisement featuring the designs of the Associated Artists (*bottom right*) appeared in *Indian Domestic Architecture* in 1885.

George Kemp retained Tiffany in 1879 to decorate his Fifth Avenue house. In the hall (*top left*) were glass tiles, as well as in the salon (*above*). The oak-paneled dining-room (*below*) had a frieze on gilded canvas.

In the Kemp library (*above*) Tiffany used interlaced designs in the transoms and set iridescent shells in the gold cove ceiling. The J. Taylor Johnston parlor (*bottom left*) had a fireplace faced with tiles. A stained glass window surmounted the fireplace in the W. H. de Forest dining-room (*bottom right*). Tiffany's firm decorated these houses in 1881.

Stanford White used Tiffany glass tiles in the dining-room of Kingscote in Newport, R. I. (1880-81) (*above*). White and John La Farge decorated the Villard house in New York (1882-83), including the music room (*below*), now used by the Roman Catholic Archdiocese of New York.

The dining-room designed by Tiffany for Dr. William T. Lusk in 1882 featured a bronze frieze, tiled fireplace and transoms of amber glass (*top*). Tiffany was probably familiar with James McNeill Whistler's Peacock Room (*center*). Samuel Colman displayed his ceramics in 1882 in his Newport library (*bottom*). Its ceiling was covered in Japanese silk.

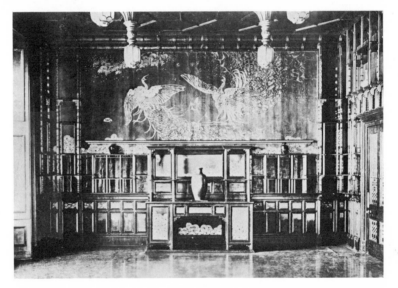

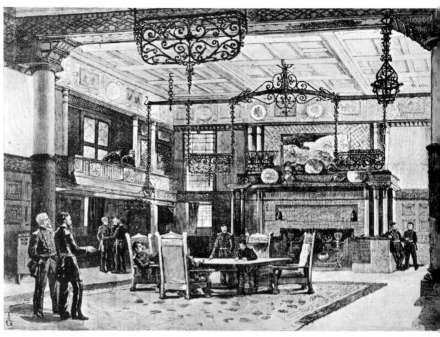

The Veterans' Room of the Seventh Regiment Armory in New York (*above*) was sketched in 1881 by Charles Graham. Tiffany had provided translucent glass mosaics (*top left*), and directed the decoration. Celtic motifs, illustrated in Owen Jones' *Grammar of Ornament* of 1856, (*left*) were plentifully employed, such as in the frieze and wainscot (*below*). The Associated Artists received a fee of $20,000 for their work in 1880 in the Veterans' Room (*opposite page, above*) Library (*opposite page, below*).

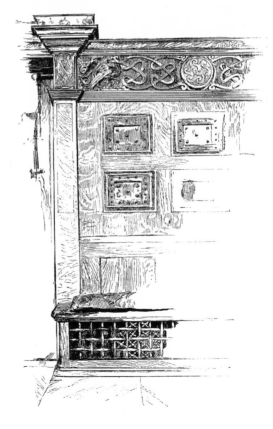

[36]

In the Rochester, New York, home of W. S. Kimball, Tiffany screened off the organ loft and staircase (*opposite page, top left*) and flanked the dining-room mantel with stained glass windows (*opposite page, bottom*). For Mark Twain's Hartford, Connecticut, home he set a window above the fireplace in 1881 (*opposite page, top right*). Tiffany provided green and silver halls of "quasi-splendor" and several stained glass windows for New York's Union League Club (*above and bottom right*).

[39]

The hall of Tiffany's apartment near Madison Square, photographed in 1882, was lighted by stained glass in the gable (*above*). The window sash was operated by a pulley and counterweight, decorated and sketched by him (*right*). Tiffany placed shelves for books and bric-a-brac the full width of the chimney-breast, covered his library walls (*below*) with panels and matting.

Above the plate rail in the dining-room hung a leather chest, drawn by Tiffany (*top*). Pumpkins, corn and a turkey-cock were painted over the hearth. The parlor (*bottom*) had Indian carvings and a fireplace topped by a spiderweb of colored glass.

[*41*]

TIFFANY & DE FOREST.
333 Fourth Avenue,
New York.

Dec. 23. 1882.

My dear Louis

I send your father a check today for $4000 to place to your account & have drawn a like sum myself. I shall only keep enough to the credit of Tiffany & de Forest to pay running expences with. I have been trying to get more rugs off on Mr Goelet & have done fairly but Mr G. has decided ideas. The Vanderbilts did not take the Kincobs for the furniture covering after all it was too expensive.

Yours very sincerely
Lockwood de Forest

New York
Dec 27th /82

Everything goes well as far I know. Work goes on at the Goelets & looks now if it might be finished soon

June 2. 1881.

319, Fifth Avenue

Dr Sir. I like the plan very much indeed. Please show to Mr Post as soon as possible. So that all buildings plans will work in together —

Yrs truly
Respectfully
W. Vanderbilt

Mr Tiffany.

Oct 22/83

Louis C. Tiffany & Co.
~~Associated Artists~~
333 Fourth Avenue.

[43]

Hon. Hamilton Fish
            Dear Sir.
            Mr. Sheldon, author
& Editor of Appleton's "Artistic
Houses", has asked us to give
him the names of houses that
we thought desirable for the
above work — Among them we
have mentioned your name & we
believe Mr. Sheldon proposes
calling upon you in person, to
gain your permission to take
photographs of some of the work
done by us in your house.
            Very truly yours
            Louis C. Tiffany & Co
            G.

The suggestions made by Tiffany to Cornelius Vanderbilt II for decorating his Fifth Avenue mansion were enthusiastically approved—except for kincobs—including the ornate Moorish Room (*opposite page, bottom*). The Stuyvesant Square drawing-room decorated by Tiffany for Hamilton Fish was photographed for *Artistic Houses*. It featured a carved mantel, Indian carved teak panels, a Moorish frieze and peacock blue plush (*below*).

In 1882-83 the Associated Artists were asked by President Arthur to redecorate the
White House. In the East Room (*above*) Tiffany supplied a Siena Axminster carpet,
decked the ceiling with a mosaic pattern in silver leaf, "in accord with the old colonial
spirit of the previous white and gold ornamentation." The State Dining Room received
a table accommodating 40 guests, fawn-colored walls and a ceiling of primrose and
lemon with a border of rosettes.

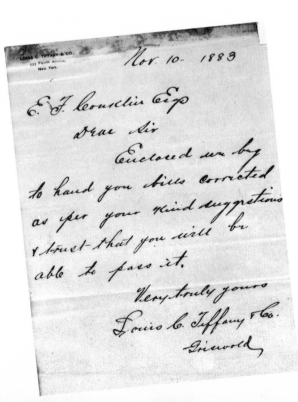

[45]

Tiffany replaced the ground glass which had separated the corridor from the vestibule with a screen of opalescent glass, its many-hued panels featuring national emblems. The ceiling was decorated with rosettes and a border of Indian brass ornamented with gold tracery and set off by crimson woodwork and palms in gilded majolica pots.

While carpenters and painters were busy with fresco colors, gold and silver leaf and bronze powder, Tiffany was busy regilding and recovering furniture, refurbishing mirrors, providing new curtains, facing fireplaces with tile and mosaic and supplying everything from ruby glass shades to pedestals for vases.

[46]

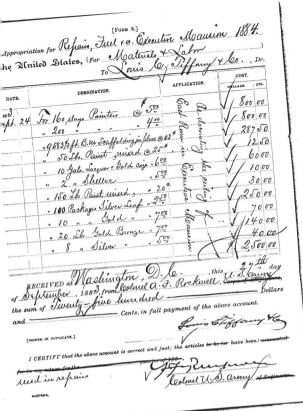

The Blue Parlor (*opposite page*) and the Red Parlor (*above*) were illuminated for public occasions by gaslight from sconces. Pendant drops of iridescent glass affixed to the arms of the gas jets produced a scintillating effect, which "impressed all Washington" with the showy transformation.

United States Patent Office.

LOUIS C. TIFFANY, OF NEW YORK, N. Y.

COLORED-GLASS WINDOW.

SPECIFICATION forming part of Letters Patent No. 237,418, dated February 8, 1881.

Application filed October 25, 1880. (No model.)

To all whom it may concern:

Be it known that I, LOUIS C. TIFFANY, a citizen of the United States, residing in the city, county, and State of New York, have invented new and useful Improvements in Colored-Glass Windows, of which the following is a specification.

This invention relates to the introduction of a new character of glass in colored-glass windows.

The improvement consists in a metallic luster being given to one surface of pieces of glass and the insertion of such glass among other pieces of colored glass in a window or mosaic. The effect is a highly-iridescent one and of pleasing metallic luster, changeable from one to the other, depending upon the direction of the visual ray and the brilliancy or dullness of the light falling upon or passing through the glass. This is the case either when such combination of glass is as a transparency or permanently in a window or in a reflective mosaic—that is to say, with a mosaic containing a reflective surface as a background, so as to reflect the light back to and through the surface of the mosaic. The metallic luster is produced by forming a film of a metal or its oxide, or a compound of a metal, on or in the glass either by exposing it to vapors or gases or by direct application. It may also be produced by corroding the surface of the glass, such processes being well known to glass-manufacturers.

In the drawings, Figure 1 represents a front view of a window containing my improvement; and Fig. 2 is a cross-section thereof, taken in the line *x x* of Fig. 1.

a a, &c., are pieces of metallic-surfaced glass, and *b b* are pieces of glass of various colors. *c c* are leaded joints running between and joining the pieces of glass to each other.

All glass in windows is, by the application of this metallic luster, made more beautiful in effect, at night producing a highly-iridescent and more lustrous effect, and when on the surface of opalescent glass the dull whiteness and spotty appearance are removed.

With opalescent glass in exteriors there is generally too strong a contrast. This is removed by the use of the metallic-luster opalescent glass in the window or windows, as hereinbefore specified.

I claim—

A mosaic or window composed of a plurality of panes of colored glass, a number of said panes, distributed among the rest, having one of their surfaces provided with reflective coatings, substantially as described, and for the purpose set forth.

LOUIS C. TIFFANY.

Witnesses:
   JAMES H. HUNTER,
   ELWYN S. MAILLER.

[*48*]

The Stained Glass Decades

THE GLASS OF FASHION

Louis C. Tiffany had, for some time, been more interested in his experiments with glass than in soothing the feelings of ruffled clients or the problems of matching swatches of kincob. The decoration of the interior of the Church of the Divine Paternity at 45th Street and Fifth Avenue in New York was to be the last collective enterprise of the Associated Artists. For this structure Candace Wheeler created embroideries copied from old ecclesiastical motifs, embroidering religious texts on wine-colored plush for the gallery and the musical score of "Old Hundred" on the hangings for the choir. But she had turned her hand to designing for commercial fabric houses such as the silk-manufacturing firm of Cheney Brothers, while Lockwood de Forest was spending most of his time in the Far East and Samuel Colman was living in Newport. As Candace Wheeler recalled, "The wave of popular decorative art [had] broken over us and receded." It was decided at this time to detach the department of artistic needlework. "The original scheme of the enterprise was continued under the name of Louis C. Tiffany and Co., its offshoot retaining the impersonal title of Associated Artists as better suited to the requirements of an enterprise under feminine control." The Associated Artists found a new location at 115 East 23rd Street and expanded their facilities to include the designing of wallpaper, while Tiffany continued to operate from their former joint studios at 333 Fourth Avenue.

"I think Mr. Tiffany was rather glad to get rid of us all," she declared, "for his wonderful experiments in glass iridescence . . . meant far more to him at the time than association with other interests." At the top of the old hotel building on Fourth Avenue were the glass rooms "where Mr. Tiffany's experiments in color went on and where he was working out his problems from bits of old iridescent Roman vases which had lain centuries underground; or finding out the secrets of tints in ancient cathedral windows, and the proportions of metals and chemicals which would produce certain shades of color. The actual melting and mixing was done in the laboratory underneath his own apartments, but the results of the study and the effects of juxtaposition were tried in the glass-loft." Tiffany worked first in tiles, stained glass and mosaic; his later experiments resulted in a distinctive type of blown glass which would ultimately become a household word.

For many centuries glass as a material, particularly colored glass, which Tiffany found had a tremendous potential for artistic decoration, was regarded as a precious commodity and treated, by the early craftsmen, with the utmost respect. Tiffany felt the quality of nineteenth-century glass left a good deal to be desired. He set about making a study of glass, ranging from that of the Middle Ages to common preserve jars, in order to determine the formulas and techniques which would best achieve his purposes.

As noted by C. Lorgues-Lapouge in *The Old Masters,* the twelfth and thirteenth centuries were notable for the stained-glass windows produced in Europe. Their radiance has rarely been surpassed, and the vivid colors, often rich reds, blues and yellows, were frequently compared to precious stones. Collection boxes in the churches helped to provide money for the making of such windows, often presented to cathedrals by guilds and corporate bodies to perpetuate symbols of their trades. Kings, noblemen, bishops and chapter-houses often presented windows "bearing their coats-of-arms, equestrian figures or allegorical compositions." Like fresco painters, according to C. Lorgues-Lapouge, the early "glass-masters" followed certain rules of composition. "Where the windows were placed low on the walls the squares often showed well-populated scenes; where the windows were high above the ground the figures were generally larger and clearly separated."

The glass-worker's intricate task in producing the widely acclaimed Chartres Cathedral windows was described by Anne Huether in *Glass and Man:* "Small pieces of differently colored glass were cut, to form, when they were assembled, the desired picture or design. Details such as drapery folds and facial features were drawn on the glass with a solution of metallic oxides. The pieces of glass were then fired in a kiln, and the design became a permanent part of the glass. After cooling, these pieces of glass were joined together with grooved strips of lead. The lead strips outlined the design, separated the brilliant colors and held the pieces of glass in place."

In his volume *Stained Glass in America*, John Gilbert Lloyd traced the development and deterioration of decorative stained glass, from the early mosaics developed by the Byzantines and the early use of glass in Romanesque and Gothic churches "as a definite art form cloaked in the mysterious aura of early Christianity." Declining as a media under the humanistic influences of the Renaissance, when the painter usurped the craft from the artisan, pictorial scenes painted on white or clear glass were often passed off as true stained glass. By the sixteenth century the skills of the painter far overshadowed the efforts of the other artisans, and by the nineteenth century painters were dividing their tasks, some specializing in flesh tints, others in folds of drapery, and lowly apprentices assigned the task of rendering simple borders. He noted the nadir of the art, when European academicians obtained "a near stranglehold on the arts" and stained glass and mosaics were relegated to "a strict craft category." But with the new industrial era came the construction of lavish new churches and the renovation of old structures, many of which required stained-glass windows in the Gothic style. Ancient glass formulas were exhumed, and lead traceries were once again evident in some windows done in a traditional style amid a spate of painted scenes illustrating Biblical events and reproductions of the works of the "old masters."

There was a scholarly impetus in Europe, including valuable research conducted in ancient techniques and traditions by Charles Winston, an English lawyer, archaeologist and connoisseur of ancient glass. Viollet-le-Duc, who was responsible for restoring many ancient French cathedrals, included a section on stained glass in a monumental volume devoted to medieval architecture. Bavarian glass firms shipped to America quantities of glass as well as workmen to produce stereotyped "Munich windows," often depicting "heroic figures under ornate canopies, bordered by pillared halls." Indeed, the popularity of European windows and the campaigns conducted in some church groups apparently deliberately deprecating American workmanship, caused alarm in American art glass establishments.

Lloyd noted a trend early in the nineteenth century toward gaudier glass, marked, in the 1870's, by the contributions made by John La Farge and Louis C. Tiffany in opalescent glass. As early as 1835 a glassworks near Pittsburgh was apparently turning out opaque glass in quantity. A glassworks in Sandwich, Massachusetts, produced early tableware of a streaked, translucent type. Before the turn of the century colorful new shades such as apple green, opaque turquoise, sunburst and peachblow marked the dawn of the "art glass" decades.

An interest in Oriental textiles and ceramics also affected the pottery and glass produced in imitation of Oriental shapes, shades and glazes. Tiffany himself had a

[51]

lavish collection. At a sale of Chinese and Japanese porcelains in New York in 1886 an eight-inch vase in the collection of Mrs. Mary J. Morgan, which served as the prototype for many copies in tint and finish, brought a record sale price of $18,000. Such art wares as Amberina, Peachblow and Burmese in warm rosy shades were highly popular. Dorothy H. Jenkins noted in *A Fortune in the Junk Pile* that the spurt of production of novelty art glass in a remarkable spectrum of colors was the answer of eastern glass firms to the growing competition of midwestern glasshouses.

An obsession with the exotic arts of the Orient, Lloyd remarked, was manifest in heavy, gaudy, decorative churches supposedly duplicating ancient edifices, particularly suited, he felt, as repositories for the opaque and opalescent glass then beginning to find favor. American opaque glass had been characterized by a streaky, cloudy appearance, with bluish tinges at the edges. Rather brittle, it had a ruddy glow when held to the light. Although glass of this type had been used for vases, pitchers and ornaments, a new type known as opalescent glass was developed by La Farge and by Tiffany, who, declared Lloyd, "publicized and popularized the form to such an extent that it took the country by storm." Opalescent glass transmits little light and produces a dead color tone, hardly considered true stained glass at all, according to Mr. Lloyd, by most traditional craftsmen. La Farge apparently began his experiments in glass in 1876 in his Washington Square studio, experimenting there with the effect of blending pre-mixed colors. In opalescent glass various streaks of color, when fused, result in a milky-textured, iridescent appearance. La Farge occasionally inserted into opalescent panels bits of bottle bottoms or "glass jewels" in order to provide accents of translucent color.

Tiffany first combined opalescent glass with antique in a window made for the Episcopal Church of Islip, Long Island. He was determined to seek a means of incorporating brilliant colors and varied texture within the glass itself. He declared some years later in an article in *The Forum* ("American Art Supreme in Colored Glass," 1893) that he was more radically consistent in his rejection of paint and brush than medieval artists. He cited as inferior windows in which craftsmen used paint to suggest modeling and details. In so doing, he pointed out, the light was kept from coming through and the windows were less jewel-like than the ancient windows, which still retained their vivid tones after many centuries. He also later recalled some of his own initial difficulties in an article published in *Harper's Bazaar* ("The Quest of Beauty," December, 1917). "Glass covered with brushwork produces an effect both dull and artificial . . . I could not make an inspiring window with paint. I had to use a medium which appealed to me . . . How many years have I toiled to make drapery glass? My chemist and my furnace men for a long time insisted it was impossible, claiming that the metallic oxides would not combine, and that was the trouble for many years. The mix would disintegrate. New styles of firing ovens had to be built, new methods . . . for annealing the glass."

The process of producing colored glass was a complex one. Tiffany recalled that the glass manufacturers of his time were not able to give him the color and quality he desired. About 1880 New York City had nine manufacturers of window glass, nine of green glass and several of fine glass. Most of these were made from silica sand, mined in great quantities in the Berkshires. Mulling over the qualities of glass in everyday use, Tiffany discovered, as he remarked in "Color and Its Kinship to Sound," a speech made to the Rembrandt Club of Brooklyn and published as an article in *The Art World* in 1917, that the glass in preserve jars had a richer, more vibrant color than window glass and, "after puzzling out this curious matter, found that the glass from which bottles are made contains the Oxides of Iron and other impurities which are left in the sand when that is melted . . . Refining the pot-metal only made weak, uninteresting glass."

As explained by Anne Huether in *Glass and Man,* glass is a substance "produced by first fusing or melting together at a high temperature certain materials found in nature, then cooling the molten mixture in such a way that the atoms arrange themselves into a disordered, or non-crystalline, pattern. The chief raw materials are sand (about 99 percent silica), soda ash, potash, limestone, lead oxide, borax and boric acid . . . Metallic oxides, added in small amounts to clear-glass formulas, are used in the making of colored glass. Skill is required to insure uniformity in color. Cobalt oxide or copper in the form of cupric oxide will color glass blue. Iron oxide gives glass a greenish color, manganese oxide produces a violet color. Gold, copper or selenium can color glass red. Coke, coal or other carbonaceous oxides make an amber color; manganese, cobalt and iron can be combined to produce black glass."

Tiffany's earliest practical experiments were in the form of decorative glass tiles used for mantels and in lighting fixtures in some of the interiors decorated by the Associated Artists. These experiments were made in the Heidt glasshouse in Brooklyn, where John La Farge was also engaged in similar work. Some tiles were opaque, others opalescent and transparent, some had a metallic, iridized surface. Frequently a marbleized glass achieved a spiral effect or a subtle blend of colors, often the result of an accidental combination. The colors ranged from opalescent white to opaque black, with bright reds, blues and greens in many combinations. Facets and irregularities were sometimes used to vary the color density. Usually square in shape, the tiles were made in a variety of sizes, generally 1-, 3- and 4-inch, with an average thickness of ⅜ inch. Swirls, four-petal rosettes, dragons, geometric and irregular patterns were made by means of a mold or by a special pouring technique. No decoration was applied after the glass was cooled and annealed. The tiles were treated so that they would adhere to a plaster or cement backing by means of random holes or applied feet. The unmarked "turtle-back" tiles were of an irregular shape and thickness, made of amber or blue glass and coated with an iridescence, and were intended for use in lamps and lighting fixtures. After 1890 the special qualities developed for Tiffany tiles were utilized largely in stained-glass windows and mosaics.

Tiffany's early experiments resulted in an application for a patent. The earliest tiles were marked "Pat. Appl'd For," and then "Pat. Feb. 8th 1881 L.C.T.& Co.," but a great many were unmarked. Tiffany applied for three patents on October 25, 1880, which were granted in February of 1881. One of these dealt with the combination of types of glass in the manufacture of tiles and mosaics, another with a kind of plating used in windows, and the third with the use of a glass with a metallic luster, which was to be utilized in many of his products.

Tiffany's earlier work in glass was largely in the field of developing an ornamental glass for windows; his famous blown Favrile glass was not produced until 1893. The making of stained and painted glass for use in churches and other public buildings was, of course, not new in America. William Jay and John Bolton had designed and executed windows for several churches in New York, Scarborough, Pelham and Scandell. "The Adoration of the Magi" was made for their father's church, Christ Church, in Pelham, which was consecrated on September 15, 1843. According to John Gilbert Lloyd, the Bolton windows at St. Mary's Church, Beechwood, Scarborough, done in 1850 "in the painted, enameled style typical of the period, do not show the usual flowery sentimentality associated with Victorian art and glass work but are more reminiscent of the 16th-century Netherlands school." The windows are made up of pieces of painted glass with little lead work. The Boltons baked the glass themselves both for the windows of the Pelham church and for the windows of the armory room in their Gothic-style home, The Priory. William Bolton, trained as an engineer, had studied fresco painting and the art of stained glass in Italy, and had won the silver medal of the National Academy of Design in 1840, his talent having attracted the notice of Washington Irving. He taught himself the art of lead-framing and fitted stained glass into traceries, winning a commission for the windows of the Holy Trinity Church of Brooklyn Heights and for the Church of the Holy Apostles in New York City.

By 1857 the J. and R. Lamb Studios were established as glassmakers in New York City and competed effectively with importations from England and Germany. Some geometric-patterned windows from opalescent glass were made for Boston's Trinity Church by John La Farge in 1876. Tiffany's first windows for a New York church, the Church of the Sacred Heart on West 51st Street, were of the bull's-eye variety. This church was built in 1876; most of the original windows were replaced in 1951.

La Farge and Maitland Armstrong, often associated with La Farge in stained-glass and mosaic commissions, were, according to Armstrong's son, Hamilton Fish Armstrong, much attracted to glass by the opportunities it afforded for luminosity and depth of color. They developed new techniques, sometimes "plating" their windows with as many as three or four thicknesses for depth and color. In this, according to the younger Armstrong, their windows differed from the windows "later manufactured by commercial artisans which gave 'American glass' such a bad name." Although Tiffany and La Farge may have compared notes in the course of their experiments in Brooklyn, they apparently did not collaborate on any project.

Techniques used at that period to manipulate glass were described in an article referring to these two outstanding artists in *Scribner's Monthly* in January, 1881. "Believing that the ancient art of making pictures in stained glass, both with and without the use of paint, might be greatly improved, two of our American artists, Mr. John La Farge and Mr. Louis C. Tiffany, have turned their attention to this art and have not only produced new effects in this field of work, but have virtually introduced a new industry of the most promising and interesting character. . . . The use of glass of varying thickness is not new, but in the new method of work this is carried out in a manner that is entirely novel, and gives effects never before attained. The hot glass, while at a red heat, is rolled with corrugated rollers, punched and pressed by various roughened tools, or is squeezed and pressed up into corrugations by lateral pressure, or is stamped by dies. The 'bulls-eyes' produced in making sheet glass, by whirling it round on a rod while still soft, are also cut into various shapes or, while still soft, are gently pressed into new shapes. . . . Next to this comes a revival and modification of the old Venetian method of imbedding bits of colored glass in sheets of clear glass. This is done by scattering filaments and irregular bits of colored glass on the table on which plate glass is made, and then pouring the hot glass (either white or colored) over the table and rolling it down in the usual manner to press the colored threads or pieces into the sheet. New styles of opalescent glass, new methods of mixing colors in the glasshouse, have also been tried, and with many surprising and beautiful results. Lastly comes one of the most original features of all, and this is the use of solid masses and lumps of glass pressed while hot into moulds, giving a great number of facets like a cut stone, or by taking blocks of glass and roughly chipping them into numerous small faces. These, when set in the window, have all the effects of the most brilliant gems, changing their shade of color with every changing angle of vision."

Roger Riordan, a Baltimore painter and reviewer, also commented on the gemlike quality of glass made by Tiffany "for special purposes, over an inch in thickness; and rough-faceted glass, looking at a distance like the unpolished stones of Indian or old Gaulish jewelry, is much employed by him." He praised Tiffany's bold handling of glass in an article for the *American Arts Review* in 1881. "The simple shapes of the lower animals and plants are easily imitated . . . the forms indicated by the leading alone or . . . rendered with an almost illusive naturalness by the choice of wrinkled, bulging or concave pieces of glass . . . Mr. Tiffany's oriental leanings are well known. He is in favor of the boldest, strongest, most telling method . . . He speaks, as nature does, through the eye to the mind and the feelings, in a manner which is too little understood at present. . . . Mr. Tiffany handles his theme as boldly and naturally as he does his material. His way of regarding his subject implies his technique. He has carried the use of pure mosaic farther, perhaps, than it has ever been carried before . . . Mr. Tiffany has shown that . . . many of the most beautiful and poetic passages of landscape can be better represented in glass than in paint. Effects of rippled or quiet water, sunset and moonlit clouds, mysterious involutions of distant hills and woods, are given with a force and suggestiveness impossible in any other material, and without at all diminishing the solidity or decorative value of the window. To do this, as will readily be supposed, requires the subtlest art."

An article by Will H. Low in *Scribner's* in 1888 referred to stained-glass windows designed by himself, as well as by Tiffany, La Farge, Frank Millet, Frances Lathrop, Edwin Blashfield, Elihu Vedder, Kenyon Cox, Maitland Armstrong and others. It is difficult to distinguish a window made in the period by Tiffany's firm from those made by his many competitors unless some of his patented iridescent glass is included in the design. His glass was used by many craftsmen who worked in a style similar to Tiffany's. Thus, windows designed by such artists as Joseph Lauber, Frederick Wilson, Lydia Emmet and Frederick S. Church, although they may have been manufactured by Tiffany and may be called "Tiffany glass," have few or no special qualities. Frederick Wilson and Edward P. Sperry were responsible for a number of figure windows and J. A. Holzer, a specialist in mosaic, had been associated with La Farge before 1886. The best Tiffany windows made prior to 1890 are generally those of purely decorative and geometric design. Examples of such ornamental use of glass may be seen in the window given by the Mitchell family to the Church of St. James the Apostle in Westville, Connecticut, in 1885; the windows of the Union Reformed Church of Highbridge, Bronx, New York, installed in 1889; the rose window in Trinity Church, Lenox, Massachusetts, installed in 1890; and windows in the Peddie Memorial Baptist Church of Newark, New Jersey, also installed in 1890. By 1892 Tiffany windows could be found in churches in twenty-four states and in the District of Columbia. Tiffany supplied ornamental windows to the Smithsonian Institution, the Arno and Arlington Hotels and several churches in Washington, D. C. The Rittenhouse Memorial window, "Lilies," in St. John's Episcopal Church in Lafayette Square is by Tiffany.

[56]

If a window is unmarked in the lower right-hand corner or if an alteration has caused the loss of a mark, information may be obtained as to the possibility of its being a window from the Tiffany workshops by reference to three lists of windows made by Tiffany's firm. These were compiled and published in 1893, 1898 and 1910. Most Tiffany windows made before 1892 were marked "Tiffany Glass Co." Those produced between 1892 and 1900 usually bear the inscription "Tiffany Glass and Decorating Co." After 1900, either "Tiffany Studios" or "Louis C. Tiffany" appeared on many windows. The first list, issued in 1893, recorded some of the churches and public buildings in the United States where Tiffany's work could be seen. Since that time more than half of the churches in New York City in which Tiffany had a hand in the decoration have been demolished. A second pamphlet, which gave a more detailed list of some sixty pages, was published in 1898. A copy of this is in the Avery Library of Columbia University. The third one, *A Partial List of Windows*, appeared in 1910, with more than 100 pages of listings. A copy of this has been preserved in the Boston Public Library. An unpublished registry of windows made after 1927 was compiled by Tiffany Studios.

Windows made for private customers are often difficult to identify. A knowledge of the type of work executed by Tiffany's firm for ecclesiastical interiors is often helpful in establishing certain recognizable features, but many of these hallmarks are so subtle that they can be recognized only by careful observation. Good examples of Tiffany-produced domestic windows may be found today at a fraction of their original cost. However, many inferior windows of the Tiffany type are also currently being offered which have little or no aesthetic worth.

The prediction made by Donald G. Mitchell at the time of the Centennial that "a window with rich designs would be a perpetual delight" was taken up by many besides those "who looked only on dingy courts." Increased vistas of stained glass embellished shops, houses, flats, even the depots of the elevated railway, "poor as the specimens may be, on every side of the city." *Harper's Magazine* had commented on the attractions of colorful glass in an article in October, 1878: ". . . the ancient and long-approved method of decoration furnished by painted glass is again taking its proper rank. Certainly the translucence of glass enables the art collector, if he carefully and fittingly uses it, to surpass all the other decorations of his room in special attractiveness. The window, being the opening to admit light, is always the first attraction to catch the eye. The deep warmth of the ruby, the tender contentment of the sapphire, the glow and coruscation of the amethyst, the brilliancy and cheerfulness of the emerald, the glitter and distinctiveness of the diamond, may all be summoned to the satisfaction of the least cultivated eye by the infinite wealth of the glass-stainer's art."

Robert W. de Forest, son of the lawyer for Tiffany & Company, was one of the first to own a Tiffany-designed window, as well as a painting by Tiffany. "The first painting I ever bought was by Tiffany's hand." He recalled the chief feature of the window as "the use of translucent quartz pebbles, which he and I picked up together on the beach at Montauk." Many critics believed Tiffany to be at his best in designs of an abstract character. John Ruskin preferred random designs and pebble-clusters to the fashionable figure windows. In "Modern Manufacture and Design" he commented that "No man who knows what painting means can endure a painted glass window which emulates painter's work. But he rejoices in a glowing mosaic of broken colour; for that is what the glass has the special gift and right of producing." Julius Meier-Graefe, a German-French art critic, publisher and dealer, admired Tiffany's marvelous mastery of technique but was not overly impressed by his designs. Herwin Schaefer, in his critical analysis of Tiffany's effect on European artists and craftsmen, declared Tiffany's designs in stained glass marked a significant departure from painted figure windows, noting a parallel step taken by the post-Impressionist painters in which soft transitions were eliminated and form was broken up and areas of color set one against the other by black leading. In the opinion of John Gilbert Lloyd, Tiffany's windows were characterized "by brilliantly colored scenes, highly realistic, artistic designs and almost a fruity use of shape and color. Constantly striving to improve his glass coloring for faces and drapery, which in Europe were painted or enameled on, he gave more life to stained glass than it had in ages. Although stylized and dated, Tiffany windows established a precedent and affected the public taste and preference for decades to come." Maurice Grosser commented that he used translucent marbleized glass in a manner not unlike modern *collage* to supply modeling and to suggest natural textures which, if "harsh in design and vapid in sentiment, were always rich in color and varied in texture." Cecilia Waern, who contributed a series of articles on American craftsmen of the nineties to *The Studio*, admired the quality and beauty of Tiffany's glass but felt there was no real need for "elaborately designed, pictorial windows with a material of this intrinsic value . . . the results still leave much to be desired. The texture is too luscious, the treatment too pictorial, the designs not important enough. The work is a . . . translation from a sketch; the medium still awaits the artist that shall make it his own. Mr. Tiffany has done his part in providing noble resources."

A THEATRICAL INTERLUDE

The impetus for the gratifying commercial success of Tiffany's firm, the prospering Tiffany Glass Company, established late in 1885, to supply windows of every description, could be traced to the intervention of Charles L. Tiffany into Louis C. Tiffany's affairs. The younger Tiffany had taken his wife and children for a holiday (his first in five years) in St. Augustine, Florida, in the spring of 1883, but it was too late for Mary Woodbridge Tiffany, who had been in poor health for some years. She died in New York, despite having undergone the open-air treatment then prescribed for diseases of the chest, on January 22, 1884. They had been a devoted couple, sharing their innermost thoughts and dreams, and Tiffany never again found anyone in whom he could have such absolute confidence. Much of his energy and ambition during the last decade of her life had sprung from the hope that a way could be found to make her strong once again. Now, after only a dozen years of marriage, Louis C. Tiffany found himself a widower, with three children, the eldest of whom was not yet eleven.

Tiffany had made his mark as a painter and as a decorator, he had begun his work with glass tiles and stained-glass windows, but he himself was not satisfied that he was on the right track in his profession. Until his father stepped in with diversionary tactics, Louis Tiffany suddenly found himself embroiled in the "gay white way." He had had by now his fill of catering to the whims of opinionated, wealthy clients. Although he was impressed by the success of Tiffany & Company, he wanted to retain his independence and he did not want to abandon art to become burdened with financial matters. Yet he was to find himself in deeper financial shoals. Tiffany's friend Steele MacKaye with whom he had worked on the curtain of the Madison Square Theater was now contemplating opening a new theater, which was to be called the Lyceum. Tiffany and his two most steady companions, MacKaye and Stanford White, were soon a familiar trio in theatrical circles. Tiffany enjoyed the enthusiastic admiration of his contemporaries and became popular with the young ladies in the chorus. He indulged for a while in fast and fancy living, but he was too energetic and too ambitious for this to last for long.

MacKaye had befriended Oscar Wilde during Wilde's tour of America. The two had hoped to build an ideal theater "according to the highest standards of aesthetics and art," but failed to raise the necessary funds for such a project. Oscar Wilde had also made his opinions known on the state of the art of decoration in

America. "Your people love art," he had declared, "but do not honor the handicrafts-man. Of course, those millionaires who can pillage Europe for their pleasure need have no care to encourage such; but I speak for those whose desire for beautiful things is larger than their means. I find one great trouble all over is that your workmen are not given to noble designs. You cannot be indifferent to this, because art is not something which you can take or leave. It is a necessity of human life.

"And what is the meaning of this beautiful decoration which we call art? In the first place it means value to the workman and it means the pleasure which he must necessarily take in making a beautiful thing. The mark of all good art is not that the thing is done exactly or finely, for machinery may do as much, but that it is worked out with the head and the workman's heart. I cannot impress the point too frequently that beautiful and rational designs are necessary in all work."

He had singled out a work by Tiffany for praise. In his review of *An Unequal Match*, which appeared in *The World* of November 7, 1882, Wilde had said, "A scene is primarily a decorative background for the actors and should be kept always subordinate, first to the players, their dress, feature and action, and secondly, to the fundamental principle of decorative art, which is not to imitate, but to suggest nature . . . and from the same master hand which designed the curtain at the Madison Square Theater I would like very much to see a good decorative landscape in scene painting." Certainly he must have learned from Steele MacKaye that this master hand had been Louis C. Tiffany's.

There had been some prior discussion between MacKaye and John La Farge, who was currently engaged in a vast church decoration project, on the decoration of the new theater, but when Tiffany offered to supply the decoration for a percentage of the profits, this put La Farge out of the picture. Their professional rivalry was to grow ever more intense. La Farge, Augustus St.-Gaudens and Stanford White were all consulted about this time on the decoration of the fortress-like thirteenth-century Gothic church of St. Paul the Apostle in New York, with massive columns framing a wide nave, octagonal pillars alternating with Romanesque, and groined arches vault-ing aisles outside the columns. La Farge, who sought to create the impression of a roof-less church, endeavored in the coloring of the clerestory windows to effect a transition from brown and various shades of green to the dark blue of a starry ceiling. Besides various windows he supplied a mural and a baptistry. Above the main portal and im-mediately below La Farge's lancet windows extended a mural, "The Crucifixion," by William Laurel Harris, over fifty-five feet high and extending almost the full width of the nave. In a series of small murals below it the Twelve Apostles were represented by twelve white lambs, and a recumbent figure of the Saviour was framed on each side by a phœnix, adopted by the early Christians as a symbol of immortality and often found in the frescoes of the Catacombs. For this church Stanford White designed several altars, including a Byzantine-style high altar of marble, onyx and alabaster, with mosaic bases for eight columns of colored porphyry supporting a golden baldachin. Kneeling angels above the high altar were complemented by four angels encircling a huge bronze sanctuary lamp designed by the sculptor Philip Martigny.

Tiffany, eager to get on with the new Lyceum Theater, had reorganized his business into a three-man firm, with John Cheney Platt and William Pringle Mitchell, the son of Donald G. Mitchell, as junior partners. The new firm signed a contract on January 6, 1885 with Steele MacKaye and Gustave Frohman of the American Theatre Building and Management Company, agreeing to furnish, for $50,000, labor and materials to be used in the decoration of the new Lyceum Theater, next to the National Academy of Design. It was the first theater to be lighted completely by electric light. Thomas A. Edison helped to install the fixtures and footlights. A new type of folding seat, which had been invented by MacKaye, was installed.

The theater opened on April 6, 1885, with the play *Dakolar*, written by Steele MacKaye. An article in the New York *Morning Journal* proclaimed, "*Wilde Outdone by MacKaye:* The Gorgeous Lyceum Theater Opens." Tiffany's touch was evident. The article commented, "It belongs to no school unless the ultra-aesthetic—the school of Wilde outdone by MacKaye . . . Everything was a departure from the hackneyed forms of theatrical decoration. The electric light from the clustered globes pendant from the ceiling is soft and pleasantly diffused. Similar lights smoulder under green sconces along the face of the gallery, like fire in monster emeralds . . . But these things are not obtrusive. A master hand has blent them into a general effect, avoiding all aggressive detail."

Had Tiffany followed Wilde's dictum that there should be a "cultured despot" in command? In his essay, "The Truth of Masks: A Note on Illusion," Wilde had declared, "Nor, again, is it enough that there should be accurate and appropriate costumes of beautiful colours; there must be also beauty of colour on the stage as a whole, and as long as the background is painted by one artist, and the foreground figures independently designed by another, there is the danger of a want of harmony in the scene as a picture. For each scene the colour-scheme should be settled as absolutely as for the decoration of a room, and the textures which it is proposed to use should be mixed and re-mixed in every possible combination, and what is discordant removed." Wilde went on to say, "As a rule, the hero is smothered in bric-a-brac and palm trees, lost in the gilded abyss of Louis Quatorze furniture, or reduced to a mere midge in the midst of marqueterie; whereas the background should always be kept as a background, and colour subordinated to effect. This, of course, can only be done when there is one single hand directing the whole production. The facts of art are diverse, but the essence of artistic effect is unity. Monarchy, Anarchy, and Republicanism may contend for the government of nations; but a theatre should be in the

[*61*]

power of a cultured despot. There may be division of labour, but there must be no division of mind. . . . In fact, in art there is no specialism, and a really artistic production should bear the impress of one master, and one master only, who . . . should design and arrange everything."

But *Dakolar*, on whose success rested Tiffany's hope of reimbursement for the lavish decoration of the interior, ran only two months. Not only was there no percentage of profits for Tiffany; there was not even enough money to pay the bills. Louis C. Tiffany and Co. took a lien on the property and sued. On August 28, 1885, the Lyceum Theater was sold at auction by order of the Supreme Court of New York. Tiffany was the purchaser, for $21,000, from which he was awarded $20,500 as a settlement and $332.26 for costs. He remained as owner until the new manager, Daniel Frohman, was able to put it on a paying basis and buy it for himself. The theater remained in operation until 1902, when it was demolished. It had set a new style in theater decoration. The first "art theater" in which principles of interior decoration were carried out, it was a reflection of the aesthetic movement which began with Whistler and paved the way for Art Nouveau. Louis Sullivan, who, as designer for the architectural firm of Adler and Sullivan, drew plans two years later for the Chicago Auditorium, may have known of the Wilde-MacKaye dream of "an ideal theater, to be fitted with the most modern improvements . . . in the same building a hotel, the profits of which would take care of any deficits in the theatrical end." Sullivan, who had studied at L'Ecole des Beaux Arts in Paris, may also have seen the Lyceum interior and the Veterans' Room and Library of the Armory. Some of Sullivan's architectural ornament featuring Celtic and East Indian motifs can be traced to such artistic interiors in vogue during the early 1880's. MacKaye, who had established the Lyceum School of Acting, the predecessor of the American Academy of Dramatic Arts, died in 1894, after failing to secure capital for a cyclorama, depicting the life of Columbus, at the Chicago World's Fair.

For Tiffany, this excursion into the theater represented the sudden loss of his savings after a decade of hard work. His work now took on a more dramatic quality and he became more than ever a showman. He considered himself a connoisseur of the theater and followed with interest the activities of such personalities as Sarah Bernhardt and Lillian Russell. He liked to organize theatrical entertainments and scenic tableaux. He provided a glass dome and window for David Belasco's studio some years later. But he had discovered that he was not satisfied after all with a career in the theater. He would have to start all over again.

Meanwhile, Charles L. Tiffany had become increasingly concerned with the "fast company" his eldest son was keeping. Annie Tiffany had married and settled down in New Haven, but the younger Tiffany children were still under the parental wing. He announced that he would build a house in New York where the Tiffanys could all live together under one roof. The "artistic" son, Louis, would be in full charge of the plans. The mansion at 72nd Street and Madison Avenue was erected before the end of 1885 at a cost of $100,000. Louis C. Tiffany selected a Richardsonian style, made a few rough sketches and retained Stanford White and the firm of McKim, Mead and White to work out the details. The house had a massive arched entrance with a grill and porte-cochere, an elevator, balconies and loggias. Tiffany reserved the top floors for a studio and apartments for himself and his children.

In a description of some of the great houses of New York before the turn of the century, Grace Mayer singled out the Tiffany mansion on Madison Avenue, once known as "The Avenue of the Gods" because of the churches dotting its length. Tiffany, in fact, decorated the neighboring St. James' Lutheran Church, at 73rd Street and Madison Avenue, which was erected in 1890. In her book about New York City, *Once Upon a City*, she described it at length, quoting the English critic Edmund Gosse's remarks. "The Tiffany house in Madison Avenue is the one that pleased me most in America." Gosse admired its vastness, "as if it had grown like a mountain," called it "a realization of an architect's dream" and thought it "the most beautiful modern domestic building I have almost ever seen."

"Commissioned, but," according to Miss Mayer, "by obstinate choice never occupied by Charles Lewis Tiffany, this Romanesque apartment-mansion bore the impress of McKim, Mead and White. Stanford White brought to it the benefit of his recent training under H. H. Richardson, and out of his collaboration with his patron artist's son (designer of the roof, with its two superimposed stories, and decorator of the whole), evolved the inspired originality of this house, superb in its many improvisations, its ornamental use of terra-cotta and the long narrow bricks of the upper floors, with their soft, broken color gradations in light brown and muted yellow . . . its portcullised entrance facing the white frame simplicity of the Lenox farmhouse, sole occupant of the block to the immediate south, with the Hunt-designed Presbyterian Hospital at 71st Street and the notable Marquand home just below, at 68th Street. The house . . . continued to shelter, among others, its original family (overlapping into the connecting 898 Madison Avenue) until the death of Louis C. Tiffany. . . . This house of many mansions, all on different planes and levels, was in accord with the ramifications of its creator's enveloping genius, for Louis Comfort Tiffany was . . . a man who, while so much of and ahead of his time, would have been at home in the days of the Medici."

Tiffany continued to occupy the top-floor studio, remodeling it in 1904, and the connecting apartment, as his town residence until the day of his death. Here, for many decades, he lavishly entertained friends and fellow artists. Here he raised a second family. The comfortable home his father provided gave him an identity, an outlet that, in part, compensated for other disappointments and losses. He was able to reorganize his own business quickly. With the help of his father's sound advice and good business judgment he was soon actively engaged once again in managing his own affairs.

GLASS FOR THE MANY

From this time on, Tiffany declared war on convention and boldly struck off on his own. The same restless impatience that had so often controlled his decisions came to the fore again. The new reorganized business was to be unique, putting to shame ordinary decorators, and proving to his friends and associates that he had not abandoned art. In time he would produce pictures in glass which he believed to be more beautiful and more lasting than any which could be rendered in mere paint. He would go beyond windows to other decorative and useful items. He had a yearning to appeal to a vast audience even larger than that beyond the footlights.

His future course now became quite clear. He would surround himself with talented young people whom he would educate as he himself had been educated —by exposure to beautiful objects. His would be an atelier like that of Della Robbia or Rubens, where he would act as the master and where they would produce beautiful objects that could be seen and enjoyed in public as well as in private places. His methods were novel, although the same system was later to be adopted by Elbert Hubbard, "The Genius of Roycroft," and by Frank Lloyd Wright and might even be considered the genesis of the concept which flowered in the German *Bauhaus* under Walter Gropius.

It gave Tiffany a basis for his claim that he was the first American industrial artist to design for the modern age. For his designs there were to be no fundamental rules, no classical formulas. Sources of inspiration could be found in the world of nature, but copying was to be discouraged. Each work was to be a unique, personal expression. Freshness and individuality were considered the "mark of truth" and the main selling-point for his products. He planned to expand from leaded-glass windows to lamps and other objects of glass and metal. This venture indeed proved new and daring enough to satisfy his independent nature and to keep him occupied for the next three decades. In it he was to find the satisfaction of providing for a vast audience the visual excitement that he himself enjoyed from the effective blending of color and form. This offered much more of a personal challenge than either painting or decorating. It was art for a museum without walls, a true art industry.

In his later years he was to expound, in the volume on his career which he more or less dictated to Charles de Kay, upon the need of the people for finely made objects of daily use and upon the "false" homage lavished on the practitioner of the fine arts over the artists and craftsmen who worked in the applied arts. "Many painters and sculptors began as craftsmen. The latter are nearer the people, for they fabricate useful objects belonging to daily life, while the artist who produces objects of the fine arts, so called, is more remote. His work usually demands on the part of the observer a longer education for its appreciation. There lies a gap between the people and objects of pure art which forces the artist-painter into a narrow sphere and compels him to seek the restricted public of amateurs and connoisseurs.

"It is this apparent exclusiveness and aristocracy in the fine arts which has given room for much error and helped impede the course of art in modern times. The inference has been drawn that objects of art without any practical end in themselves, objects without direct usefulness, are necessarily of higher value than such commonplace things as tools, utensils and weapons, table ornaments and furniture, objects used as personal decorations. These last are regarded as non-esthetic and therefore inferior to things of pure or fine art like a symbolical picture, a heroic statue, a church window. As a crowning touch to this tendency to establish a system of caste in the realm of esthetics we get the cry 'art for art's sake' along with some of the most childish and insincere grotesques the world has ever seen."

He foresaw a new importance for the arts and crafts. He freely admitted he had followed first one road, then another, in art "without heeding the formulas of his fellows," who, he said, "seemed always singularly enraged if one of the fraternity deviated from the unwritten rules of the gild." There were also new art patrons, he believed. "In place of the church, the king, the noble, the millionaire, we have the broad masses, educated as well as the foregoing on the whole, if not better than they, and perhaps less open to prejudices and conventions, more unsophisticated, less self-conscious, readier to give ear to any new message that may come from far or near.

"Art for the people, if we may judge by the past, is sure to be freer from tradition than that of the bygone schools and is likely to have a larger element of the useful. In other words, the arts and crafts will gain, relatively speaking, on the fine arts. Already are legislative halls, railway stations and opera houses liable to be not only costlier but more beautiful than the palaces of the rich, even than the homes of religion. One sees a definite stream setting away from easel pictures and household marbles toward as beautiful walls, hangings, furniture and table-silver as the age can produce. While there is still a great and increasing demand for mural painting, owing to the erection of municipal and governmental buildings whose architecture demands such adornments, the field for painters has broadened out so tremendously

[65]

during the past half century that the old limitations imposed by artists on their own gild have gone by the board. As to those who cling to the view that art lies only in the hands of painters and sculptors, their patrons are tending to become relatively fewer as time goes on. No profession is more overcrowded. Clients do not keep increasing; it is rather the other way."

The justification for Tiffany's own wide diversification was underlined still further. "His (Tiffany's) taste in color has found expression in a thousand articles of applied art; these, occupying prominent places in households, have exercised a happy influence on the taste of citizens . . . The fact that things of daily use like lamps, flower-vases and toilet articles reach a wider public than do paintings and sculpture makes the 'decorative' arts more important to a nation than the 'fine' arts. Hence the value to a community of artists who devote their talent to making things of use beautiful. They are educators of the people in the truest sense, not as school-masters laying down the law, but as masters of art appealing to the emotions and the senses and rousing enthusiasm for beauty in one's environment."

An Artist-Artisan Institute was founded in the late nineteenth century by John Ward Stimson, a painter and writer, and was sponsored by, among others, Tiffany's former associate, Candace Wheeler. Stimson's school, which provided a stimulus toward the development of the arts and crafts movement in America, was an early effort toward training the industrial worker as an artist and toward persuading the artist to turn his attention to industrial needs. Stimson's lectures and a review of the work of the Institute were compiled in a textbook entitled *The Gate Beautiful*. The New York Society of Craftsmen, founded in 1905, represented the individual artistic craft worker and sought to bring before the public craftsmen of note who aimed to make useful articles beautiful as well as mechanically and technically perfect.

Frank Lloyd Wright, Sullivan's pupil, "foresaw a possible salvation for the craftsman in his humbly learning from the machine," and declared in 1901 in *The Art and Craft of the Machine*, "Rightly used, the very curse machinery puts upon handi-craft should emancipate the artists from temptation to petty structural deceit and this wearisome struggle to make things seem what they never can be." To William Morris, production by machinery was "altogether an evil." To Walter Crane, Morris' disciple, the desirable aim was "to turn our artists into craftsmen and our craftsmen into artists." Actually, the arts and crafts movement, according to Nikolaus Pevsner, author of *Pioneers of Modern Design*, "brought a revival of artistic crafts-manship, not of industrial art."

A PROPER SETTING

The English architect C. R. Ashbee maintained a school and guild of handicrafts where students executed designs under his personal supervision, as described in the German publication *Dekorative Kunst* in 1898. Before establishing the ideal American atelier that Tiffany envisioned, where he could imbue his assistants with his personal concepts of beauty, which would be embodied in beautiful objects, he decided it was time to set his own household in order. The second Mrs. Tiffany was Louise Wakeman Knox, a cousin of Julia de Forest and the daughter of a Presbyterian minister. They were married on November 9, 1886, and she was readily accepted even by the devout Congregationalists of the Tiffany family. The new Mrs. Tiffany was a quiet woman, a devoted wife and a good mother. She gave a great deal of time to charitable activities and never interfered in her husband's business.

Following his marriage Louis C. Tiffany threw himself into his work with renewed vigor, much to his father's satisfaction. His own golden wedding a few years later was perhaps the proudest moment in the life of Charles L. Tiffany. Louis was back on his feet again, there were new grand-daughters, including a set of twins. One child, named for Annie Olivia Tiffany, lived only four years. Louise Knox Tiffany did her best to show equal affection for both her own children and her stepchildren. Tiffany painted her with the vast 72nd Street studio as a background. The interplay of curved, sensuous forms, creating a sense of growth and warmth, makes his portrait of his wife an outstanding example of Art Nouveau painting in America. Rendered in Whistlerian, thin, warm tones, it captured the essential quality of the flickering light which he embodied in the myriad glass objects produced under his careful supervision.

The studio was photographed at the time of the elder Tiffanys' golden wedding, November 30, 1891, when they were given an anniversary window featuring a golden horn of plenty by Louis and Louise Tiffany. In an article in *Interiors* (December, 1957), Edgar Kaufmann, Jr., marveled at its rich polyglot nature. "What a mixture there is: rugs and pelts, pots, oil paintings, peasant chairs and porch wicker, multitudes of lamps, an ostrich egg, a vast wrought-iron bracket, tiers of balconies and clusters of columns accent a room rounded as if by the sweep of some giant hand, whose fingertips curved the arches and ribbed the chimney in clay. A master rhythm yet pervades—the eye if dazzled is not lost. The rugs and hanging lamps are not mosque-like any more than the architecture is Byzantine; this is a free development of interlocking traditional themes—a *passacaglia* for the eye. No mere revivalist could have spun this shimmering web, yet no one ignorant of the great spatial adventures of the past could have conceived the task either."

[67]

In *The Art Work of Louis C. Tiffany*, a monograph written in 1912, illustrated in 1913, and published privately by Tiffany in 1914, the rich details of the interior were recalled by its decorator. "Harsh lines of the roof-tree were overcome by the use of concrete and plaster ... All the flues for chimneys had to find their exit through the roof. To meet this difficulty they were assembled in the center of the studio and the stack to which they converged was made one of the chief decorative features. With brick and concrete this stack was modeled into a shaft as easy of line as the bole of a great tree. On four sides fireplaces were hollowed out so that the wide and lofty studio is lighted up at night in every direction by smouldering log fires ... At night the glow from the hearths lights up the brightest of the vases and bowls and plaques, gleams with dull, rich notes on copper and bronze and throws wide spaces of the irregular apartment into deep shadow . . . Great windows of dull greenish-yellow glass in the sloping roof filter the daylight. At night suspended lamps of Japanese bronze and Favrile glass, of many shades of red, rose, yellow and creamy white, are foiled against the blackness of the high roof-ceiling. An organ loft, above the main entrance to the studio, is full of growing flowers and large Oriental vases. Colored tiles and the cinnabar red so much loved by the Japanese, iridescent glass and shelves full of keramics in subdued tones meet the eye in every direction."

Below this studio on a grand scale were a great ballroom, a dining room and a breakfast room. The spacious, high-ceilinged rooms provided an ideal arrangement for balls and receptions. Tiffany filled the house with beautiful things. In the words of the monograph's anonymous scribe: "Loving the objects for their own sakes, he added one to the other because he could not bear to exile any." However, the account continued, "his fine taste avoided the error of so placing them that they interfered with the ease of living among them."

The ballroom contained wall cases on each side of a broad hearth containing rare Oriental porcelains and examples of Tiffany glass. A Persian-style niche featured a glass mosaic with a floral design and a composition of peacocks "surpassing in richness of tones any single other ornament." The dining room featured a massive table, sideboards on which silver was displayed, a wide hearth with a severely treated mantel filled with various *objets d'art*. In the breakfast room were windows filled with glass that simulated flowers and twining plants. The jambs and casement of frames of a bay window were decorated with Japanese sword guards, a part of Tiffany's extensive collection.

No visitor to Tiffany's abode could fail to appreciate the luxuriant atmosphere of what might be called a "decorative jungle." Cecilia Waern noted in *The Studio* that his studio contained "the whole street-front of a house in India combined with a truly gorgeous American window, with lamps, chains, plants of many lands.". It seemed like a dream to Alma Mahler Werfel, who recalled her visit to Tiffany's 72nd Street house in her book, *And The Bridge Is Love*.

"Shortly after the founding of Mahler's orchestra we received a card from Louis Tiffany. He wrote that he was afraid of people; could he attend rehearsals unseen? Mahler granted the request and so we were invited to a party at Tiffany's.

"We drove to his mansion with Mrs. Havemeyer, walked up a palatial flight of stairs and up another flight between walls with complete Sudanese Negro huts built into them on each side. At the top at last we found ourselves in a hall so vast it seemed boundless. Suspended in the dusk we saw luminous colored glasses that shed a wondrous, flowery light. An organist was playing the prelude to *Parsifal*.

"We thought we were alone. A black chimney with four immense fireplaces, each ablaze with flames of a different hue, rose in the center of the hall. We stood transfixed.

"A man with a fine head appeared, murmuring unintelligibly—it was Tiffany, who never spoke—and before we could get a good look at him, let alone answer, he vanished.

"He seemed enchanted, like everything in that place. The chimney soared into infinity. No ceiling was visible, but high above us there were Tiffany glasses set in the walls, transparent and illuminated from outside. We spoke in whispers. We felt as though one might fly into Paradise through these panes of flowery light. The organ fell silent; suddenly a hum of muffled voices indicated a large company. Servants passed soundlessly, carrying trays of beautiful, champagne-filled glasses. We saw palms, divans, lovely women in oddly iridescent gowns. It was a dream: Arabian nights in New York."

VISTAS OF GLASS

In order to provide such a luxurious Arabian Nights atmosphere by night Tiffany conducted a thriving business by day, attending to all orders promptly. The Tiffany Glass Company discouraged individual clients, catering primarily to architects and rapidly building a reputation for providing stained glass windows of the finest quality. The firm had been officially incorporated, on December 1, 1885, with Tiffany as president, Pringle Mitchell as business manager, John Du Fais as secretary, Benjamin F. McKinley and John Cheney Platt as trustees, to "provide the manufacture of glass and other materials and the use and adaptation of the same to decorative and other artistic work of all kinds." On December 15, 1886 a sum of $50,000 was paid for "the business, good will and firm assets of the late firm of Louis C. Tiffany and

[*69*]

Company." The stock value was set at $105,000 and divided into 1,050 shares, the certificate being prepared and filed by Henry W. de Forest for the firm of De Forest and Weeks. On March 24, 1887, the capital stock was decreased to $90,000 and divided into 900 shares of $100 par. Henry W. de Forest was named chairman of the board. Although the company did not show a profit it continued to grow and was reorganized under the name of the Tiffany Glass and Decorating Company in 1892. A report filed by the Tiffany Glass Company on January 27, 1892, showed a capital stock of $90,000 and assets valued at $239,407.64, consisting of "its plant and stock in trade used in connection with the manufacture of glass and the transaction of a general decorating business." Receipts for 1891 amounted to $450,833.74, but expenditures totaled $454,633.34.

Many leading architects gave Tiffany orders for various kinds of interiors and for stained-glass windows, which became more and more popular as the century moved toward its end. Stanford White, who had favored La Farge until they had a disagreement over the decoration of the Church of the Ascension in New York, awarded his glass work to Tiffany after 1888. Among the architects who employed the services of Tiffany's firm were Thomas Hastings of Carrère and Hastings, who had met Tiffany when working for the Herter Brothers in the decoration of the Seventh Regiment Armory in New York, Charles C. Haight, J. C. Cady, W. Halsey Wood, William A. Potter and Robert H. Robertson. When the millionaire Henry M. Flagler decided to develop Florida as a resort, the firm of Carrère and Hastings was given the job of designing the Ponce de Leon Hotel in St. Augustine, with Bernard Maybeck as one of the designers and Louis C. Tiffany as the decorator. The Ponce de Leon was opened early in 1888, and its acclaim led to many more such orders. Many of the features of this hotel served as sources of inspiration for Tiffany when he later designed a palatial country estate for himself.

The commercial success of his firm necessitated the regular services of additional designers to meet the great demand for stained-glass windows. Tiffany did not regard himself as adequate as a painter of figures, but many painters skilled in rendering anatomy and draperies sought such commissions. All commissions Tiffany considered important were, however, given his personal attention and often made according to his design. Among his fellow artists Tiffany's reputation was beginning to decline and he was to be increasingly accused of commercialism. His foremost rival, John La Farge, was having some trouble making ends meet. After an exhibition in England, where his work was acclaimed, his efforts found greater favor in America. St. Peter's Roman Catholic Church in New York City had declined to accept either his "Madonna" or "St. John," and his canvases in a Japanese manner found no buyers. After studying the stained glass in ancient French cathedrals he executed a window,

"The Presentation in the Temple," for the Church of the Ascension, painted frescoes for the chancel of St. Thomas' and decorated the Brick Church, all in New York City. He also provided windows for William K. Vanderbilt and for Whitelaw Reid and ornate ceilings for Cornelius Vanderbilt.

By the late 1880's, Tiffany found that in addition to the vogue for windows the demand for mosaics seemed to be growing apace. This in part reflected a Byzantine revival sparked by Sardou's play *Theodora*, starring Sarah Bernhardt in Paris and New York as Justinian's empress. Tiffany had experimented with mosaics as early as 1880 while engaged in decorating the Union League Club, but the techniques associated with the Byzantine-revival churches of this era were first utilized in mosaic decorations made by J. A. Holzer for the Osborne Apartments on West 57th Street in New York City, which were completed in 1886.

The Tiffany mosaic technique, which utilized iridescent glass, mother-of-pearl and transparent tesserae backed with gold or metal leaf, was undertaken in its preliminary stages within the studio and later mounted directly on a wall. "Pieces of glass were selected, cut out and assembled upon the working drawing, then reassembled, face downward, upon a table and covered with cement mortar to form a slab with the glass imbedded in its surface . . . the mortar backing, being white, reflected the light through the glass in a softly luminous effect." Cecilia Waern, writing for *The Studio*, felt that to many Tiffany's ornate mosaic and inlay work was "overripe and heavy, with a tendency to somewhat cloying sweetness." Between 1889 and 1893 Tiffany's firm was asked to decorate the interiors of at least five churches, two in New York City, one in Troy, New York, one in Providence, Rhode Island, and one in Boston, Massachusetts. In all of these, mosaics were used extensively, under the supervision of J. A. Holzer. Windows were also designed by E. P. Sperry and Frederick Wilson. Tiffany himself had little to do with these interiors except to approve their designs.

His decorating business continued to operate during the eighties and nineties, but on a lesser scale than when Candace Wheeler had been associated with him. In 1896 the firm decorated the new library for Pratt Institute in Brooklyn. According to a contemporary description of the new building, which had been designed by William B. Tubby in a "Renaissance palace revival style," the Tiffany Glass and Decorating Company produced a "particularly attractive *ensemble*, with oak woodwork, softly tinted walls and ceilings in soft yellows, creams, buffs, terra-cottas and yellow-greens, marble columns with yellow shafts and red pedestals and the entrance-hall and corridors paved with stone mosaic." This library contained the first children's room.

During the last decade of the century Tiffany was devoting most of his time to a few special commissions and to the affairs of his expanding business. One decorating commission in which he took an active personal part was the decoration of the Henry O. Havemeyer house. The other projects which appealed most to him were special windows.

The architect for the Havemeyer mansion at 848 Fifth Avenue was Charles Coolidge Haight, who had worked with Tiffany in 1884 on the renovation of the Leonard Jerome house at Madison Avenue and 26th Street when it was adapted for use by the Manhattan Club. The Havemeyers had specified that they wanted interiors by Tiffany. Samuel Colman, a friend of Mrs. Havemeyer's, came out of semi-retirement in Newport to work with his former associate. Mrs. Havemeyer proved to be Tiffany's most sympathetic client, and the result was one entirely to his taste. The decoration was in a style similar to that used by Tiffany in his Kemp salon a decade earlier. Here were the same Indian chairs and tables, wrought-iron hangings, Japanese wallpapers and Chinese bric-a-brac, but this time they were more effectively blended.

In her book *The Proud Possessors*, Aline B. Saarinen provides a description: "Mrs. Havemeyer was thrilled that the Byzantine chapels of Ravenna inspired 'our white mosaic hall and ten pillars at the entrance of our gallery,' and that the staircase derived from the one in the Doges' Palace. . . . The walls of the music room were covered with Chinese embroideries. On the blue and gold Chinese rugs stood special, richly carved furniture rubbed with gold leaf and varnish to look like the ivory *inro* that inspired it. The furniture and the woodwork in the library were based on Viking designs and Celtic motifs. In order to stain the oak woodwork the exact color of a Japanese lacquer panel he admired, Mr. Colman invented a system of acid staining that intrigued Mrs. Havemeyer so much she busily diverted herself for many years experimenting with it. . . . The library ceiling was a sensation. . . . In his Newport studio Mr. Colman fashioned a mosaic design of multicolored silks, outlined them with heavy braid and framed panels with carved gold moldings. . . The two-story upstairs gallery . . . became a topic of animated conversation by virtue of its 'golden' or 'flying' staircase. A narrow balcony with an alcove ran around the second story of the picture gallery. The spectacular staircase was suspended, like a necklace, from one side of the balcony to the other. A curved piece of cast iron formed the spine to which, without intermediate supports, the stair treads were attached. The sides of this astonishing construction, as well as the balcony railing, were a spider web of gold filigree dotted with small crystal balls."

"Nothing could achieve such a unified concept in an interior," the Parisian art-dealer Samuel Bing exclaimed when he saw it. Although the elements were derivative, the effect was not one of clutter. Working principally with Oriental forms, Tiffany had been able to define their basic shapes and used them to achieve an effective blend of East and West, which was precisely what Bing was advocating in his monthly publication, *Artistic Japan*, published in three languages from 1888 to 1891. Bing had displayed Japanese ceramics at the Paris Exposition of 1878, and as a leading importer of Oriental art had offices in Paris, New York, London and Berlin.

While Samuel Colman was putting the finishing touches to the Havemeyer house Tiffany turned his attention to the large memorial window commissioned by Simeon B. Chittenden of Brooklyn to be given to the new library of Yale University in memory of Chittenden's daughter Mary Hartwell Lusk, the deceased wife of Dr. William T. Lusk. Tiffany made for it a full-size cartoon in oil on canvas. Thinly painted in subtle tones, it shows his planning in terms of light rather than form, of fluid color rather than sharply defined areas. The completed window, thirty feet long and five feet high and containing more than twenty figures, was installed in time for Commencement Week of 1890, in a building designed by J. C. Cady.

A contemporary report in the Boston *Post* was glowing: "No one can stand in this room without a profound feeling of satisfaction that America produces such window work as that of Louis Tiffany. It is truly a wonderful production of this man of thought." The opalescent glass was admired for its subtle gradations. The detail in the wings of the angels and the sunset sky shows a cloisonné-like use of leads to enhance the contours and delineate the design. Sweeping curves, echoed and re-echoed, provide a continuity of surface and pattern which denies the forms of the figures and the effect of space. A similar basic contradiction may be found in the academic figures painted by Puvis de Chavannes, a contemporary French artist.

In 1889 Tiffany, on a summer holiday abroad, was astonished to find a window by La Farge displayed in Paris and being hailed as a masterpiece. Tiffany felt that he had missed his chance for international recognition. Better late than never, he went straight to the shop of S. Bing, from whom he had purchased many Oriental treasures, and informed the proprietor that he himself was about to produce a window for display. Bing's shop had always attracted artists, particularly those in search of new materials and techniques. Van Gogh had been a frequent visitor in the eighties, spending hours there browsing through Japanese prints. By 1890 it had become a meeting-place for members of the group who called themselves the *Nabis*. Bing, who fancied himself a critic, encouraged young painters to frequent his shop and derive inspiration from the arts of Japan. To him the lesson to be learned from the Japanese was that "Nothing exists in creation, be it only a blade of grass, that is not worthy of a place in the loftiest conceptions of Art. . . . Under such influences the lifeless stiffness to which our technical designers have hitherto so rigidly adhered will be relaxed by degrees, and our productions will become animated by the breath of real life that constitutes the secret charm of every achievement of Japanese art."

Bing was delighted that Tiffany had come to him and agreed to make all the necessary arrangements. Thus began a close association which was to have a lasting effect on the careers of both men and which was to influence the taste of a generation of artists in Europe and America. Both Bing and Tiffany admired the ideas of William Morris but differed with his concept that the machine was evil; they believed mass production could be harnessed to multiply beautifully designed objects. Within a few years Tiffany's efforts in this direction would link his name with Morris' as highly influential in the "useful arts." Gardner C. Teall would write in an American periodical, *Brush and Pencil*, in September, 1899, "We know what such men as William Morris have done for the useful arts, how they led them to a lasting companionship with the fine arts . . . In America Mr. Louis C. Tiffany has probably done the most of anyone practically toward forwarding a feeling for the beautiful as applied to our necessities. . . . Mr. Tiffany's work is a lesson to every craftsman. . . . He has not been content with the mere discovery of things, but, like Morris, he has spent quite as much energy in applying his art." Bing himself later described the burgeoning Tiffany organization as "a great art industry, a vast establishment combining under the same roof an army of artisans of all kinds united by a common current of ideas. It is perhaps by the audacity of such organizations that America will prepare a glorious future for its industrial art."

Another aspect of the Paris Exhibition of 1889 left a deep impression on Tiffany. There he saw the glass vases of Emile Gallé of Nancy, which utilized many novel organic effects of floral and foliage motifs to suggest rather than to copy nature, and which seemed to preserve the unique character of the medium. While Tiffany painted flowers and flower-markets in Germany he began to work out the design for a "Four Seasons" stained-glass window, which he intended to produce without the use of pigments. It would, he was confident, be a masterpiece that would put the La Farge window to shame. This window, when completed, was to be exhibited several times in Paris as well as in London, and eventually returned to Tiffany. Four cartouche-shaped scenes were banded by pearl and twisted bands with circular openings, known as guilloche. The center space was filled with cellular shapes. At the top was an eagle with widespread wings and at the bottom were five vases out of which leafy scrolls issued to form a frame. Each panel measured more than three feet square.

When Bing made a survey of American art and architecture, for the French government, he was sumptuously entertained by Tiffany. The exchange of ideas resulted in an expansion for both. They agreed that they should redouble their efforts to promote a new kind of art, to make available to the public objects that would be beautiful as well as useful and that could be produced in quantity. Each man had an abiding confidence in the other. They respected each other as businessmen, and both were sure of their values and their ability to discriminate in matters of beauty. They spent many long evenings in Tiffany's studio, discussing mutual interests. Bing could describe the work of Van de Velde and *Les Vingt* in Brussels and a group of designers in Glasgow. Tiffany, in turn, could inform Bing of the work of Richardson and Louis Sullivan. Bing's report to the French government showed a remarkable appreciation of the work of these two architects.

Both Bing and Tiffany were looking for a new and unconventional means of interpreting their times. They believed that the future belonged to those who were most creative and original in their interpretation of the rapidly expanding complex society in which they were both actively involved. Leadership, they believed, was all that was needed to bring this to the fore, and they were both experienced in the education of clients. They convinced each other that there was, indeed, no limit to their potential as "taste-makers." From these meetings seems to have stemmed Tiffany's conviction that he was a genius.

Bing discussed with Tiffany a project which would link his name with French artists of note. An order was placed for ten windows to be made of Tiffany glass, with designs by French artists selected by Bing. Paul Ranson designed two. Pierre Bonnard, Eugene Grasset, Henri Ibels, Ker-Xavier Roussel, Paul Serusier, Henri de Toulouse-Lautrec, Edouard Vuillard and Felix Vallotton each produced one. Some three years later, when they were shown at the annual *Salon du Champ-de-Mars*, Tiffany supplied for Bing a brochure proudly proclaiming American stained glass supreme and Tiffany's colored glass superior to all Medieval glass, a statement that one French critic called a "*bizarre manifeste.*" Tiffany, in any case, felt himself much indebted to Bing, whom he named as his exclusive European distributor, not only for having helped to promote his work but even more for helping to establish a link between himself and French painters who seemed to be working in a parallel direction. This liaison encouraged him to work boldly and to seek new means of expression.

Bing was largely responsible for prodding Tiffany into producing a display for the forthcoming World's Fair to be held in Chicago. Tiffany's former colleague Frank D. Millet was serving as director and coordinator of all painted decorations and Candace Wheeler had been appointed director of the Women's Building. Bing felt that the six paintings by Tiffany accepted for the art section were hardly sufficient to display Tiffany's versatility. Although no specific provisions had been made by the fair officials for a display of ecclesiastical art, arrangements were soon made to use a portion of the space reserved by Tiffany & Company in the Manufacturers and Liberal Arts Building for the Tiffany Glass Company and its products.

Tiffany's exhibit, consisting of a chapel, a light room and a dark room, was not ready for the opening of the fair in October of 1892, but was first shown in New York and later shipped to Chicago, where it became one of the main attractions. Wilhelm Bode, the director of the *Gemaldegalerie* of Berlin, reported that the opalescent windows, a main feature of Tiffany's chapel, received more attention from visitors than any other product of American industrial art. The Tiffany Glass Company exhibited as a whole was marked by continuity of design and a wide variety of materials. In an illustrated brochure, published July 25, 1893, Tiffany's aim was stated as "the introduction of new and original ideas . . . equal in merit with the best that has been done."

The chapel represented the apex of Tiffany's Neo-Byzantine ecclesiastical interiors. It has been ranked with Sullivan's "Golden Door," made for the Transportation Building, as one of the two most original contributions to the Columbian Exposition. It is hard to imagine its pristine magnificence, as it stands in ruins. Neither the theatricality of the over-all effect nor the precious treatment of materials may appeal to modern tastes, but the subordination of detail to the unity of the design makes this one of the finest monuments of its kind. The altar was a simple rectangle of white marble, with a white and iridescent glass mosaic front. Behind the altar, the reredos was composed of a pictorial iridescent glass mosaic of blues and greens representing peacocks and vine scrolls. It was one of the most intricate and effective of all the mosaics by Tiffany, and since it was set into black marble, the iridescent effect must have been one of maximum brilliance. A jeweled filigree tabernacle, which was placed above the altar, provided richness, but the mosaic was the focal center of the whole ensemble by its very nature and color. Surmounting it was a series of concentric Romanesque round arches—the ciborium—decorated with relief interlaces overlaid in gold. These arches were supported by clusters of columns with carved capitals the shafts of which were completely covered by glass mosaic of reds, greens and browns in random patterns. Light was admitted by a series of twelve stained-glass windows, including "The Entombment," and an elaborate cruciform bejeweled sanctuary lamp was suspended in the center of the domelike space. A matching set of ritual pieces was made from designs by Tiffany, who personally supervised the execution of his plans.

Entering the chapel may very well have been an experience similar to that encountered by the people of Ravenna when their own Byzantine mosaics were new. The chapel was opulent without ostentation, the static structural forms made vibrant with luminous color. Tiffany later remarked that well nigh a million pieces of glass mosaic, in which opalescent glass predominated, "made up, with pearls and semiprecious stones, the several parts of the niche." The religious symbols included emblems of the four Evangelists in pearl and semi-precious stones and an inscription in mosaic referring to the eucharist. The peacock, he later commented, was a bird found in "late Roman and therefore Christian churches, not withstanding its bad repute as the bird of Juno and the emblem of vanity. It was in truth a bird beloved of the nations about the Mediterranean, who imported it from India. The early peoples held it in high esteem because it seemed to symbolize the sun with its wheel of brilliant, eyed feathers, and it commended itself to the Hindus because it hailed the coming of the rains and because its clamor notified them of the presence of the dangerous big cats, the tiger and the leopard." Inlaid mosaic inscriptions on five lower steps signified the five wounds of Christ, and on the upper three the Trinity.

He elaborated later on the principles underlying his use of rich color for mosaics like those used as durable substitutes for wall paintings and carpets from the fifth to the ninth century under the later Roman and Byzantine emperors. "In mosaics, almost as much as in stained-glass windows, there is necessary to their eminence a feeling for rich color which must be innate since it cannot be acquired. The sense must be delicate also, because it depends on the surroundings and the light, whether brilliant colors or dull, whether simple designs or complicated, shall be employed. When a mosaic floor is unearthed on the site of a Roman temple or villa we have no means of determining under what conditions as to lighting the artist carried out his task. We have the same difficulty, but perhaps to a less degree, with ancient sculpture and architecture. We must try to imagine what effect they had when entire, when clothed with colors, for both temple and statue were painted, while the effigies of gods and goddesses were often decked out with robes and ornamented with crowns, fillets, earrings and chains of gold. A very false idea of classic art grew up during the Renaissance period . . . an idea that it was cold from lack of color. An artist who would like to employ the richest materials in architecture, sculpture, painting and decorative arts finds . . . the mistakes made in former centuries concerning ancient art hard to combat."

Tiffany's chapel was undeniably effective, and it became a symbol of American ingenuity which could rival and even surpass anything that could be produced abroad. A wealthy Chicago widow, Celia Whipple Wallace, was so impressed by Tiffany's work that she arranged for the chapel to be donated to the Romanesque-style Cathedral of St. John the Divine in New York. It had remained in Tiffany's Fourth Avenue studios from 1894 to 1897. It was installed in the crypt of the cathedral and used for all services from January, 1889, until 1911, when the main choir was opened.

Tiffany's "dark room" for the Columbian Exposition was decorated in different shades of a single color, ranging from pale yellowish greens to dark, rich bluish greens. It included fixtures and lamps which were "entirely novel and, at the same time, artistic," utilizing glass "of a very peculiar tone and filigree work finished in various metallic colors." The "light room," which was done in silver and opal, contained two stained-glass windows, one entitled "Feeding the Flamingoes," with a statuesque female figure among birds of exotic plumage, the other entitled "Goldfishes." It was lighted by an electrolier "composed of metal and mother-of-pearl, enriched with filigree work" and "carrying out a design entirely new in its conception." Some of the fixtures in the display made use of the new iridescent glass with which he had been

[77]

experimenting and which he would soon put to use in various forms of Favrile glass.

To keep up with the unprecedented demand for stained glass, Tiffany found it necessary to retain the extra workmen he had hired to produce his chapel. The Fourth Avenue studios were expanded by the purchase of two adjoining buildings. Between 1893 and 1897 the Tiffany Glass and Decorating Company turned out as many windows as had been made under his direction prior to 1893. According to John Gilbert Lloyd, there were some 211 glasshouses in 1880, with some 24,000 employees and an output valued at $21,000,000. Congress set the tariff rate at 45 percent *ad valorem* in 1883, 35 percent in 1894, and restored it to 45 percent in 1897. The National Ornamental Glass Manufacturers formed an organization in 1903, later known as The Stained Glass Association of America.

Many wealthy Americans and institutions, however, preferred to import their works of art—paintings, statuary, stained-glass windows. Otto Heinigke, a worker in stained glass for several decades, once asked, "Why is it that a liberal American will pay $25 per square foot and 40 percent in addition to the price of setting to a foreign maker, with years to carry out the contract?" In the opinion of Samuel Bing, such a deprecatory attitude toward American artists was a threat to their survival. Stanford White had by now abandoned the elements of American Colonial tradition in favor of classic façades. Tiffany, who was always proud of America's artistic heritage, publicly appealed for support of "a truly American art." In an article entitled "American Art Supreme in Colored Glass" in *The Forum*, July, 1893, he declared, "Today this country unquestionably leads the world in the production of colored glass windows of artistic value and decorative importance." A complaint on the lack of appreciation of American efforts voiced by another glassmaker of this era, Ludwick von Gerichten, was noted by John Gilbert Lloyd in *Stained Glass in America:* "Nine out of ten priests are prejudiced against American houses and not altogether unjustly, as most American houses who have tried to equal the European execution of the work sent here had to inevitably learn they had to lose money doing so, owing to the low tariff, and not wishing to do that, naturally relapsed into the state of doing the best they could for the money allowed them, and as that was not enough, it gradually reduced the general standard, and created the impression that nobody in this broad land of Uncle Sam's could do good work."

Tiffany, however, stoutly affirmed his faith in American windows in his article, which referred to his efforts to include examples of his windows in the display space available at the World's Fair. "You will look in vain in the great 'White City' on the shores of Lake Michigan for a department in the Exposition devoted exclusively to exhibiting the results of the development in this particular art . . . Those of us in America who began to experiment in glass were untrammeled by tradition and were moved solely by a desire to produce a thing of beauty, irrespective of any rule, doctrine or theory beyond that governing good taste and true artistic judgment. At first very little attention was paid to mere form. Color, and color only, was the end sought. The first requisite was obtained through the aid of modern chemistry, the last by chipping the glass in such a way as to give irregular faceted surfaces, until a material was obtained which rivaled the painter's palette in its range of tones and eclipsed the iridescence and brilliancy found in the Roman and Egyptian glass. . . .

"The American development of the art, or the American method of making colored glass windows, is, of course, still in its infancy. If there is one point of superiority in the work done by the artists of the Middle Ages it is in their wonderful knowledge of the proper distribution of color. Yet I maintain that the best American colored windows are superior to the best medieval windows . . .

"That our knowledge of glass is greater than the past cannot be denied. Our range of color is far in excess of the palette of the 13th century. The mechanical contrivances that are used in the construction of windows and in preparing the leads are greater in number than those at the command of the medieval glazier. This, together with the skill of hand acquired through the rigid training of our modern art schools, places us in such a position that if we do not make better windows than we ever have made, it will only be because the public is not yet ready to receive them."

Many of Tiffany's colleagues felt that this was perhaps an exaggerated claim, but Tiffany felt that by this article he had asserted his leadership. La Farge, whose lectures on color at the Metropolitan Museum of Art were later published in book form, published about this time a booklet, "The American Art of Glass: To Be Read in Connection with Mr. Louis C. Tiffany's Paper in the July Number of *The Forum*." He took issue in particular with Tiffany's dismissal of tradition and what he called "mere form."

The controversy generated a rash of articles by other artists and competitors, including Caryl Coleman, an admirer of Tiffany's work, who provided a mural for St. Peter's Roman Catholic Church in New York City, which had declined to accept works by La Farge, as well as contributions on the subject by Frederick Stymetz Lamb and by Charles R. Lamb. An article by Theodore Dreiser, "The Making of Stained Glass Windows," appeared in *Cosmopolitan* in 1899. A series of articles on Tiffany and his work by Cecelia Waern appeared in *The International Studio* in 1897 and 1898.

There was yet another aesthetic controversy often debated in print. After the tide of heroic figures engulfed the market, there were some who did not hesitate to speak out against the unselective use of stained-glass figure windows in the already overornate churches and public buildings of the day. Ralph Adams Cram, a prominent church architect, felt that stained glass must be used in a disciplined way. John Gilbert Lloyd quoted one statement by Cram: "Next to music, stained glass may make the most poignant and emotional appeal, but it cannot do this unless it holds faithfully within the fixed law of its being. In the first place it is not a picture but a space of translucent wall, possessing neither linear nor aerial perspective . . . Space composition is fundamental, also line composition. In these respects it approaches nearer Chinese or Japanese art than that of the west . . . A stained glass window is a unity, almost a communal organism, and no color stands by itself. It is the interplay of living light that gives the old work, as at Chartres, its transcendent glory . . ."

Cram, as early as 1894, took as a target the profuseness of ecclesiastical decoration. "The church may be carved into rivalry with a Japanese ivory ball, it may be painted with all the colors of the paint box . . . and yet it may not possess one breath of art, one line of beauty." A few years later he elaborated upon this point of view in *The Gothic Quest*. "In the United States two very great artists, John La Farge and Louis Tiffany, had invented and perfected a new style that, however ingenious it may have been and however widely popular, was based on entirely new principles wholly at variance both with those that held during the great five hundred years of the Middle Ages and with the whole ethos of Christian art. Besides, we ourselves thought it very ugly." Although Samuel Howe, one of Tiffany's former employees, stated passionately in *The Craftsman*, "I love opalescent glass . . . because for a few years it was the material with which what thoughts I had found a ready means of expression," Cram demurred. "Probably the majority of people like Hoffman Bible pictures done in opalescent glass, glittering and richly wrought pulpits of lacquered brass, gold leaf and Dutch metal gummed on jigsawed fretwork, yet even a unanimous consensus of opinion could not make these things other than what they are—abominable."

Still another controversy, aired in the pages of *The Craftsman*, affected Tiffany's workshops. This was the question of appropriate subject matter in church windows. Tiffany found himself under attack for promoting the use of landscapes, which were more and more in demand for homes, chapels, etc. Frederick S. Lamb asked, "We are told that the artist should be satisfied with the language of form and color and that subject is of minor importance. If this is true the American artist has achieved success, but is not the subject, and its selection, of vital importance to any work of art?" Tiffany's major competitor in the landscape-window field was David Lang of Los Angeles, a former employee who supplied landscape windows in the Tiffany manner to clients who engaged the architectural firm of Greene & Greene to design their homes. Many landscape windows supplied by Tiffany to purchasers in the East and Midwest were designed by Agnes F. Northrop, a favored pupil, who accompanied him on a European trip. One large landscape window was executed for a chapel in Ohio. A marked trend toward simplicity was evident in the decoration provided by Tiffany for the Wade Memorial Chapel of the Fair Lawn Cemetery in Cleveland, Ohio, in 1899. Except for the opalescent window, the colors used in the interior were subtle and restrained, with an architectural clarity and a rectilinear simplicity carefully proportioned and effectively integrated throughout. The structure was designed by a local firm of architects, Hubbell and Benes. The mosaics on the wide wall, representing "The River of Life," were designed by Frederick Wilson.

The popular jewel-medallion type, "in the manner of the thirteenth century," made by Tiffany since the 1880's, was the kind of window chosen by Stanford White for his Madison Square Presbyterian Church. These windows were later installed in the Mission Inn, Riverside, California. Later examples of medallion windows were placed in the Congregational Church of Fairfield, Connecticut, and the Old Blandford Church in Petersburg, Virginia. The Virginia church, erected in 1735, became a Confederate shrine, featuring fifteen Tiffany designs incorporating state seals and a cross of jewels. Three memorial windows were ordered from Tiffany by the American Red Cross for the Assembly Hall of their national headquarters.

Through the years various Tiffany divisions offered a variety of windows and memorials on such a large scale that Tiffany finally purchased his own granite quarry in Cohasset, Massachusetts. The last ecclesiastical interior in which Tiffany himself took an active interest was the redecoration of a Brooklyn church. This incorporated opalescent mosaics and a figure window. A redecoration of the building, which had been completed in 1842 from designs by Richard Upjohn, was ordered in 1916/17 by the children of Alexander and Margaret Orr as a memorial, at a cost of over a quarter million dollars. The new chancel window, made at a cost of $100,000, portrayed "The Adoration of the Magi." Made without the use of pigment or enamel or vitrifiable color of any kind, except that which was embodied in the glass, the window, which was said to have appeared as a huge glowing jewel, was completely destroyed in a fire on February 26, 1939. Many of the original pieces of furniture and ritual objects were saved, however, and workmen reconstructed the pulpit and chancel, with their softly glowing mosaic inlay, and a large opalescent panel behind the altar. The Tiffany window was subsequently replaced by a La Farge window.

In many years of supplying a variety of stained-glass windows Tiffany's firm survived the rise and fall of a number of popular styles, but the pull toward "pure Gothic" for churches and public buildings ran counter to his own leanings. Although Tiffany had not suffered during the wave of Neo-Classicism, for instance, Louis Sullivan's fame had waned. After completing the Carson, Pirie, Scott building in Chicago in 1899 he was reduced to designing modest bank buildings in Minnesota. Sullivan, however, had something trenchant to say about the penchant for Gothic "restorations."

The firm of Cram, Goodhue and Ferguson was awarded the contract to design new buildings in the Gothic manner for the U. S. Military Academy at West Point. George B. Post, who had worked with Tiffany on a Vanderbilt mansion in the 1880's

[*81*]

selected a Gothic style for the buildings of the College of the City of New York. Frederick S. Lamb called for a return to the Gothic style in an article in *The Craftsman*, to which Sullivan tendered a "Reply to Mr. Frederick Stymetz Lamb on 'Modern Use of Gothic.'" In this he declared, "Corruption has gone so far that it is time for a reaction. Not a trivial reaction from classic to Gothic, but a fundamental reaction from irresponsibility to responsibility; from irrational to rational ideas; from confused to clear thinking. It is time for the nightmare of our feudalism to end and for us to awaken to the reality of healthful life." Tiffany and Sullivan both received an accolade in *The Craftsman* in December, 1902, from Professor A. D. F. Hamlin, a professor of architecture at Columbia University, who observed, "Personally, I hail the revived use of forms borrowed from Gothic architecture because we have so many kinds of buildings to which they are artistically applicable, and they thus enlarge the resources of modern design. So also do I hail the emancipating influence of the so-called 'Art Nouveau' (whereof Tiffany and Sullivan are the true first prophets), in spite of the architectural nightmares to which it has given rise in France, Germany and Belgium."

Neither Louis C. Tiffany nor his opponents, who advocated a return to the Gothic style, could accept the "purist" approach, which totally denied the value of ornament and decoration and which was beginning to manifest itself among architects and designers in Belgium and Germany. The austere "International," or *Bauhaus*, style which developed and flourished in the years following World War I, soon had the effect of undermining, for almost half a century, all attempts to elevate the decorative arts to a level of greater artistic importance. The "purist" use of materials, as advocated by the functionalists, virtually denuded architecture for some years of almost all ornamental accessories, although some architects returned to the use of decorative elements such as mosaics, ornamental grillwork and sculptural features to enliven surfaces and open spaces.

A few artists sought to revive the traditional elements of the old Gothic windows. William Willet's Gothic window, made for the First Presbyterian Church in Pittsburgh, was said to be the first antique medallion window in America. Ralph Adams Cram commissioned Willet to execute a chancel window for Calvary Episcopal Church in Pittsburgh, which he had designed in the Gothic style. This window was installed in 1908. A protégé of Cram, Charles J. Connick, began a long campaign of educating public taste, during the stained-glass "boom" of the nineties, to an appreciation of better stained glass, after leaving a career as a cartoonist for a Pittsburgh newspaper to work in an opalescent art glass shop. The author of *Adventures in Light and Color*, he designed windows for the Princeton University Chapel and for the Church of St. Vincent Ferrer in New York City. Connick wryly recounted Tiffany's adroitness in inserting one of his landscape windows in a Gothic chapel. "A gifted young American [Cram] was the architect of a lofty Gothic chapel [the Russell

[*82*]

Sage Memorial Chapel in Far Rockaway, Long Island] that was inspired by the best periods in England and France. He dreamed of a great stained glass window in its chancel wall opening. . . . He planned to search England for the best artist-craftsman he could find and to commission him to design and make that window. But he dreamed too long, for as he dreamed, a super-salesman of an art-glass emporium [Tiffany] did his stuff, and a great landscape window burgeoned forth in those slender Gothic openings . . . That young architect was a man of character. His convictions were strong and clear; so was his vocabulary. The echoes of his ringing words still shake the walls of art-glass emporiums." Mrs. Russell Sage, apparently, never regetted her decision. At the time the chapel was dedicated, scant attention was paid to the architecture, but the landscape window was described at great length. "It is said to be the largest and most expensive window that Tiffany's have ever turned out. It is 25 feet in height and 21 in width and is said to have cost $35,000. It is designed to symbolize life—infancy being represented by the meadows and old age by the trees, gnarled but ever lifting their branches higher."

Soon thereafter Cram found an opportunity to even the score. The death of Bishop Henry Codman Potter in 1908 resulted in a re-evaluation of the building program for New York's Cathedral of St. John the Divine, which he had begun in 1892. He had approved the plans of the firm of Heins and La Farge to construct the cathedral along modified Romanesque lines and he had accepted the gift of the Tiffany chapel. The firm of Cram, Goodhue and Ferguson was retained to draw up new plans, and they subsequently changed the style to Gothic. In 1911, when the nave was built, the Tiffany chapel was sealed off from further use, much to Cram's delight. In 1916 Tiffany repossessed his chapel and moved it out to his Long Island home, where he consecrated it as "a temple of art, not a place of worship," and dedicated it to Henry Codman Potter. In the same month that the dismantled chapel was enroute to him a newspaper feature revived interest in its donor: "Long Missing Jewel Queen Found in a Hut. Mrs. Celia Whipple Wallace, Chicago's diamond queen, who gave the $50,000 Tiffany Chapel to St. John's Cathedral, fortune exhausted by charities, lives in a lonely cottage at Savin Rock, near New Haven."

But while Cram was engaged in closing up the Tiffany chapel its designer was watching the finishing touches put on a mammoth vista in stained glass, the drop-curtain for the National Theatre in Mexico City, some thirty years after his first modest venture for the Madison Square Theater. The building itself was begun in 1904 by Adamo Boari in a style blending classic and Art Nouveau in a most unusual manner. The contract for the glass curtain was awarded to Tiffany in 1909, and he retained the painter and stage designer Harry Stoner to make the design. Stoner was sent to Mexico to inspect the new building and to familiarize himself with the Mexican landscape. The resulting scenic design, representing a panoramic view of the

Valley of Mexico with its majestic mountain peaks as seen from the President's Palace, was translated into glass by workmen at the Tiffany Furnaces at Corona and required twenty workers more than fifteen months to complete. When finished, it consisted of 200 panels containing in all nearly a million pieces of glass, each panel three feet square, and when assembled, weighed a total of 27 tones. Its estimated value was $250,000. It was first exhibited in New York in April, 1911, and then shipped to Mexico City, to be installed in the Palace of Fine Arts. More of an accomplishment in engineering than a work of art, it is operated by hydraulic pressure and counter-balances and only seven seconds are required to raise or lower it.

There were many other large-scale commissions. For the Catholic cathedral in St. Louis, for instance, designs were supplied by Artistide Leonori in Rome, and from them Tiffany workmen set and installed 300,000 square feet of glass mosaics, which covered most of the wall space. There was still another large glass mosaic mural which was to bear Tiffany's imprint—the execution of a design by Maxfield Parrish for "The Dream Garden," for the Curtis Publishing Company building in Philadelphia, Pennsylvania. In 1911 Edward Bok, editor of *The Ladies' Home Journal*, had engaged Edwin A. Abbey, Howard Pyle and Boutet de Monvel successively to make a design for the mural, but each had died before producing a sketch. He then organized a competition of six leading muralists but eventually rejected all of their efforts. In his book, *The Americanization of Edward Bok*, he related the resolution, quaintly referring to himself in the third person:

"Bok was still exactly where he started, while the building was nearly complete, with no mural for the large place so insistently demanding it. He now recalled a marvelous stage-curtain of glass mosaic executed by Louis C. Tiffany of New York for the Municipal Theatre at Mexico City. . . .

"He sought Mr. Tiffany, who was enthusiastic over the idea of making an example of his mosaic glass of such dimensions which should remain in this country, and gladly offered to cooperate. But try as he might, Bok could not secure an adequate sketch for Mr. Tiffany to carry out. Then he recalled that one day while at Maxfield Parrish's summer home in New Hampshire the artist had told him of a dream garden which he would like to construct, not on canvas but in reality. Bok suggested to Parrish that he come to New York. He asked him if he could put his dream garden on canvas. The artist thought he could; in fact was greatly attracted by the idea; but he knew nothing of mosaic work and was not particularly attracted by the idea of having his work rendered in that medium.

"Bok took Parrish to Mr. Tiffany's studio; the two artists talked together, the glass-worker showed the canvas-painter his work, with the result that the two became enthusiastic to cooperate in trying the experiment. Parrish agreed to make a sketch for Mr. Tiffany's approval, and within six months, after a number of conferences and an equal number of sketches, they were ready to begin work. Bok only hoped both artists would outlive their commissions!

"It was a huge picture to be done in glass mosaic (15 feet in height and 49 feet in length). The space to be filled called for over a million pieces of glass, and for a year the services of thirty of the most skilled artisans would be required. The work had to be done from a series of bromide photographs enlarged to a size hitherto unattempted. But at last the decoration was completed; the finished art piece was placed on exhibition in New York and over seven thousand persons came to see it. The leading art critics pronounced the result to be the most amazing instance of the tone capacity of glass-work ever achieved. It was a veritable wonderpiece, far exceeding the utmost expression of paint on canvas."

Tiffany himself commented on "The Dream Garden" in a brochure published by the Curtis Publishing Company. "I have been studying the effects of different glasses to accomplish perspective, and effects of color of different textures, of opaque and transparent, of lustrous and nonlustrous, of absorbing and reflecting glasses.

"The mosaics of the past, although of the greatest beauty, were all made to copy pictures or flat decorations, and these modes of mosaics would not have answered this purpose.

"When Mr. Maxfield Parrish's painting was shown to me, with all of its beauty of suggestion, I saw the opportunity of translating it into a mosaic which would bring, to those who could see and understand, an appreciation of the real significance of this picture.

"In translating this painting so that its poetical and luminous idealism should find its way even to the comparatively uneducated eye, the medium used is of supreme importance, and it seemed impossible to secure the effect desired on canvas and with paint. In glass, however, selecting the lustrous, the transparent, the opaque and the opalescent, and each with its own texture, a result is secured which does illustrate the mystery, and it tells the story, giving play to imagination, which is the message it seeks to convey.

"As a matter of fact, it is practically a new art. Never before has it been possible to give the perspective in mosaics as it is shown in this picture, and the most remarkable and beautiful effect is secured when different lights play upon this completed mosaic.

"It will be found that the mountains recede, the trees and foliage stand out distinctly, and, as the light changes, the purple shadows will creep slowly from the base of the mountain to its top; that the canyons and the waterfalls, the thickets and the flowers, all tell their story and interpret Mr. Parrish's dream.

"I trust it may stand in the years to come for a development in glass-making and its application to art which will give to students a feeling that in this year of nineteen hundred and fifteen something worthy has been produced for the benefit of mankind, and that it may serve as an incentive to others to carry even farther the true mission of the mosaic."

The collaboration with Maxfield Parrish on "The Dream Garden" stimulated Tiffany to return to painting, and for a time he began to work in a manner influenced by Parrish's style. In his design for "The Bathers," a window planned for exhibition purposes but eventually installed in Tiffany's own home, Tiffany realized what had been one of La Farge's unfulfilled ambitions, the execution of an elaborate figure window made entirely of colored glass.

The demand for stained glass in America was sustained even through the twenties, when some 900 stained glass studios were in operation. Tiffany Studios, an outgrowth of the Tiffany Glass and Decorating Company, continued until 1938, when its remaining stock was disposed of and arrangements were made for Payne-Spiers Studios to complete any unfinished orders for windows. By this time, despite decades of European competition, there was a growing recognition of the quality of American stained glass. Tiffany had once proclaimed the supremacy of American stained glass and he had rapidly expanded his own early experiments into a full-scale business. American glassmakers, in time, banded to form an influential body which insured protectionist tariff provisions. Charles Connick, who as Cram's champion had once called Tiffany a "super-salesman for an art-glass emporium," became a leading spokesman for the stained glass industry in the years when the name of Tiffany was no longer a glittering hallmark but almost forgotten. Connick's remarks on the scope of the art glass business echoed what Tiffany had, in fact, seen was inevitable and necessary, and had set about putting into effect several decades earlier. John Gilbert Lloyd quoted Connick's admission in his *Stained Glass in America.* "If we are to undertake big commissions we must have help, and we must have larger shops and studios, and so—whether we like it or not—we must enter the world of business . . . we are citizens of the world . . . we cannot do our work in ivory towers. We have to pay rent, wages and that arrogant and rapacious monster known as Overhead."

part two
ILLUSTRATIONS

Louis C. Tiffany
AS A DESIGNER OF STAINED GLASS
WINDOWS AND MOSAICS

The Associated Artists eventually disbanded: Candace Wheeler's embroidery department was detached, as she had anticipated, and she turned to the designing of silks, (*right*) while Tiffany became increasingly immersed in his experiments with glass in the "unusually light" loft at the top of 333 Fourth Avenue.

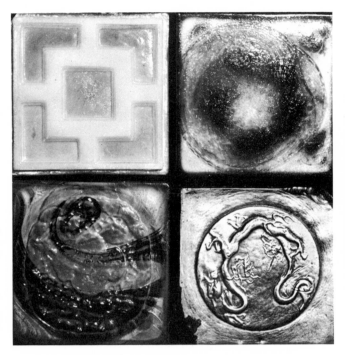

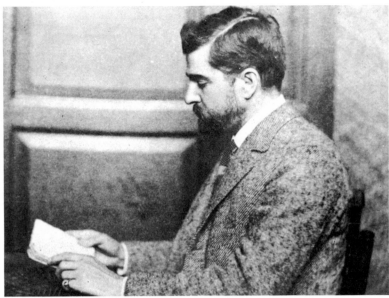

Tiffany, shown (*above, right*) as he looked in 1886, often incorporated his early glass tiles (*left*) in his decorative schemes for interiors. Ornamental glass windows had become the height of fashion, and Tiffany's firm supplied them in quantity for homes and public buildings. J. J. Lefebre's oil, "Girl Reading," (*bottom left*) was copied by Tiffany in glass (*bottom right*).

[*89*]

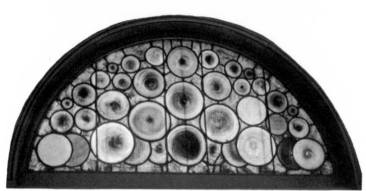

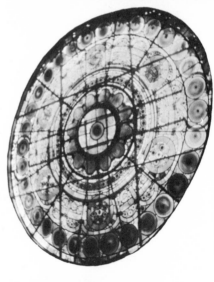

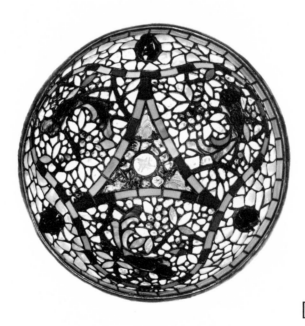

[*90*]

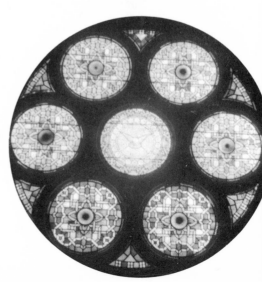

(*Opposite page*): William J. and John Bolton made the "Adoration" window (*top left*) for Christ Church, Pelham, N. Y. in 1843. Tiffany's "bull's-eye" semicircular window (*center, left*) was made for the Church of the Sacred Heart in New York in 1876; his "St. Mark" (*top right*) for the Episcopal church of Islip, L. I., in 1878; two circular windows, one for Trinity Church, Lenox, Mass., in 1890 (*center right*) and one for the Union Reformed Church, Highbridge, Bronx, N. Y. in 1889 (*bottom right*). Tiffany also made a hanging globe (*bottom left*), now in a European collection.

(*This page*): John La Farge provided windows for Trinity Church of Boston, decorated in 1876 (*top*), collaborated with Stanford White on the decoration of The Church of the Ascension (*bottom left*) and The Church of St. Paul the Apostle (*bottom right*) in New York. Tiffany made windows for the Peddie Memorial Baptist Church, Newark, N. J., in 1890 (*center left*).

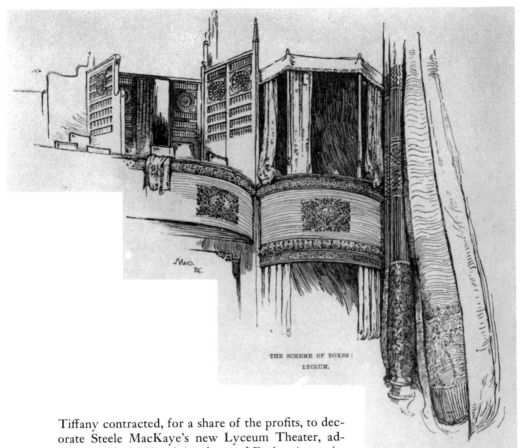

THE SCHEME OF BOXES :
LYCEUM.

Tiffany contracted, for a share of the profits, to decorate Steele MacKaye's new Lyceum Theater, adjacent to the National Academy of Design (*opposite page, above*). He made a watercolor of the stage (*opposite page, below*). The Lyceum interior was described as "Wilde Outdone by Mackaye." A detail of the boxes is drawn (*above*). Louis Sullivan's interior for his Auditorium Theater in Chicago (1887-1899) is shown (*below*).

The Romanesque Tiffany mansion at 72nd Street and Madison Avenue, with its loggias and *porte-cochere*, was sketched by Tiffany (*above*), photographed (*right*) in 1885. Ceramics were displayed above one tiled fireplace (*bottom left*), his collection of Japanese sword-guards above another (*bottom right*).

Tiffany's parents were photographed in his top-floor studio in 1893 (*top right*). He painted his second wife here in 1896 (*left*), emphasizing the bole-like hood of the four-sided fireplace and the exotic plants and hanging lamps (*bottom*) which gave it an "Arabian Nights" air.

(*Opposite page*): Alphonse Mucha's poster of Sarah Bernhardt in the role of a Byzantine empress (*far left*) typified the popularity of Byzantine motifs, particularly the art of mosaic. Tiffany supposedly modeled his "Head of Joseph of Arimathea" (*top right*) after his own father. The watercolor design (*bottom right*) was for a mosaic "Christ Blessing The Children."

(*This page*): Tiffany's glass mosaic, "Fish," (*top right*) was made in 1908. The pulpit of inlaid marble and glass mosaic (*bottom*) was made for St. Michael's Church in New York by Tiffany 1895-97.

[97]

J. A. Holzer designed the altar and chancel for St. Paul's Church of Troy, N. Y. (*above*) in 1893, adding the baptistry (*bottom right*) in 1897. His window for Christ Church, Rye, N. Y. (*bottom left*) was made in 1896.

...any designed the rose window and chancel arches for ...First Presbyterian Church of Bath, N. Y. (*top right,* ...ils *top left*) in 1897 and decorated the library of Pratt ...tute in Brooklyn in 1898 (*bottom left*). Tiffany's firm ...lied the reredos and "The Last Supper" mosaic for the ...ton Springs Sanitarium, Clifton Springs, N. Y. (*right*) ...901. J. A. Holzer provided mosaic decorations for the ...ago Public Library (*bottom right*) in 1898.

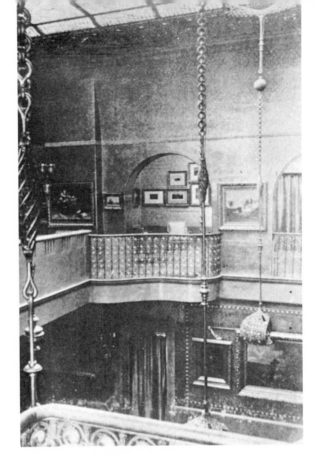

Tiffany and Bernard Maybeck were the decorators for the Ponce de Leon Hotel in St. Augustine, Fla. (*opposite page, top*), built in 1885-87. Samuel Colman came from Newport to work with Tiffany on the interiors for the H. O. Havemeyer house in New York in 1890-92. The drawing room is shown (*opposite page, below*). Tiffany found Mrs. Havemeyer to be a highly sympathetic client. The filigree suspended staircase (*below*) and hanging lamps (*above*) elicited many favorable comments from visitors to the mansion.

Among the lighting fixtures designed by Tiffany for the Havemeyer house was the Byzantine-style pebble and glass chandelier (*above*). The Tiffany Glass Company, incorporated in 1886, (*right*) subsequently expanded to provide a wide variety of decorative items.

Tiffany utilized a pageant of figures in his oil, "Allegory of Spring," in 1890 (*above*) and in a series of memorial windows commissioned by Simeon Chittenden for the Yale Library (*below*) in 1889. A figure from the "Education" window cartoon (*below*) is shown in enlarged detail (*right*).

[*103*]

(*This page*): Shown (*above left*) is the cartoon for the "Art" window, (*below*) the central portion of the "Education" window, installed in the Yale Library in 1889.

(*Opposite page*): After seeing a stained glass window by La Farge hailed in Paris in 1889 Tiffany designed "The Four Seasons" (*top left*). It was exhibited by Bing, who later commissioned ten windows of Tiffany glass from French artists, including Pierre Bonnard (*top right*), Paul Ranson (*bottom left*) and Henri G. Ibels (*bottom right*).

[105]

Major attractions of the Chicago Exposition of 1893 were Louis Sullivan's "Golden Door" for the Transportation Building (*opposite page, bottom left*) and Tiffany's resplendent Chapel (*opposite page, top left*). French architects awarded the door three medals, claiming Sullivan alone among Americans understood what the École des Beaux-Arts taught. A series of stained glass windows, a glass-topped baptismal font (*above*) and a benediction candelabra (*right*) also displayed the versatility of the Tiffany Glass and Decorating Company. The Tiffany Chapel in Chicago was visited by more than 1,400,000 people.

[108]

Figure windows on Biblical themes vied in popularity with floral and landscape subjects. The Middle Collegiate Church of New York selected a figure window (*opposite page, top right*) copied by Tiffany's firm from Heinrich Hoffman's 1880 lithograph, "Mary at the Tomb of Christ" (*top left*). David promising Bathsheba that Solomon would succeed him was the subject of the watercolor for a window, (*opposite page, bottom right*) suggested for the Marble Collegiate Church of New York. "The Entombment" was painted by Tiffany for a window in his Chapel (*opposite page, bottom left*). He signed the mats of the floral and landscape designs (*top and center*). The landscape design (*bottom*) was made in 1912 for a window in the Pittsburgh residence of R. B. Mellon.

The Wade Memorial Chapel, Cleveland, Ohio, (*top left*) was decorated by Tiffany in 1899; its "River of Life" mosaic was designed by Frederick Wilson. Tiffany supplied a landscape window for the Gothic-style Russell Sage Memorial Chapel in Far Rockaway, L. I. (*bottom left*). The landscape window designed by him in 1920 for L. D. Towle of Boston (*bottom right*) was acquired by the Metropolitan Museum of Art in 1925.

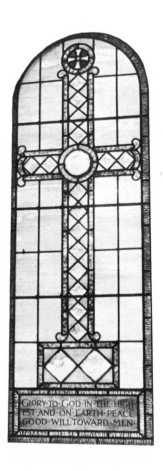

The Old Blandford Church of Petersburg, Va., a Confederate shrine, ordered several windows, including the Tennessee memorial (*top right*) and "Cross of Jewels" (*center*) from Tiffany. The American Red Cross headquarters in Washington, D. C. installed a large triple-paneled window (*below*) in 1918, designed by Frederick Wilson.

The Chittenden memorial window (*above*), with detail (*below*), was made by Tiffany for the Plymouth Church in Brooklyn Heights, N.Y. in 1890, the medallion window (*right*) for exhibition purposes about 1892. The rose and medallion windows made by Tiffany for Stanford White's Madison Square Presbyterian Church were later removed to the Mission Inn, Riverside, Calif. (*opposite page*).

[*112*]

Tiffany provided an "Adoration of the Magi" window (*left*) for Christ Church, Brooklyn, in 1917 as well as an altar of inlaid mosaic, with an iridescent panel above (*bottom right*). The glass panel for the door of the Sigma Phi House in Berkeley, Calif. (*bottom left*) was made by David Lang for Greene & Greene.

SIGMA PHI

The ecclesiastical department of Tiffany's firm provided a variety of monuments and memorials, including the window (*above*) and George M. Cohan mausoleum (*top right*) in Woodlawn Cemetery in 1917. The watercolor design of 1895 (*right*) was for a pair of bronze and glass memorial doors.

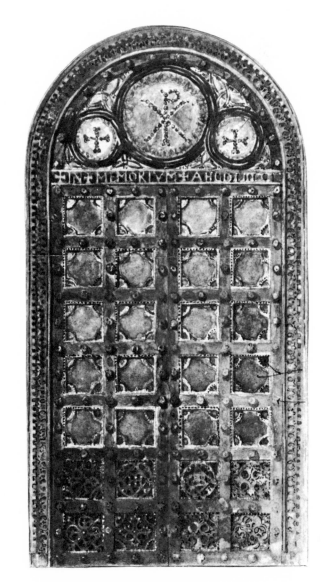

For the National Theater of the Palace of Fine Arts in Mexico City, Tiffany provided a huge glass curtain in 1911 (*above*). For it Harry Stoner painted a view of distant snow-capped mountains, as seen from the President's Palace (*below*).

"The Dream Garden" a mosaic which was the collaboration of Tiffany
and Maxfield Parrish, was installed in the Curtis Publishing Company
building in Philadelphia in 1915 (*above*, and *below*).

UNITED STATES PATENT OFFICE.

TIFFANY GLASS AND DECORATING COMPANY, OF JERSEY CITY, NEW JERSEY,
AND NEW YORK, N. Y.

TRADE-MARK FOR DECORATIVE GLASS.

STATEMENT and DECLARATION of Trade-Mark No. 25,512, registered November 13, 1894.

Application filed September 26, 1894.

STATEMENT.

To all whom it may concern:

Be it known that the TIFFANY GLASS AND DECORATING COMPANY, a corporation organized under the laws of the State of New Jersey, and having an office in the city of Jersey City, in said State, and also having an office and doing business at No. 333 Fourth avenue, in the city and State of New York, has adopted for its use a trade-mark for decorative glass or vitrified bodies manufactured by said corporation and used in making colored or stained glass windows, mosaics, glassware, or used in conjunction with other substances in manufacture or the arts, of which the following is a full, clear, and exact specification.

The trade-mark of said TIFFANY GLASS AND DECORATING COMPANY consists of the unadorned capital letters in Roman type but of different sizes, "T G D Co" surrounded by two circles of different sizes and arranged as shown in the accompanying fac-simile. Within the inner and outer circle are the words "Tiffany Favrile Glass Trade-Mark Registered." These words may be varied by inserting between the words "Favrile" and "Glass" some modifying word descriptive of particular kinds of glass manufactured by said corporation, thus making the phrase read "Tiffany Favrile Fabric Glass," "Tiffany Favrile Sunset Glass," "Tiffany Favrile Horizon Glass," "Tiffany Favrile Twig Glass," "Tiffany Favrile Lace Glass," &c.; but any or all of the particular words of modification or description may be omitted and the various accessories of this trade-mark may be otherwise varied without materially altering the character of the trade-mark of which the essential features are the monogram of the letters "T G D Co" and the word "FAVRILE."

This trade-mark has been continuously used by said corporation since its incorporation in February, 1892.

The class of merchandise to which this trade-mark is appropriated is glass or vitrified substance and the particular description of goods comprised in such class on which it is used by the said TIFFANY GLASS AND DECORATING COMPANY is a hand made glass or vitrified body invented and used more particularly for the making of colored or stained glass windows, mosaics, glassware, &c., but also used in conjunction with other substances in manufacture and the arts. This substance may be either homogeneous or various in color. It may be wrought or blown in such forms as a skilled artist-artisan may see fit to force or lead the molten metal. It may therefore be either flat, foliated, convoluted, cylindrical, globular or cubical, of one color or many, laminated, floriated or foliatious.

This trade-mark is usually affixed to the goods by stenciling on the box containing said glass or by printing the trade-mark in black or colors upon labels attached to boxes containing said glass, but it may also be applied directly as a brand to the goods themselves or in any other suitable manner to packages or boxes in which said glass is packed. This trade-mark may also be applied in a suitable manner to cards, letter-heads, advertisements, or other notices which advertise said glass to the public.

Dated September 25, 1894.

[L. S.] TIFFANY GLASS & DECORATING
COMPANY,

By PRINGLE MITCHELL,
Vice-Pres.

Witnesses:
CARYL COLEMAN,
JOHN L. WILKIE.

DECLARATION.

State of New York city and county of New York ss:

PRINGLE MITCHELL being duly sworn deposes and says, that the TIFFANY GLASS AND DECORATING COMPANY the applicant named in the foregoing statement is a corporation duly organized under the laws of the State of New Jersey. That deponent is the vice-

---

Tiffany's statement and declaration of his "trade-mark" for decorative glass, registered in 1894, a media with which his name would be increasingly identified.

[*118*]

"Summer," a panel of Louis C. Tiffany's "Four Seasons" window of 1892. *Courtesy of Hugh F. McKean.*

A window from the Heckscher house and furniture formerly in Laurelton Hall (*top left*) formed a part of the Museum of Contemporary Crafts' retrospective Tiffany exhibit in 1958. "Feeding The Flamingoes" (*top right*) was exhibited in Chicago in 1893 and later installed in Laurelton Hall. The "Butterflies" window (*bottom left*) was made about 1900. The pebble-cluster window (*bottom right*), like all the other items on this page, is in the McKean collection at Rollins College, Winter Park, Florida.

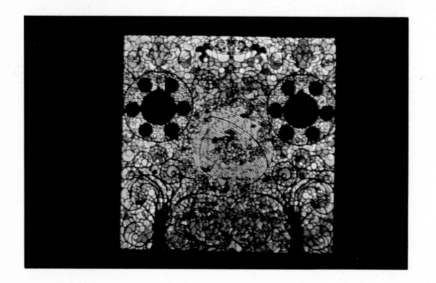

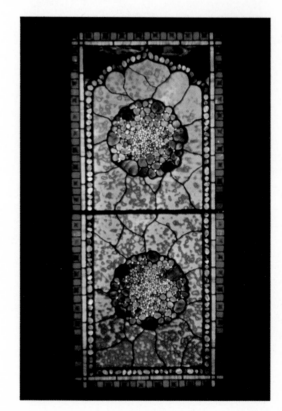

The figure window (*top left*) "Girl Picking Gourds," designed by Frank Brangwyn, was made without the use of pigments. It was exhibited at the Grafton Galleries in London in 1899. The memorial window (*top right*) in the All Angels Episcopal Church, New York City, was installed before 1897. A detail of a medallion window in the First Church of Christ Congregational Church, Fairfield, Conn., installed in 1915, is shown (*left*). Tiffany Studios showroom samples for lampshade designs, "Yellow Tulip" and "Woodbine" patterns, are shown (*below*).

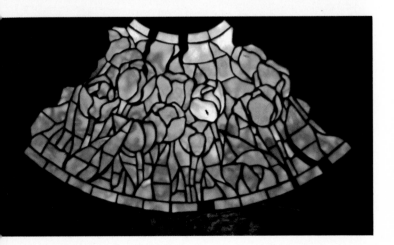

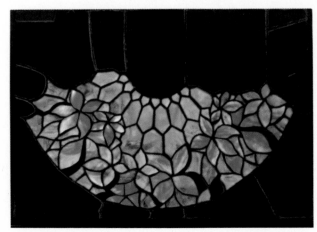

The dragonfly appears on both a mosaic plaque and a mosaic lamp with a shade (*top right*) designed by Clara Driscoll, which was awarded a prize in Paris in 1900. The popular wisteria-tree lamp (*opposite page, bottom left*) has a shade designed by Mrs. Curtis Freshel and a tree base designed by Louis C. Tiffany. Other lamps made by Tiffany Studios include a table lamp with a bronze and glass base (*top left*) and a lotus lamp with leaded glass shade and bronze base (*opposite page, top*) *courtesy of The Chrysler Art Museum.* The 12-branched candle-lamp (*opposite page, bottom right*), is owned by the author. Also shown (*below*) are a melon-shaped paperweight-type vase with millefiori flowers and a purple enameled covered jar decorated with pink flowers.

Shown (*right*) are a group of Tiffany vases, *courtesy of Helen Eisenberg*, and (*below*) a group of Tiffany vases *courtesy of J. Jonathan Joseph*. The jeweled altar cross (*opposite page, top left*) was made for the 1893 Chapel. In the peacock necklace (*opposite page, top right*) the central mosaic is of opals, amethysts and sapphires, the side pieces enamel on gold repoussé with opals, rubies and emeralds. The articles of jewelry (*opposite page, center right*) were exhibited by the Museum of Contemporary Crafts in 1958. The necklace, pendant, cufflinks, bracelet and pin (*opposite page, bottom*) are in the author's collection. This jewelry is all marked with the stamp of Tiffany & Company.

In the author's collection are the group of Tiffany vases and salt cellar (*top left* and *bottom left*). The opaque copper-red iridescent vase with "Art Nouveau" overlay design (*top right*) was signed by Tiffany himself in 1898. The vase (*bottom right*) has a swirled design and red glass overlay.

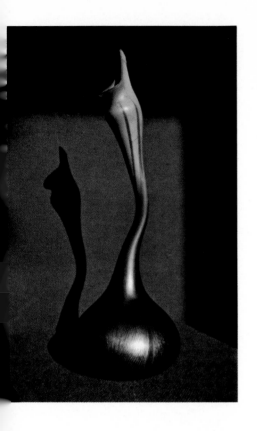

Shown (*top right*) are a punch bowl mounted in silvered bronze, made by Tiffany in 1900 for exhibition in Paris, now in the author's collection, and (*top left*) a goose-neck rosewater-sprinkler vase of peacock glass, also made in 1900. The group of vases (*bottom left*) and the iridescent golden rose bowl (*bottom right*) are also in the author's collection. All signed by Tiffany, they show a variety of techniques and colors.

The marbleized green bowl with gold thread overlay (*top left*) was purchased for the Musée des Arts Décoratifs in Paris from S. Bing in 1894. The iridescent plate (*top right*) with a peacock-feather design and the iridescent volcano, or lava ware, bowl (*center right*) 6-5/16″ high, are in the collection of the Metropolitan Museum of Art. The iridescent blue vase (*bottom left*) is known as a jack-in-the-pulpit design and is in the Corning Museum of Glass. Of the two vases shown (*bottom right*) the smaller opaque blue and green iridescent vase with varicolored bosses is in the Design Collection of the Museum of Modern Art, New York; the larger one, inset with stones, was exhibited at the Paris Salon in 1906 and is now in the Musée des Arts Décoratifs of the Louvre.

Shown (*top left*) are two flower-form vases and a goblet, an iridescent four-footed vase with a feather pattern (*bottom left*), a green translucent vase with a wave and feather motif and four miniatures (*bottom right*). The golden iridescent vase with lilypad design (*top right*) was made and signed by Tiffany for his sister, Mrs. Alfred Mitchell of New Haven. It is now owned by the author.

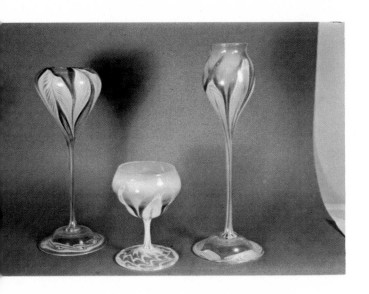

Laurelton Hall is shown (*above*) shortly before it was destroyed by fire; (*below*) a detail of a dragon tile by Tiffany formerly mounted above the entrance, now in the author's collection.

part three

"Good Art In Our Homes"

FAVRILE GLASS

After 1900 Tiffany's name began to be associated with art glass even more than with stained glass or mosaic. As he became better known to the public, his standing as an artist was frequently a matter of debate—was he more interested in art or was he more interested in commercialism? Tiffany himself never believed he had abandoned art in favor of the marketplace; to him the profit motive was not the major factor in the commercialization by which his career was increasingly marked. He simply wanted, he stated time and time again, to provide good art for American homes, to offer objects of quality for the widest possible audience. He was convinced that his concept of beauty was absolute and self-perpetuating and that once his designers and workers had been properly trained by him and steeped in his principles they could continue to produce beautiful objects by the carload—with a minimum of supervision.

He was eclectic in adapting earlier styles to his purposes, basing some of the shapes for his designs in glass, for instance, on ancient Middle Eastern, Iberian and Islamic forms. In his aesthetic approach Tiffany consistently held to a traditional

[*119*]

criteria not too far from Burke's definition of the cardinal principles of beauty, which were first stated in 1756 in his essay "On The Sublime and Beautiful," later reprinted in book form in New York in 1892. These qualities of beauty, "as they are merely sensible qualities," were: "First, to be comparatively small. Secondly, to be smooth. Thirdly, to have variety in the direction of the parts; but fourthly, to have those parts not angular but melted as it were into each other. Fifthly, to be of a delicate frame without any remarkable appearance of strength. Sixthly, to have colors clear and bright, but not very strong and glaring." In an article written for *Country Life in America* entitled "The Gospel of Good Taste," Tiffany rested his hopes for better art on the ability of the common man to understand and share his views. "It is all a matter of education, and we shall never have good art in our homes until the people learn to distinguish the beautiful from the ugly . . . We have too many rules now; most of them should be discarded. We should avoid all extravagances of ornament and seek simplicity. We should study classic art, and learn that the simplest things are the best, learn also to avoid glaring contrasts of color and over-elaboration."

Like other Art Nouveau artists, Tiffany advocated the use of new and unconventional forms and techniques within traditional concepts, but he was often unable to achieve a successful synthesis. His own generation, while it could tolerate the "new look" of the Art Nouveau movement, with its swirls and exotic ornament, found it difficult to accept the revolutionary art of the young generation of artists who created a totally new concept and swore by startling criteria. Today, with an increased emphasis on personal visual experience, Tiffany's aims can perhaps be more readily accepted and many of the articles created by him or under his supervision according to his principles of beauty better appreciated as works of art in their own right.

Encouraged by Bing and heartened by the reception of his designs at the Chicago Fair, he confidently set out to provide for the households of America objects of everyday use which he felt would enrich the lives of the people by their beauty. About the time Tiffany's chapel was sent to Chicago in 1893 he established his own glass furnaces from which would come quantities of his world-famous Favrile glass—in Corona, Long Island. Expert glassblowers and workers were hired, some from abroad, some from the Boston and Sandwich Glass Company of Sandwich, Massachusetts, which had gone out of business after a long and costly strike in 1887 and 1888.

The results of the first successful glassblowing experiments at Corona were shipped by Tiffany to Bing in Paris, who was delighted by Tiffany's success in America and pleased by the attention given to his windows and to his earliest vases and bowls. Bing considered the vase to be the highest form of expression in glass and declared his amazement that "after all the accomplishments of the Venetians, of Gallé and others, it was still possible to innovate, to utilize glass in a new way that was often opaque and mat, with a surface that was like skin to the touch, silky and delicate." To Bing, Tiffany's art glass stood out among the other popular glasswares of the period as truly unique. He wrote a rapturous description of a peacock-feather vase for an exhibit of Tiffany ware at the Grafton Galleries in London. "Just as in the natural feather itself, we find here a suggestion of the impalpable, the tenuity of the fronds and their pliability . . . Never, perhaps, has any man carried to greater perfection the art of faithfully rendering Nature in her most seductive aspects. And, on the other hand, this power which the author possesses of assigning in advance to each morsel of glass, whatever its color or chemical composition, the exact place which it is to occupy when the article leaves the glassblower's hands—this truly unique art is combined in these peacock's feathers with the charm of iridescence which bathes the subtle and velvety ornamentation with an almost supernatural light."

A single piece of ornamental glass began, of course, as an iridescent ball of glass from a furnace, slightly dilated by the initial inspiration of air. Bing described the process. "The workman charges it at certain pre-arranged points with small quantities of glass of different textures and different colors, and in the operation is hidden the germ of the intended ornamentation. The little ball is then returned to the fire to be heated. Again it is subjected to a similar treatment (the process sometimes being repeated as many as twenty times) and, when all the different glasses have been combined and manipulated in different ways, and the article has been brought to its definite state as to form and dimensions . . . the motifs introduced into the ball when it was small have grown with the vase itself, but in differing proportions; they have lengthened or broadened, while each tiny ornament fills the place assigned to it in advance in the mind of the artist."

Brochures supplied by Tiffany provided scant information on the exact process used in Tiffany glass, declaring only that Tiffany "obtained his iridescent and lustre effects . . . by a careful study of the natural decay of glass . . . and by reversing the action in such a way as to arrive at the effects without disintegration." In comparing glass which had developed a natural iridescence after centuries of lying buried in the earth and the antique pitted type of Tiffany's iridescent ware, known as Cypriote, it is apparent that the later pieces have a remarkable versimilitude. The lustrous patina fitted the lavish taste of the nineties, with all its fondness for luster, irregularity and richness of detail. Such an effect was described by Tiffany in his patent application of 1880, "The effect is a highly iridescent one and of pleasing metallic luster, changeable from one to the other, depending upon the direction of the visual ray and the brilliancy or dullness of the light falling upon or passing through the glass."

Tiffany did not state that he had invented the means for producing iridescent glass, but did describe the method he used in the patent claim filed in 1880. "The metallic luster is produced by forming a film of a metal or its oxide, or a compound of a metal, on or in the glass, either by exposing it to vapors or gases or by direct application. It may also be produced by corroding the surface of the glass, such processes being well known to glass-manufacturers." Gold chloride was used both in suspension in the glass and sprayed on the surface before cooling. The gold in the glass was brought to the surface by a reducing flame. The effect could be intensified by the use of a spray which etched the surface, creating a satinlike texture. Twenty-dollar goldpieces were placed in a solution of nitric and hydrochloric acid, which was heated and thinned for use in a spray.

Sir David Brewster (1781–1868), a Scotch physicist, was the first to experiment with the iridescent patina produced by the decomposition of ancient glass. He patented his colorful kaleidoscope in 1817. In the latter decades of the nineteenth century wide interest was generated in the ancient glass objects, naturally iridescent, which were being evacuated by archaeologists working at many sites in the Middle East. Modern iridescent glass was first made in Bohemia and in Venice before 1880. According to Anne Huether's *Glass and Man*, Ludwig Lobmeyr exhibited the first iridescent glass to be produced commercially at an exposition in Vienna in 1873; European craftsmen were among the first to see and be influenced by Tiffany's work in this field, since samples were sent abroad even before they were introduced to the New York market.

Almost the entire glassblowing production of the Corona Furnaces' first year— 1894—was reportedly shipped to various museums. Some 38 items were sold to the Smithsonian Institution in Washington, D. C., 50 were sent to the Musée des Arts Décoratifs in Paris (this division of the Louvre had purchased a single example from S. Bing on June 3, 1894), 23 were reportedly sent to the Imperial Museum of Fine Arts in Tokyo, and 56 were presented to the Metropolitan Museum of Art in New York City as the gift of Henry O. Havemeyer, to be followed in subsequent years by other examples presented by an anonymous donor and by the Louis Comfort Tiffany Foundation to complement the original collection. According to Tiffany, collections went to various other museums, the Art Institute of Chicago, the "South Kensington Museum" (the Victoria and Albert Museum in South Kensington stated that there was no record of pieces having been presented by him, but that some pieces were purchased by the museum in the closing years of the century), the Royal Museum in Berlin, the Cincinnati Museum of Art and the Boston Museum of Fine Arts. The Art Institute of Chicago declared it had no record of any such gift made at this time. The Cincinnati Museum stated that no pieces of Tiffany glassware were acquired in 1894, but that in 1897 Alfred T. Goshorn purchased 29 pieces and a stand. The Boston Museum of Fine Arts stated that the pieces in their collection did not come during the 1890's as Tiffany's gift but as a bequest many years later.

Not until early in 1896 did Tiffany feel he was ready to launch his new product on the market. This he did by means of an exhibition in his Fourth Avenue studios to which the press was invited. *The New York Times* called the glass "curious and entirely novel, both in color and texture." The New York *Herald* called the variety of shades "almost bewildering." The *Commercial Advertiser* described the display as "a fine arts museum in itself, with all the attributes of form, beauty and design . . . the effects are spontaneous; there is no artificiality about them."

Bing, as Tiffany's friend as well as European distributor, held the first major public exhibition of Tiffany glass at his shop at 22 Rue de Provence, which had been transformed from a showroom of Oriental *objets d'art* into the Salon de l'Art Nouveau by the architect Louis Bonnier and the English painter Frank Brangwyn. Perhaps at the suggestion of Louis C. Tiffany, and certainly with his knowledge and encouragement, Bing's business took a new direction. The shop's grand opening, on December 26, 1895, was the first representative exhibition of what has come to be known as Art Nouveau. Besides the ten Tiffany glass windows by French artists which Bing had commissioned and some twenty pieces of Tiffany blown glass, there were also examples of glass by Gallé, jewelry by Lalique, furniture by Lemmen and Van de Velde, paintings by Anquetin, Besnard, Bonnard, Brangwyn, Denis, Ibels, Khnopff, Menzel, Pissarro, Ranson, Roussel, Serusier, Signac, Toulouse-Lautrec, Vuillard and Zorn, sculpture by Bourdelle, Meunier, Rodin and Vallgren, prints and drawings by Beardsley, Mary Cassatt, Carriere, Walter Crane, Eckmann and Whistler, posters by the Beggarstaff brothers, Mackintosh and Will Bradley. Louis C. Tiffany was to be known after this as the foremost American representative of Art Nouveau, which has recently been recognized as the first and formative stage of the modern movement in art.

Tiffany's blown glass "so attracted the attention of European connoisseurs that in many of the museums of Europe . . . small collections were gathered together as object lessons for local craftsmen . . . Tiffany's works were the first by an American artist to be known and imitated even in provincial regions of Europe." Karl Koepping (1848–1914) produced glass vessels of "exquisite fragility and slenderness" in Germany by 1895. Examples of Austrian and Bohemian glass copied after Tiffany's vases were exhibited at the opening of a new exhibition building for the Vienna *Sezession* in 1898. Graf Harrach of Neuwelt, Bohemia, made copies of Tiffany's flower-form vases, which were particularly popular in Europe. Gustav Pazaurek, in his treatise on glass, *Moderne Glaser*, reproduced a Harrach vase which was a veritable duplicate of a Tiffany vase in the Havemeyer collection at the Metropolitan Museum of Art. He objected to Tiffany's use of iridescence and luster, which he felt were against the very nature of glass because they robbed it of its "finest quality, its absolute transparency." Pazaurek contrasted the art of Venetian glassmakers, who traditionally relied on the material itself for effect, with the mode of the Cisalpine glassmakers, who relied on cutting and engraving for effect. He singled out the work of the French designer Emile Gallé, with its delicacy and fantastic colors, as a good model for German glassmakers. Gallé rejected the "perfect" look of machine-produced glass and used flower and leaf forms imaginatively in his vases, also experimenting with bubbles and other imperfections in the glass itself.

The styles of Tiffany and Gallé were contrasted by Greta Daniel in "The Decorative Arts," in *Art Nouveau*. "Tiffany's art, like Gallé's, originated with technique . . . Unlike Gallé, who cut decorations from various layers of colored glass superimposed on each other, Tiffany's technique was to control the way in which the layers of color were made to flow either transparently or opaquely over each other, bringing about an abstract play of line and color. . . . His colors and forms suggest the quality of a mood as summer is suggested by the pearly iridescence on the wings of a butterfly." She rated Tiffany's products above those in the ceramics field of the Rookwood and Grueby workshops as reflecting the "American master of the New Style," and found his designs remarkably inventive. "He would often go back," she commented, "to traditional Oriental and European prototypes for the shapes of bowls and vases, but most of the forms he used were uniquely his own and extraordinarily inventive and unconventional as the iridescent colors with which they were decorated. Graceful images of exotic flowers on attenuated stems, twisted fruit forms or lumps of oddly shaped glass with casual openings created a dream world in which proportion and detail had been strangely transformed. In Tiffany glass the exotic and the irregular became the norm. When Tiffany combined metal with glass he produced objects in which structure and decoration were eloquently integrated."

Max Ritter von Spaun created Tiffanyesque vases at the factory of Johannes Loetz Witwe of Klostermuhle, Austria, beginning in 1898 and continuing in production until after 1918. These were declared to have good color effects and forms, but although they had a luxurious surface they were said to lack "the beautiful velvet softness of the opaque glasses of American origin." A further comparison of the products of Tiffany's most prolific European imitator was made by Professor Herwin Schaefer: "While Tiffany's glass has a silky texture and sheen, Loetz vases often have a cheap, metallic glare." He felt that the Austrian forms were more forced and contrived, although he felt Tiffany also was capable of clumsy forms, "particularly in his combinations of glass and metal."

With few exceptions the glass of Tiffany's competitors, according to Stuart Feld, "lacked the inventive design and inherent quality of material that characterized Tiffany's productions." The earliest American imitator was Martin Bach, Sr., who had been among Tiffany's glassworkers at Corona in 1894 and who set up his own plant in 1901. He and his partner William Overend, also previously employed by Tiffany, formed the Quezal Art Glass and Decorating Company in Brooklyn, which began to market iridescent glass in 1902. Martin Bach, Jr., was later engaged by Baccarat-born Victor Durand, who set up an art glass division in his Vineland Flint Glass works, established in 1897 in Vineland, New Jersey. The art glass made here has come to be known as Durand glass. The glass known as Kew Blas, produced by the Union Glass Company of Somerville, Massachusetts, was more opalescent than iridescent and was coated smoothly with clear glass. Such items as vases, candlesticks, creamers and pitchers were available in shades of deep blue, green, rose, gold and bronze. The pressed glass known as taffeta or carnival glass, with an inferior iridescent effect in imitation of Tiffany glass, was obtainable in golden orange luster tones or in purple and blue-green shades. There were, of course, many other kinds of art glass, both American and European, on the market.

In terms of both quality and quantity, the glass that was most like that of Tiffany was Frederick Carder's Steuben glass. Aurene was the trade name of Steuben's iridescent glass, which was first produced in 1904. This was an iridized glass with which Carder had experimented in England before establishing the Steuben Glass Works in Corning, New York. It was a metallic glass with a high metal content that remained in suspension as long as it was subjected to an oxidizing flame, but on contact with a reducing flame precipitated to the surface to form a shiny, semi-opaque metallic film. Iridescent hues, often gold or brilliant blue, the glistening surfaces alternating with deep shades of ordinary glass, were described as making pieces which were "akin to painting in their effects and to sculptural modeling in their method." The shapes were identical to those produced earlier by Tiffany. Decorative loops and swirls might be applied and the surfaces sprayed with a solution of stannous chloride to give them a sensuous, velvety texture.

Tiffany instituted a lawsuit against Steuben in November, 1913, which was settled out of court and discontinued in March, 1914. There was, in fact, very little basis for such a suit. In applying for a patent in 1880 Tiffany himself had used the phrase, in connection with iridescence, "such processes being well known to glass manufacturers." There was no infringement of methods. Carder had, on his own, developed a type of iridescent glass which was often indistinguishable from Tiffany's. Carder maintained in court that the glass manufactured by the plaintiff "having a golden iridescence and other color effects, is similar to or identical with glass and glassware manufactured in the United States and in Europe by processes and formulae known and used for many years prior to the organization of the plaintiff's company."

In general, the glass produced by or under the supervision of Louis C. Tiffany has a recognizable quality of style and workmanship that cannot be duplicated. Its

[125]

secret lies not so much in a chemical formula as in Tiffany's taste, his sensual feeling for form and color, the residue of his travels and experiences and of his many years of experimentation with and study of the unique properties of blown glass. Each genuine example embodies Tiffany's concept of beauty as an expression of harmonious variety achieved by a controlled technique. Yet perhaps the single factor which markedly differentiates Tiffany glass from that of his competitors was the freedom with which it was handled. It is a tribute also to the virtuosity of the craftsmen who worked for Tiffany that, without monotony or repetition, they could produce a full range of blown and decorated glass without violating the character of the material and without sacrificing the principles of good design.

Accidental qualities were prized and often effectively embodied in the glass to enhance the finished product. Edgar Kaufmann, Jr., observed in an article in *Interiors* (February, 1955), "Accident, the casual effect, was, furthermore, his approach to ornament; iridescence, acid etching, flowered or marbleized patterns that swell, stretch and converge according to the craftsman's puff and twist at the glass." Hugh McKean, a major collector of Tiffany ware, commented, "Here are 'free forms' sometimes thought of as originating in the School of Paris. The clean line of modern art is here too. There are fresh shapes and colors and textures here, the creation of Mr. Tiffany. In this art there is the daring and adventure of creation. These qualities keep art always new and always modern."

Tiffany's blown glass was known as "Favrile," the distinctive trademark chosen by Tiffany or one of his associates and registered in 1894. It was described as "a composition of various colored glasses, worked together while hot." Perhaps it was Tiffany's chief glassblower Arthur Nash who conceived of the name which would become a household word. An 1896 brochure stated that the word was derived from the Old English "fabrile," meaning "belonging to a craftsman or his craft." It was presented as "a material produced by what is believed to be a new formula, the outcome of a number of experiments instituted by and carried on by Mr. Louis C. Tiffany."

According to Albert Christian Revi, Arthur Nash and his son Leslie were responsible "for all the designs, glass formulas and decorating techniques, while Douglas Nash was entrusted with the distribution of the factory's wares in the better shops." In his *Nineteenth Century Glass*, Revi referred to other Tiffany factory locations, Jersey City and Hoboken in New Jersey, as well as the "Tiffany Furnaces" of Corona. His account of the Nashes' part in the development of Tiffany's Favrile glass attributes to them a major share in the operation of the business. To Leslie Nash he attributed Favrile Fabrique, a process for coating copper-mesh screen with glass for lampshades, the development of the peacock iridescent ware (for which he received, according to Revi, a partnership in the "Tiffany Furnaces"), and the

[*126*]

development of Cypriote glass, "an ingenious imitation of the nacreous and pimpled surface texture sometimes found on ancient specimens of glass." (It is more likely that Mr. Revi meant Arthur Nash, since both peacock and Cypriote glass were produced by Tiffany before Leslie Nash reached the age of fourteen.) Revi's version of the Tiffany-Nash set-up is as follows: "At first the Nashes encountered tough sledding to make ends meet at the factory, but Leslie Nash developed several very useful artistic and commercial products that brought the company onto firm financial ground—in spite of Mr. Tiffany's efforts to run the works on a philanthropic basis. Leslie introduced the manufacture of fine metalwares like bronze, copper and combinations of rare and semi-precious metals. He purchased huge metal stamping machinery to make the fine fittings for Tiffany glassware and other products . . . Mr. Tiffany's withdrawal of his financial support at a most crucial period was quite a shock to the Nashes, especially so when for the first time in years they were finally writing their ledgers in the black."

Although the Nashes admittedly received little or no credit in the promotion efforts of Tiffany's firm, to Arthur John Nash certainly belongs some of the credit for the superior quality of much of Tiffany's blown glass and some of the remarkable effects created by the manipulation of a variety of glasses. He was the only man ever employed by Tiffany who was allowed to sign his own pieces. (Glass made by Douglas and Leslie Nash from 1919 to 1928 is either not marked or marked simply "Nash.") While Arthur Nash was a superb manager, it is to Tiffany and his gaffers that the unique quality of the designs which distinguish Tiffany ware must be attributed. Perhaps without Tiffany's courage, support and entrepreneurship the Nashes could not have achieved the success they did. Arthur Nash, who was born in Stratford-on-Avon in 1849, had been a partner with Sir Edward Webb at the Whitehouse Glass Works at Stourbridge before coming to America. Leslie Nash, who claimed that his father was the sole inventor of Favrile glass and that he and his brother were the only persons who had the formula—secret from father to son—recalled, "Dad came to America, New York, as I remember it must have been, either July or August, 1892. Sometimes I think 1891 because glass was made in December '92 or '93 and the factory had to be built. . . . I was only eight years old and that is a long time ago." Apparently a fire in Nash's glasshouse had forced him to seek assistance elsewhere. Leslie Nash's memories of Tiffany were somewhat bitter. "You would have loved Dad—just the kind of a man a man likes to meet—direct, bright, full of energy, well-read, educated to perfection. To watch him work in the lab was a pleasure. . . . why try to rob a guy who gave so much and received so little? I don't know how it is that man craves honors and praises unless his mind is filled with ego."

Thomas Manderson, Tiffany's first gaffer, was a wizard with a blowpipe. He

[*127*]

could blow life into an ordinary piece of bottle glass and then, working with his son as a decorator, by applying varicolored rods, which were fused into the surface, he could proceed in a way that made it impossible for the ornament to contradict the shape. The glassblowing techniques were the same as those commonly used at such glass centers as Murano, but the results in the Corona laboratory were quite different. Tiffany, the Mandersons and the Nashes did not seek to produce either a pseudo-Venetian or a Victorian art glass, both then highly popular. These men achieved a mutual respect and understanding and the products of their collaboration reflect this synthesis. The best of them rival the jewel-like brilliance of the finest mosaics or stained glass windows. Many can be called gemlike in quality and color. The use of opaque, opalescent and iridescent glass in most of the blown pieces contributes to this rich effect and makes them unlike any previous style except, of course, that of the Tiffany windows.

The vases and bowls made before 1896 have an elegant simplicity, with, in most cases, the decoration imbedded in the surface of the glass. The only exceptions are those which have designs cut into the surface by a lapidary wheel, sometimes with a cameo effect. Tiffany and Nash employed a highly effective technique which was quite in the stream of sensuous art forms popular among Art Nouveau artists and illustrators and in the vein of contemporary symbolist literature, exemplified by Oscar Wilde's play, *Salomé*, "a fascinating mixture of exotic images and violent passions," Baudelaire's *Fleurs de Mal* and Huysmans' *Against the Grain*. The two found that glass, while hot and in a semi-fluid state, could, because of its high surface tension, be made to take on symbolic forms suggestive of vital organs or of organic abstractions with Expressionistic implications. The exquisite satiny or skinlike texture of the Tiffany pieces, which imparted a highly sensuous quality, was apparent from the earliest exhibitions of Favrile glass. Bulbous, pear and gourd shapes predominated, with combed or marbleized combinations of a variety of colors creating flowing lines of growth or force. An iridescent surface often provided additional variety.

The early pieces were not meant for sale and were not signed. Those which were numbered bear the prefix "X." Any later pieces not meant for sale also were marked with an "X" engraved near the base. A paper label was affixed to the base at the pontil mark, which appears on any piece of free-blown glass and marks the spot at which it was held by the blower. The pieces which were first offered for sale had two paper labels affixed to the base, one with a simple registry number and the other with the monogram of the Tiffany Glass and Decorating Company. As labels are quite perishable, some pieces of Tiffany blown glass made as early as 1894 or 1895 exist but no longer bear any identifying marks. These, however, are quite rare and of a quality that is readily recognizable.

From the time early in 1896 when a numbering system was instituted there were almost no exceptions. Each individual blown piece was inspected and marked before being annealed. Therefore, only very few pieces were smuggled out without being registered. However, pieces which were cracked or damaged in the showroom were sometimes sold at half-price. Tiffany once referred (in a letter written in 1926) to the numbering system used. "Each article of Favrile glass is marked with the Tiffany name or initials, and all unusual pieces bear a number, the letters of the alphabet being used first as a prefix, later as a suffix to the numbers." Pieces which were not unusual were simply given lot or pattern numbers with no letter designation.

This system, when coordinated with a change in the wording of the label, which was effected in 1900, makes it possible to date most unusual examples with a fair degree of accuracy. Those which have prefixes from A to N were produced from 1896 to 1900, those with a prefix from P to Z from 1901 to 1905, those with a suffix from A to N from 1906 to 1912 and those with a suffix from P to Z from 1913 to 1920. The prefix "X," meaning "not for sale," and the prefix "O," which indicated special orders, for use by family or friends, were assigned to some exceptional pieces. Some were, of course, pieces made for exhibition only. Those which Louis C. Tiffany liked particularly he signed with his own hand. Those which he wished to keep for himself were marked "A-Coll."

Stuart Feld, in a bulletin of the Metropolitan Museum of Art, presented another interpretation of the numbering system used by Tiffany. Feld may, however, have been influenced by misnumbering in the accession numbers used by the Metropolitan Museum of Art in listing their collection of Tiffany glass. His conclusion that the numbers on pieces refer to correlation between number and design could also account for the similarities of numbers of similar types that might well have been produced at about the same time.

By 1898 the Tiffany Glass and Decorating Company was storing between 200 and 300 tons of glass in the basement of its Corona plant, classified into some 5,000 different colors and varieties. Several thousand articles, no two exactly alike, were produced each year. The remarkable variety makes classification of shapes and styles of vases and bowls extremely difficult. The range was vast, from a clear crystal through a rainbow of shades to an opaque black, from restrained simplicity to wild eccentricity. Complex and elaborate techniques were developed to improve the quality, with no thought given to expense.

AT THE CREST

While the craze for Tiffany glass lasted, Louis C. Tiffany, as president of the bustling Tiffany Glass and Decorating Company, was in his glory. He was his own boss, with more than a hundred skilled workers in his employ. He was free to design and to experiment. His family was well provided for, with his son at Yale and his oldest daughter Mary married to Graham Lusk, the son of the Tiffany family physician. Charles L. Tiffany was proud of his son's accomplishments and pleased that, as a result, he was lauded as a patron of the arts. He was confident that his only grandson, Charles L. Tiffany II, would someday take his own place in the family business. That was a part of the bargain. Graduated from Yale in 1900, he had always known and never objected to the fact that he was being groomed for an executive position in Tiffany & Company. Charles L. Tiffany II later became vice-president and vice-chairman of the board of the jewelry firm, effectively maintaining policies established by his grandfather.

Every morning, after breakfasting with his wife and younger daughters, Louis C. Tiffany would walk with his children to school before calling at the Fourth Avenue studios to inspect work in progress. If no new orders demanded his attention and things were going smoothly he would proceed to Corona, where he enjoyed spending most of his time. There he could personally direct the operation of transforming ordinary sand into shimmering works of art, each one different from the next.

Most of his employees liked and respected him. To them, as to his family, he was a paternalistic tyrant. He was always there but never in the way. He did not waste words, but was as generous with praise and encouragement as with criticism. He knew what he wanted and was often able to show how it might be obtained, but was never satisfied with anything less than perfection. He was sympathetic and understanding but always managed to have his own way.

He had developed during his years in the decorating business a facility for working with others, including skilled women, and he was able to direct the work of his assistants in such a way as to make each of them feel important. He frequently encouraged women to take active roles in the business. Mrs. Clara Driscoll, who came to work for him in 1887, was trained as a designer. She later organized a women's glass-cutting department and in 1900 won a prize in Paris for her design for a dragonfly lamp. By 1904, she was one of the highest-paid women workers in the United States, earning a salary of more than $10,000 a year.

[130]

Tiffany paid good salaries but never gave advances. If he discovered that anyone in his employ was making purchases on credit or had gone into debt, this was sufficient grounds for dismissal. He had learned a bitter lesson from the Lyceum Theater failure and had seen Steele MacKaye come to a tragic end, a victim of credit financing. He wished to be kept informed of all personal problems and often gave help where he could, but on a strictly cash basis.

In his leisure hours Tiffany customarily spent his evenings either in entertaining or being entertained. He deplored the fact that his second wife did not enjoy going out more often, as he himself felt more at home than ever in the theater. He found that his own work and his vast, unknown audience gave him something in common with the actor, who, by his creative performance onstage, brought joy into the life of strangers. Tiffany felt that he was contributing to an artistic renaissance which would usher in a new era of enlightenment. But this was the decade of the "gay nineties," and he enjoyed them to the fullest.

By the turn of the century Louis C. Tiffany was, at the age of fifty-two, world-famous. A lesser man might have been content to rest on his laurels. But his father, a vigorous eighty-eight, was still personally directing the affairs of Tiffany & Company, and he encouraged his son to expand still further if he wished. Louis C. Tiffany had by this time acquired a country estate, The Briars, on Long Island. Here he spent his summers, directing his gardeners and painting flowers. He was close enough to his factory to commute to Corona if necessary. He might, instead, choose to read aloud from articles in current periodicals containing flattering references to him and his work. He was more relaxed in this era than he had ever been before and increasingly allowed his sensuous feelings to emerge both in his designs and, before long, in a home far more sumptuous than The Briars, which was subsequently used by his married daughter and her growing family.

The Briars, a home in the Colonial manner, was decorated in a style far simpler than that chosen by Tiffany for his 72nd Street studio. In another group of interiors designed by Tiffany in the nineties the treatment of walls and placement of doors and fireplaces featured the same *kamoi* division which he had utilized in interiors since the decoration of the Armory in 1880, but in this case the lines were thinner, the woodwork lighter and the ornamentation more restrained. Where leaded glass was used in doors and windows it was organized into proportional rectangles. The frieze decorations were more a series of repeat patterns than a system of interlaces. The sense of continuity in these rooms, as they looked when photographed in 1900, was complete down to the last detail, including andirons, rugs, bric-a-brac and electroliers, all of which had been carefully selected for size, shape and relative proportion. Only the hanging "stalactite" Favrile glass globes in the dining room provided a clear contrast to the rectilinear structural definitions. In the library an irregular oval desk in the center of the room was effectively placed to animate the space; in the billiard room the angular solidity of the billiard table imparted a strong masculine character. The furniture was produced by a furniture firm under Tiffany's supervision. Although some pieces bear a resemblance to the French Empire style, the effect is surprisingly modern.

The general trend toward simplicity in interior decoration was pointed out by Candace Wheeler, who had retired from an active role in business, in her book *Principles of Home Decoration*, published in 1903. "The principles of truth and harmony which underlie all beauty may be secured in the most inexpensive cottage as well as in the broadest and most imposing residence. Indeed, the cottage has the advantage of that most potent ally of beauty—simplicity. . . . It is the principle, or requirement, of geometric base in interior design which, coupled with our natural delight in yielding or growing forms, has maintained through all the long history of decoration what is called conventional flower design."

In 1901 came a personal milestone—the birth of Tiffany's first grandson, William T. Lusk. In the same year he was accorded an honor that meant more, perhaps, to him than all his prizes and medals. He had always been somewhat self-conscious about his lack of a college education. Through the years he had had continuing associations with Yale University, even before his son enrolled there. Donald G. Mitchell had been one of the early and active supporters of the Yale Art Gallery in the 1860's. Tiffany had supplied the decorations for the Wolf's Head Society in 1883, he had designed the Williams window for Yale's Battell Chapel in 1888 and the Chittenden window for the library in 1890. Tiffany's son-in-law, Graham Lusk, had taught at the Yale Medical School. It was probably Robert W. de Forest, a Yale graduate of 1870, who proposed that Tiffany be considered as decorator for the Yale Bicentennial. The two men worked together on a committee. The affair was rated a huge success. The entire campus was adorned with orange Japanese lanterns, blue flags and evergreens. These were hung from posts and bars that lined the streets and screened many of the buildings. The effect was as impressive at night as during the day, and many who were in New Haven for this celebration felt that this was Tiffany's most effective job of decoration. Yale showed its appreciation by awarding him an honorary master of arts degree in June of 1903.

After the death of Charles L. Tiffany on February 18, 1902, at which time Charles T. Cook became president of Tiffany & Company, to be succeeded in 1907 by John C. Moore, Louis C. Tiffany purchased outright from the estate the 72nd Street house. He then began to make plans for a new mansion for himself. Before the end of the year he had purchased a tract of 580 acres at Oyster Bay, Long Island, with an extensive shoreline facing Cold Spring Harbor. On this property stood an old-fashioned resort hotel called Laurelton Hall. On April 11, 1903, the Brooklyn *Daily Eagle* announced: "Louis C. Tiffany has decided that Laurelton Hall as a hotel shall be closed to the public. He purchased the well-known property not long ago and has already set a large force of men at work constructing a large dwelling-house near the present hotel structure." The hotel was torn down and the new structure completed in August of 1904, less than four months after the death of the second Mrs. Tiffany.

When the chimes in the clock-tower of Laurelton Hall first rang out, Louis C. Tiffany was not there to hear them—he was away on a summer holiday. The scandalous circumstances surrounding the death of Stanford White had convinced Tiffany that the strictest parental discipline was necessary. He became even more of a domestic tyrant, insisting on absolute punctuality and the observance of all kinds of formalities for the seventeen-year-old twins, Julia and Louise Comfort, usually known as Comfort, and Dorothy, thirteen. He disapproved, in turn, of each of his daughters' fiancés. Craving the limelight, he ceaselessly sought publicity for his own concepts of beauty and art. His reputation for being something of an eccentric seems to have begun at this time.

Business matters, however, also clamored for his attention, and new departments proliferated. After the death of Charles L. Tiffany, the 333 Fourth Avenue building which had housed Louis C. Tiffany's early glass experiments was sold and all departments formerly operating there were relocated at Madison Avenue and 45th Street in a structure which had been designed for the Manhattan Athletic Club. This now became the Tiffany Studios. Then, in 1905, Tiffany & Company also made a move further uptown, to occupy a handsome building at Fifth Avenue and 37th Street which had been designed for it by Stanford White. Both Tiffany & Company and the Tiffany Studios carried products of the "Tiffany Furnaces." The new departments which had been developed by Tiffany included a department of metalwork, an expanded decorating service incorporating a complete furniture firm, as well as departments of enameling, jewelry and ceramics.

When he felt the mosaic and stained-glass window departments and the glass-blowing division were well in hand, Tiffany began to cast about for new areas in which to expand. The department of metalwork had been set up in the closing years of the nineteenth century. He had designed some objects which were cast in bronze for use in the Seventh Regiment Armory, but it was not until the Corona Furnaces were completed that any such objects were offered for sale. More than a decade of experience as a decorator had provided Tiffany with a wide experience in the field of lighting fixtures and enabled him to develop a distinctive style that was both practical and decorative. He had also designed gas sconces for the White House, electric lights for the Lyceum Theater and massive chandeliers for the Havemeyer house.

Tiffany's lamps were first offered to the public in 1895. Like the vases of the period, they were generally bulbous in shape. The bases of his bronzes were marked with the monogram of the Tiffany Glass and Decorating Company and the model number. Tall-stemmed bronze candelabra in a Queen Anne's lace pattern and "dandelion" lamps were made before 1900, but the same or similar molds were used after 1900, when the designation "Tiffany Studios, New York" replaced the earlier marking.

Lamps produced from special designs for the Tiffany Glass and Decorating Company had been exhibited in the Women's Building at the Chicago Fair of 1893. Tiffany bronzes exhibited in Paris in 1900 included kerosene lamps, the dragonfly lamp designed by Clara Driscoll, Tiffany's dandelion lamp, a spider-web desk set and several bases for tall, slender bud vases.

By the end of the nineteenth century artificial light had been made more widely available by means of Edison's incandescent bulbs, the earliest of which had been blown at the Corning Glass Works in Corning, New York. Hanging and standing lamps and electroliers, priced at more than $100 apiece, were soon popular items of sale at the Tiffany showrooms. Tiffany did not originate models of lamps with leaded glass shades, but those made in his studios, along with bronze bases which were sometimes combined with glass, were of the finest design and quality of workmanship. These shades achieved great popularity and were extensively copied both in America and abroad. The Tiffany Studios mark was placed on either the top or bottom rim of the shade.

The most famous Tiffany lamp, the lily-cluster design with morning-glory shades, won a grand prize for Tiffany at the Turin Exhibition of 1902. The original design was made up to contain eighteen bulbs, but the same basic shape was adapted to lamps in green or gilt bronze containing from three to twenty bulbs. Between 1902 and 1914 Tiffany left the designing of leaded glass for lamps largely to others, while he devoted himself to projects which he felt would contribute to the glorification of his name and the perpetuation of his concept of beauty.

The leaded glass lamps sold as rapidly as they were produced and his business interests flourished. He was constantly introducing new patterns, most of which were designed by his employees. The well-known Wisteria lamp, which was designed in 1901, was created by Mrs. Curtis Freshel. The lamps varied in size from 7 to 36 inches in diameter and ranged as high as $750 in price. Patterns made under the supervision of Clara Driscoll included such motifs as Ivy, Pansy, Daffodil, Rose (in either yellow or red), Geometric, Leaf, Orange Petal, Geranium and Butterfly. Other types included the Weight-Balance, Cushion-Back Globe, Scarab, Snail, Turtle-Back and Linen-Fold. The Spider-web lamp had a base covered with glass mosaics. Two designs by Tiffany, one incorporating a Queen Anne's lace motif, were patented in 1914 and 1918.

Among the items made by Tiffany Studios after 1900 were such articles as desk sets, ash trays, enameled boxes, jewelry, tableware and ceramic lamp bases. The desk sets were made in more than ten different patterns and included plain sets, combinations of glass and bronze, enamel and inlay of glass or mother-of-pearl. The first of these to be shown was the "pine-needle" design, which was exhibited in Paris in 1900, followed by the popular "grapevine" pattern. These featured stamped and openwork metal with a backing of marbleized glass, usually amber or green in color, with the metal etched to produce a greenish patina. Matching accessories consisted of such objects as bill files, blotter-ends, book racks, trinket boxes, calendar holders, scales, paperweights, letter racks, letter openers, clips, etc., ranging in price from $4.00 to $20.00 each. Other patterns offered in metalware were Zodiac, Crab, Bookmark, Ninth Century, Venetian, the costly Byzantine (an inkstand was priced at $55.00), Abalone, Chinese and American Indian, which was introduced in 1909.

A bewildering array of household items, some made of Favrile glass and metal, were produced under the Tiffany trademark; among these were cigar lighters; cigar, cigarette and tobacco boxes and jars; smoking sets and stands; inkstands; jardinieres, mantel and traveling clocks; thermometers; twine holders; photograph frames; pen-holders; penwipers; pincushions; pin trays; sealing-wax trays; dishes for nuts, bonbons, olives, fruit, nuts, berries, salad, ferns; compotiers; epergnes; marmalade jars; salt cellars; decanters; finger bowls; punch bowls; flower holders; cologne bottles; vinaigrette bottles; pitchers; syrup jugs; tankards; goblets; cups; plates; plaques and seals.

For a few years the decorating department was operated under several different plans. In 1898 it absorbed the Schmitt Brothers Furniture Company by creating a system of interlocking directorates, with Pringle Mitchell and John Platt on the boards of both corporations. Pringle Mitchell died, however, two years after this step was taken. On April 2, 1900, the Allied Arts Company was formed to take in both the Tiffany Studios and the Schmitt Brothers Furniture Company. Thereafter the name "Tiffany Glass and Decorating Company" was no longer used. Tiffany Studios absorbed the Allied Arts Company, including the furniture shop, in 1902. The Schmitt Brothers remained in the firm until 1907, when they again set up on their own. Under the new plan the firm proposed to supply industrial artwork and useful and ornamental articles in glass, metal, wood and other materials, and undertook to provide whatever was necessary pertaining to the exterior and interior fitting, furnishing and decorating of buildings of every description, including carpets, rugs and other fabrics.

The decorating service of Tiffany Studios carried a full line of Oriental rugs, "artistic furniture" and "quality reproductions" and an assortment of fabrics which could be used for draperies, curtains, bedspreads, etc., made up in patterns harmonizing with Tiffany glass and metal ware. Tiffany took a keen interest in the work of the department. René de Quelin, who described himself as head designer and manager, wrote that Tiffany's "ideas for decoration and glass were mainly expressed by quick, rough color memoranda that could only be understood or interpreted by artists who surrounded him." Charles de Kay later commented, in *The Art Work of Louis C. Tiffany*, on his contributions: "One need not be surprised, then, to find that Louis C. Tiffany has been tempted to make excursions into the field of the loom through the charm of textile work, in order to obtain rugs, carpets and hangings which will express his particular color sense and harmonize with certain given interiors. While he has never set up looms of his own, he has devoted a good deal of time to the dyeing and finishing of textiles woven elsewhere, taking loom works of a neutral shade and giving them art value under his personal superintendence. In this way he has made them vie with paintings for their color charm and greatly surpass paintings in purely decorative effect. Some exhibit changes of tint as they fall in folds and catch the light; their shadows are full of unexpected colors."

The enameling department was set up with a staff of four young women—Miss Julia Munson and Miss Patty Gay, and two apprentices—in a small laboratory in Tiffany's 72nd Street mansion. It was then moved to the building on 23rd Street which had once housed the embroidery department of the Associated Artists, and in 1903 was given more spacious facilities at Corona, with Miss Alice Goovy in charge.

The first Tiffany enamels were exhibited in Buffalo, New York, in 1901 and were immediately acclaimed in the pages of *The Craftsman*. Samuel Howe supplied an article on his erstwhile employer. "Mr. Louis C. Tiffany has, for some years, been carrying on elaborate experiments in enamels and pastes, applied, for the most part, to lamp bodies, small boxes, vases and the like. He has produced an astonishing range of color, surface and gradations of transparency and translucency, from the absolutely clear to the completely opaque, and by applying his compositions to the surfaces of repoussé copper, has attained most interesting results."

According to Julia Munson, Tiffany's role in designing various objects, including enamels and jewelry, consisted of making suggestions of usable forms in nature and of supplying occasionally a rough pencil sketch, or perhaps selecting a suitable model from his vast collection of Oriental and Near Eastern pieces. He could supply specimens of Chinese cloisonné or Japanese sword guards for any desired purpose. The designers under him were generally given the job of working out the suggestions in terms of the material to be used. In the case of enameling, the final stage consisted of spraying on a characteristic iridescent surface before cooling.

Enamel remained for a while a popular medium for Art Nouveau ornament and was frequently used for jewelry, at which Tiffany also tried his hand. By 1902, *The Studio* noted, "little by little it was being abandoned in favor of tones such as onyx, agate and malachite . . . which can be cut in different ways and whose color gives fine effects infinitely preferable to those of inferior enamels." As fashionable New York jewelers, Tiffany & Company through the years had provided an array of opulent pieces, including elaborate testimonial swords with scabbards of gold studded with rubies, diamonds and sapphires. Tiffany, as the art director and vice-president of Tiffany & Company, was not limited to enamels or even to onyx. He could easily afford to obtain the rich tones he liked by using any number of precious or semi-precious stones in his unique jewelry.

When Louis C. Tiffany was vice-president of Tiffany & Company, a separate artistic jewelry department was established, with Julia Munson in charge. Relatively few pieces were made for this department, and many of them were quite expensive. However, the department did not show a profit. Some smaller and less expensive pieces were made and eventually sold, but production of this kind of jewelry was finally discontinued in 1916.

The "ruthless mixture of precious, semi-precious and worthless materials" had suddenly become fashionable about 1895, but it went out of vogue just as suddenly, some fifteen years later. At the Paris Salon of 1906 a few notable Tiffany pieces were exhibited. One brooch, "a marine motif, half crab, half octopus, with writhing feet split into two or more special ends," set with opals, sapphires and rubies, attracted particular attention. The design had been sketched in pencil on a piece of cardboard and is characteristic of Tiffany's style—semi-abstract, Art Nouveau in form, with a sensuous and disturbing expression of young shapes, possibly young, growing ferns, which seem about to unwind.

Charles de Kay acknowledged, speaking for Tiffany in *The Art Work of Louis C. Tiffany*, the rich inspiration of gems and nature plus the influence of the enamels of China and Japan, Byzantium and the Italian Renaissance. "A painter born with a sense for color must revel in the deep-set richness of hue offered by precious gems and the tones so lavishly presented by nature in marbles, onyx, malachite and car-nelian; in various shells; in pearls, opals and coral; in old amber and tortoise shell; the flower-like colors of jewels, hues rivaled only by sunsets, rainbows and the northern aurora." Indestructibility and seeming fragility were the qualities sought.

One of Tiffany's earliest designs was based on what he called a "charming weed," the "unpretending wheel" of the wild carrot, or Queen Anne's lace. This unusual brooch was formed of a number of small white or delicate mauve flowers, centered with a garnet, the lace being of white enamel on silver. A dragonfly enameled and set with opals on a platinum base made an unusual hatpin. A blackberry spray was made with berries of garnets and carnelians and leaves of enameled gold outlined in silver. A girdle of silver ornamented with opals had berries of opals. In a cluster of clover blossoms, flowers of hammered gold overlaid with yellow enamel were sprinkled with diamond dewdrops, contrasting with leaves and stems of repoussé and filigree silver overlaid with green enamel. A peacock necklace had a gold center-piece with a mosaic of opals, amethysts and sapphires, decorated on the reverse with flamingoes. On the sidepieces, which were enamel on gold repoussé, were opals, rubies and emeralds. Below a pendant of the necklace hung a single ruby, selected for its exact shade. Fullblown dandelions, spirea and four-o-clocks were other flower forms which were adapted into unusual pieces.

Among the designs produced by Tiffany judged most worthy of mention by *The Craftsman* were a clover-blossom tiara, a coiffure ornament in the form of a cluster of blackberries, a necklace and a girdle. "The necklace suggests the metal work of the Etruscans," an account of an exhibit stated, "but in this piece a new art has lent a charm unknown to the old work. The translucence of the green and blue enamel upon silver, the deep color quality of the sapphires, the sheen of the garnets set at the center of the flower forms, combine to gratify the eye as the intense, unrelieved yellow of the Etruscan gold could never do. The girdle uses as its motif the bitter-sweet. Its boldness counterfeits the hand of Lalique himself, while its delicacy makes it suitable for personal adornment and use rather than a museum piece. It is a masterpiece of American craftsmanship and at the same time an artistic creation of great value."

Bold and unusual settings for gems, semi-precious stones and glass had long been of interest to Tiffany. Roger Riordan had commented in the early 1880's on his penchant for Frankish or Gaulish ornamentation, some of his "rough-faceted glass looking at a distance like the unpolished stones of Indian or old Gaulish jewelry." Herwin Schaefer perceived a derivation from old jeweled Visigothic votive crowns, which had been exhibited at the Cluny Museum in Paris, in the sanctuary lamp made for Tiffany's chapel. He also noted similarities to the work of early Medieval gold-smiths, Ottonian book covers and crucifixes in Tiffany's lamp bases, decorative plaques, the crucifix and tabernacle door of the chapel, with its cabochon stones, spirals of filigree, mother-of-pearl and colored glass, and an ante-pendium, a wall-hanging embroidered in gold and studded with precious stones. Graham Hughes noted a similar strain in Louis Sullivan's "colossal jewels," his large-scale architectural metalwork decorations.

Tiffany scorned to rely on "safe," neutral tints and expressed himself clearly on the necessity for close supervision of textures and colors for the rich effects he wanted, whether for an ornament or a carpet. As he expounded his opinions to Charles de Kay, it was the part of a rounded artist to know "when to apply hot and cool colors, rich and pale tones, how to run the gamut of colors in the most diverse branches of art, according to the place the object in question was meant to occupy. "When one examines the textile objects in exhibitions of the arts and crafts one observes a great timidity among the artisans with regard to color. A similar reliance on neutral tints may be seen in architecture, sculpture, jewelry, pottery, even mosaic; so one comes to the conclusion that the public dislikes strong coloration, or, at any rate, that the workmen and workwomen think the public does. The impression one gets is lack of courage, an obscure feeling that color is a danger; and perhaps that feeling is based on a real lack of temperament in the public and in workmen, which makes them unable to distinguish between deep, strong coloration and gaudiness. Perhaps it springs from a lack of naïveté, a presence of self-consciousness which combine to depress and sterilize art. Certainly our climate invites to sumptuous colors. It is therefore incumbent upon leaders in the arts to counteract this weakness on the part of the public by making people familiar with works full of powerful color and accustoming them to something richer and more virile than the drabs and greys and anemic color schemes of the past. It is only fair to say that, consciously or unconsciously, Louis C. Tiffany has powerfully helped to educate the public in this respect."

The Tiffany & Company "Blue Books," the hard-bound catalogues or price lists in deep blue and gold, revealed a wealth of "fancy items" from which to choose in the art jewelry and regular jewelry departments, from "scarabs" and lorgnon chains to intricate necklaces. The "scarabaei" were offered in lapis-lazuli, Amazon stone, rock crystal, amethyst, glazed steatite, sard, carnelian, jasper and faïence, with or without cartouches. Tiffany Favrile beetles were often mounted in scarf pins, sleeve links, studs, watch guards, belt pins, belts and charms, as well as lorgnon chains. Also available were bracelets, buckles, brooches, charms, collars, corsage ornaments, cuff links, cuff pins, earrings, hair ornaments, hatpins, lorgnons, watch chains, necklaces, pendants, rings, scarf pins, stoles of beads, many enameled and set with precious and semi-precious stones.

Prices quoted for some of the items ranged from about $10.00 for a small repoussé box to more than $4,000 for a necklace or pendant. Some of the boxes and inkstands, including those containing gold and precious stones, bore the name of Louis C. Tiffany or were stamped "Tiffany Furnaces." The jewelry, however, carried only the mark of Tiffany & Company and is therefore difficult to authenticate as the work of Louis C. Tiffany. The presence of enamel may provide a clue. If opals or other semi-precious stones are cut and mounted for their color values and harmonious effect instead of for their brilliance and if the over-all design is consistent with other products of Tiffany Studios, it is probable that the piece is one of those made in the department established by Louis C. Tiffany. With few exceptions, pieces of Tiffany art jewelry are still treasured by the original owners or their families.

Tiffany proudly showed the Art Nouveau designer and poster artist Alphonse Mucha through his studios when he visited America in 1903-04 to paint portraits of Maude Adams, Ethel Barrymore and members of the Rothschild family. Here, he wrote home, he "saw them working from my design," which may have been for jewelry. When Mucha was married in Paris in 1906, Tiffany sent him an extravagant wedding gift, silver from Tiffany & Company.

Favrile glass dinner services proved a highly popular item. Matched pieces of blown-glass tableware were made after 1901 in several sets of varying proportions in stems and base. More than a dozen related shapes—Queen, Prince, Victoria, York, Colonial, Manhattan, etc.—were available in gold or the more expensive blue iridescent glass. The stemware and tableware were sometimes engraved, the Grapevine pattern being most frequently selected. (A matched set of 48 pieces was recently sold at a price more than double the original cost for the table setting.)

After 1905 the ceramics department began to produce a variety of vases and bowls similar to the enamelware. The artisans had previously obtained lamp bases from the Grueby Faience Company of Boston and fitted them with shades of Favrile glass. Tiffany Studios began to make their own pottery only after the failure of the Grueby firm. The pottery proved more difficult to coat with iridescence, however, and was not as actively promoted as the enamelware. Tiffany & Company's china and pottery departments carried Rookwood ware, made in Cincinnati, samples of which could also have served as models for the Corona craftsmen.

Each example of Tiffany pottery was unique. Some were molded, others were thrown. Shapes and decorations were fused to suggest plant and flower forms, such as fuchsias and creepers, in a free expression of organic growth. Decorations and colors were produced in the clay itself or evolved in the firing without the use of applied paints or enamels. Some lamps had porcelain bases, with plastic clays used as ornamentation. The earliest of the vases used for lamp bases was a deep ivory shade, sometimes shaded with brown. Later, shades of green, from a delicate tint to a deep, dark hue, were used. Some were white, devoid of glaze; others coated with a thin sheet of bronze. There was a variety of shapes and glazes, from soft to rough. A mat glaze often gave an added crystalline effect. Each piece had the initials "L.C.T." carved into the base.

With the years of expansion came a change in policy. The number of individual and unique objects was generally curtailed. Matched sets of stemware, place settings, finger bowls, lighting fixtures, lamp shades, lamp bases and desk sets were produced in quantity and actively promoted. That these were of the most subtle design and of the finest material justified, in Tiffany's mind, his belief that he was the world's foremost industrial artist. But others had begun to feel differently. In an article which first appeared in *Art et Décoration* and which was reprinted in *The Craftsman* in 1903 there was the observation that "the name of Tiffany promised us an admirable display, but we must confess to have been deeply disappointed. . . . There is absolutely nothing to observe among these pieces—heavy, yet weak in form and with vivid, yet inharmonious coloring. . . . We are indeed far from the exquisite specimens of Mr. Tiffany's earlier manner, in which the gamut of rich golds sang so superbly. We trust that the artist may return to his first method."

Unfortunately, this wish was not to be realized. The artist was too busy filling his father's shoes and managing his own affairs. He protested in *The Forum* that managers of large expositions often neglected to prepare their halls with suitable day and night illumination for the "proper exhibition of stained glass." He was still managing to acquire various international honors and awards—or to announce that he had. He won various medals and prizes at the St. Louis exposition of 1904, the Jamestown Tri-Centennial of 1907, the Seattle exhibit of 1909 and the San Francisco exhibit of 1915. In 1897 the Museum of Fine Arts in Boston was credited, in a Tiffany brochure, with owning a collection of Favrile glass which, in fact, it did not. The Field Columbian Museum, later the Chicago Museum of Natural History, was credited with a collection, although actually the Tiffany glass was merely on loan. However, Tiffany had donated the collections of the Imperial Museum and the Fine Arts Society of Tokyo.

Tiffany was eager to increase his own importance. He did not for a moment doubt his own values, but he was beginning to realize that he would never convert all of his countrymen to his concepts of beauty. More and more he came to depend on others for designs which artisans of the Tiffany Studios could convert into fast-selling items of merchandise. Some of his former assistants became his competitors. J. A. Holzer left the Tiffany mosaics department to establish his own studio and executed several major commissions, including one for the Alexander Commencement Hall in Princeton, New Jersey, and for the Chicago Public Library and the Marquette Building in Chicago. Holzer was succeeded as foreman by Joseph Briggs, who was to outlast even Tiffany.

THE QUEST OF BEAUTY

For a few years Tiffany concentrated his energies on making his new country estate, Laurelton Hall, one of the showplaces of the century. The process of decoration was somewhat delayed as the result of a dispute over beach rights with the former owner, Dr. Oliver L. Jones, who temporarily cut off the electricity on the Tiffany property. The work was completed in the spring of 1905 and the Tiffany family moved in. Dr. and Mrs. Graham Lusk then took over The Briars, where they raised their three children.

The house had been completely designed by Louis C. Tiffany without reliance on any professional architect. The construction alone cost nearly $200,000. It was a steel frame building with walls of a single course of brick covered by a thick coat of stucco. The layout was an asymmetrical one, with a small stream running through the center of an enclosed court containing a clear glass fountain. Tiffany worked out his elevations by modeling them in clay, producing an almost Expressionist combination of simplified Art Nouveau forms with Islamic overtones. The Mission-Moorish aspects of the Ponce de Leon Hotel in St. Augustine, Florida, were also suggested to some extent. It was utterly unlike anything ever done before or since.

During the decade following its completion, Laurelton Hall became one of the most publicized domiciles in America. Illustrated feature stories appeared in many newspapers and magazines, including *House and Garden* (September, 1906), *International Studio* (1907/08), *Town and Country* (September, 1913) and *House Beautiful* (January, 1914). Two writers, Samuel Howe, a former Tiffany employee, and Charles de Kay, a relative by marriage after 1911, were kept busy expounding in print the praises of the house and the gardens that surrounded it. When fully decorated and landscaped the estate was valued in 1910 at nearly $2,000,000.

The main entrance at the upper level, which led into the court, was recessed behind four columns of granite topped by floral capitals of ceramic mosaics suggesting formalized poppies. Three bell-shaped glass lanterns were suspended in the spaces between the columns. Blue iridescent glass tiles on the lintel above provided a recurring color note. The same blue glass, in transparent form, served as a domed skylight over the court. K'ang Hsi lions, which guarded the entrance, were glazed a brilliant, fluctuating turquoise blue.

On the far side of the court one could step out onto a high terrace which faced east, overlooking Cold Spring Harbor. Here a giant rock crystal in a small pool served as the focus for the stream. From the court one could enter either the living room or dining room. These two areas provided a strong contrast in feeling, similar to the light and dark rooms he had designed for the Chicago Fair of 1893.

The living room was a sheltered and dimly lighted area with a variety of stained-glass windows, all of Tiffany's own design, which he had saved for his own use. The earliest, "Eggplants," had been made in 1880, "Flowers, Fish and Fruit" in 1885, "Feeding the Flamingoes" for the Chicago Fair. His "Four Seasons" window was cut into separate panels and set into a wall. The largest window, "The Bathers," done after he had worked with Maxfield Parrish on "The Dream Garden" mosaic panel, was not installed until 1914. Tiffany had planned to exhibit it in San Francisco but was not satisfied with the arrangements the fair officials had made for proper lighting.

At the other end of the living room, three steps down, was a large cavelike fireplace complete with bearskin rug. The lighting fixtures, suspended from heavy iron yokes, contained shades and globes of a type of turtle-back tile developed by Tiffany some years earlier. Rounded joints between the walls and ceiling, instead of moldings, created a continuity of space that was entirely Art Nouveau, if in a somewhat heavy-handed, highly romantic mood. The total effect was both theatrical and overpowering.

The dining-room which ran the full width of the house, was in striking contrast to the living room. The colors were light and the trim thin and angular. Clear glass panes at each end let in daylight, from floor to frieze. Of all Tiffany's interiors, this dining-room was the simplest and the most dignified. A severe rectangular fireplace was faced with green marble, with a thin mantel and three clocks, one for the day of the week, one for the hours of the day and one for the days of the month. The furnishings were simple and sparse and the ornament restrained. Wisteria was featured in some stained-glass panes of the glass-enclosed veranda at the west end of the room. The arrangement of the thin rectangular panels of clear glass in order to achieve an indoor-outdoor effect presaged many modern glass-curtain walls.

Two other rooms at this level were a Chinese octagonal room in which a number of fine Oriental antiques were displayed and an American Indian room containing a collection of Northwest Coast Indian baskets acquired in 1912. The upper floors were furnished with Early American furniture.

During his lifetime Louis C. Tiffany continued to make additions, such as a gatehouse and his chapel of 1893, which was installed in 1916. Heating proved to be a major problem, which was solved only by the erection of a coal-burning power plant with a smokestack decorated to look like a Moorish minaret. The landscaping centered around an informal "hanging garden" on the shorefront side of the house and included a wealth of exotic and tropical plants. The little stream of water cascading over a series of falls terminated in a large Chinese-dragon fountain which seemed to repeat the main contours of the house. To anyone looking up from the shore, the house appeared like a great Mission church or mosque; the rounded copper roofing of both the structure and the tower, bulging out over the banded windows, produced

[143]

a mushroom-like contour that can only be characterized as fantastic. Similarly daring and unconventional forms can be found in the works of Gaudi in Spain and of Taut in Germany, but nothing comparable to it was built elsewhere in this country during the first quarter of the twentieth century. It was the largest and most important achievement of Art Nouveau in America. Its major weakness was that it failed to achieve a synthesis of structure and form.

In the summer of 1908 Tiffany left his Long Island showplace to go abroad with his children. They sailed up the Nile on a rented yacht. This was the first of several extravagant gestures, which included various fêtes and a book eulogizing his career and justifying his concepts of beauty.

When Tiffany's second daughter Hilda died at the age of thirty in a sanatorium at Saranac Lake of the same disease that had claimed her mother, all of the feelings that he had suppressed for years once again surged to the fore. A lonely man, he sought distraction. He had already lost two wives and a daughter and soon was to lose the remaining daughters by marriage. On December 10, 1910, Julia became Mrs. Gurdon Parker, the wife of an architect, and on April 20, 1911, Comfort became Mrs. Rodman de Kay Gilder when she married the son of Richard Watson Gilder, a writer and art critic. Dorothy was married to Dr. Robert Burlingham on September 24, 1914.

Der Geniale Tiffany was not tall and his beard was sometimes poorly trimmed, but he was always well groomed and there were many women who found him attractive. One young lady named Ethel Syford wrote an article in praise of Tiffany which was published in the *New England Magazine*. Tiffany promptly invited her to visit his New York studios. From the moment they met, Miss Syford became an ardent admirer, displaying her devotion with enthusiasm. In return for her attentions, her article was reprinted by Tiffany in booklet form.

There were also some married women and widows among his admirers. There was a good deal of talk about Tiffany and the wife of his chemist, but he managed, for the most part, to keep this aspect of his private life from the public eye, successfully avoiding scandal. He was regarded largely as an eccentric, mostly because of his beard and the strange cut of his clothes. He was suddenly stricken in his sixties with what seemed to be a kidney ailment, was confined to bed and required a nurse in attendance at all times. Although he recovered rapidly, he refused to permit the three attractive young nurses who had been hired to attend him to leave. He invited each in turn to stay on and one, a Miss Sarah Hanley, accepted his offer. She was Irish and a devout Catholic with very little education. She remained at his side until the day of his death. Tiffany taught her to paint and built a home for her on his property at Oyster Bay. Her paintings were accepted in several exhibitions in New York.

In an effort to impress his ideas on influential segments of the public Tiffany delivered his first public lecture on October 24, 1910, to the Society of Illuminating Engineers at Johns Hopkins University. Entitled "The Tasteful Use of Light and Color in Artificial Illumination," it was subsequently published in the *Scientific American* in April, 1911. It was brief, adding little to what he had already said time and time again to his colleagues and friends. He read the speech slowly and dryly, as nervous as a schoolboy. But as soon as it was over he was flushed and happy. In a few years he would even muster up enough confidence to address an audience of several hundred at a mammoth celebration of his birthday. The limelight had a perennial appeal for him. Armed with a master's degree, honorary or not, from Yale University for his part in providing the decorations for the bicentennial, he decided he could very well become a noted arbiter and educator; not a dry, scholarly professor but more in the manner of a P. T. Barnum—with taste. He could be counted on to put on the kind of lavish spectacle and display that would long be remembered as a superior aesthetic experience.

It took time to work out all the necessary details, but it was decided that a great costume fête would be given on February 4, 1913. Joseph Lindon Smith, an artist who had preserved in meticulous detail some of the treasures of the ancient past discovered in excavations by archaeologists, was retained as the director of Tiffany's sumptuous re-creation of the splendor of ancient Egypt, with himself in turbaned magnificence as an Egyptian potentate. Tiffany supervised the arrangements, including the catering by Delmonico's, but at the time of the performance mingled with his guests at a reception at the 72nd Street mansion before the show. The sets and costumes for the affair were designed by Mrs. Edward P. Sperry, the widow of an artist who had worked for Tiffany, John W. Alexander and Francis Tonetti.

Ruth St. Denis, in a short-skirted costume of East Indian cloth, performed an East Indian nautch dance to music composed for the occasion by Theodore Steinway and played by members of the Philharmonic concealed in the wings of a temporary stage set up in the Madison Avenue showrooms. The role of Cleopatra was assumed by Hedwig Reicher and that of Mark Antony by Pedro de Cordova. There were some professional extras, but in the main friends and members of the family and the staff were pressed into service.

The New York Times called it "the most lavish costume fête ever seen in New York." But somewhere along the line the avowed educational purpose was lost. There was too much champagne and not enough pure aesthetics. The Favrile vases so carefully arranged onstage were perhaps not properly related to the sensuous contortions of the dancers. There were many young socialites and tradesmen who were not quite ready to absorb Tiffany's aesthetic principles and who turned the affair into a wild party. Beauty was transformed into revelry. In restrospect, the effect was not quite as artistic as Tiffany had envisioned.

On February 17, 1913, the day after an illustrated feature on the Egyptian fête had been published in the Sunday papers, another event was reported which had a far greater impact on the art world in America. This was the opening day of an exhibition held at the 69th Regiment Armory at Lexington Avenue and 25th Street, only a block away from the Fourth Avenue studios in which Tiffany had begun his career forty-four years earlier. The exhibition was the famous Armory Show, at which the public got its first look at the works of Matisse and the Fauves, Cubism and German Expressionism.

It created a sensation. On the day that Tiffany went to see for himself what had caused the furor, he drove past the empty building that was a silent reminder of the ambitions of his youth. Then, as he inspected what was the "very latest" in art, he found one work to be uglier than the next! He was rather surprised to find so many American artists represented and was relieved that he had not been asked to participate—or so he told himself. The worst of it was to find that Arthur B. Davies, whose paintings he had admired, was in charge. Somehow he suddenly felt old for the first time. Something had been put over on him. He assured himself that it couldn't be important since he had not been in on it. It couldn't be that he had lost touch, that he had outlived his times! Or could it?

At any rate, he was positive it was all ugly. He had declared himself on this subject in 1910: "The great thing in art—the thing that has helped me more than anything—is the practice of looking at the beautiful and shutting out the ugly. If the ugly is there, I don't look at it." He would speak out again against those "modernists." The shock with which he regarded the efforts of the younger generation of artists might be compared, oddly enough, to the sensation he himself had provided some forty years earlier when he began to experiment boldly with form and color in glass. He simply could not accept the fact that the world of art had passed him by and now looked upon his work as a relic of the gilded age, the stained-glass decades.

At this point, he was beginning to feel the tide of public taste turning from him and the singular products which were produced from his designs and under his direction. But perhaps he could try another tack. Now, more urgently than ever, he felt he had to promote the concepts he was convinced were right, the ideas that could justify his entire career. This time he decided there was to be a hand-picked guest list

[146]

of 150 persons who, he felt, were true intellectuals with a quality of genius, like himself, those who believed as he did and who couldn't be fooled.

The invitations were sent out, asking the favored few to visit Laurelton Hall on May 16, 1914 to "inspect the spring flowers." A special train left New York at four o'clock in the afternoon. From Oyster Bay the party was driven by car to Laurelton Hall so that they would arrive about an hour before sunset. Dinner was a veritable feast of peacocks served by young ladies in ancient Greek costume. The host's three grandchildren were also pinned up in togas to add to the effect. After dinner everyone witnessed a display of varicolored lights coordinated with selections from Bach, Beethoven and Brahms played on the organ. Promptly at eleven o'clock the cars arrived to transport the guests back to the city. The affair had the dignity that the Egyptian party had lacked, but it was still not quite enough. It was too evanescent, too quickly forgotten in a world on the eve of a world war.

Tiffany's next move was to launch something of a more enduring, yet subtly instructive, nature. This was the completion of a memorial volume, which was, in fact, still another piece of shrewd promotion. Tiffany had already invited Charles de Kay, a respected Knickerbocker and originator of the Authors' Club in 1883, to write the text based on a series of personal interviews. De Kay's name, however, would not appear as author; it was to be all about Tiffany and his ideas of beauty. Even the names of many loyal friends who had done so much for the success of the business had to be omitted. Only a brief mention could be made of a few associates such as Donald G. Mitchell and George Inness. There was no time for careful research, for the checking of facts or dates. The illustrations, some hastily captioned, of Tiffany's princely surroundings and of his various designs were, Tiffany felt, far more important than the text, set down by de Kay in 1911–1912.

Tiffany himself wrote the table of contents to make sure it would be properly inclusive. The eight chapters of *The Art Work of Louis C. Tiffany* were entitled: "Tiffany the Painter," "Tiffany the Maker of Stained Glass," "Favrile Glass," "Enamels and Jewelry," "Textiles and Hand Stuffs," "A Decorator of Interiors," "A Builder of Homes," and "As Landscape Architect." The Spanish painter Sorolla was commissioned to paint a portrait of the bearded, hatless Tiffany in his garden, to serve as a colorful frontispiece. The false modesty of the foreword, which implied that the book was produced by request of his children, remained a standing family joke.

The book, printed on heavy, creamy paper and bound in red and gold, was ready in time for Christmas. It was published, at Tiffany's expense, by Doubleday, Page & Co. Only 502 copies were printed, and of these only 300 were distributed. The book was never sold, only given to those whom Tiffany felt were "deserving." The copy sent by him to the mural painter Edwin Blashfield was inscribed: "I have always felt that you were one who was interested in the work of others and I therefore send you this book with much pleasure. Louis C. Tiffany. Xmas 1914."

Tiffany did not consider himself wasteful or extravagant. He felt that what he did with his wealth brought pleasure and understanding to others. He paid his own way and abhorred debt. He accumulated a fortune, very little of which came from his father's business, except for what he drew as vice-president of the firm. Tiffany Studios was his own enterprise; he ran it with efficiency and insisted on absolute punctuality. He made a point of visiting each department at least once a week, and was in on the initiation and completion of every important job for many years. He saw to it that besides the brochures on windows there were other persuasive advertisements, as well as handsomely printed booklets on expensive paper with such titles as *Collection of Notable Oriental Rugs* (1906), *Memorials in Glass and Stone* (1913) and *Character and Individuality in Decorations and Furnishings* (1913), all available at the Madison Avenue showrooms. The more than 200 employees held their employer in high esteem, and Tiffany rarely took advantage of this. Until the outbreak of hostilities in Europe in 1914 he was in the habit of spending summers abroad and enjoyed escorting a group of his favorite employees to points of interest in England and France. He liked to relax in Germany for several weeks. He liked the German people and particularly admired their industry and efficiency. During the war he often expressed his opinions on this touchy subject in a way that was embarrassing, but there was never any doubt of his patriotism. He was, in fact, a dye-in-the-wool Republican and proud of having redecorated the White House for President Chester A. Arthur but had nothing to do with his Oyster Bay neighbor, Theodore Roosevelt.

As still another step in his deliberate campaign for self-glorification, Tiffany once again asked the artist Joseph Lindon Smith to produce a lavish spectacle to celebrate his birthday in February of 1916 which would be sure to be "featured in the press as the artistic sensation of the social season," surpassing the Egyptian fantasy he had arranged for him a few years earlier.

Joseph Lindon Smith's widow, Corinna Lindon Smith, has recalled in her memoirs, *Interesting People: Eighty Years with the Great and Near Great*, some of the difficulties incurred in staging this birthday masque, "The Quest of Beauty." In his allegory Joseph Lindon Smith endeavored to symbolize Tiffany's career as a painter, decorator and master glass craftsman, employing the theme that "art was the search for beauty and the effort to express it in many mediums through the ages." He visualized the masque as a symphonic poem, played to a soft musical accompaniment, with forty-five characters and changing color effects in scenery and costumes, from brilliant hues to somber interludes, from darkness to pale starlight, from the rosy glow of dawn to sunset. He had no difficulty in obtaining Tiffany's permission to employ a Hamburg lighting expert to supervise the manipulation of the complex new "dome" system. Some thirty-three reds, for instance, were used instead of the standard half-dozen. Tiffany made only one comment when his artistic director observed that the cost ($15,000 for lighting alone) was probably prohibitive for a private entertainment: "Do you have such a technician in mind?" A contract was sent off at once.

Tiffany, who was to make a speech on the goal of the artist, had promised the leading roles of Fire and Beauty to two of his protégées, a *première danseuse* of the ballet of the Metropolitan Opera and an actress soon to make her debut on Broadway. Fire, in a wild dance, was to exhaust her rage at primitive man's presumption in daring to make a decorated bowl of his own, and then tear a living flame from her side, a symbol of the inextinguishable divine fire. Beauty, wife of the chief barbarian, beholding the fire burning brightly in the world's first bowl made by an artist, was to aid him in the realization of his ideals, invoking all materials—metals, minerals, woods, gems, semi-precious stones, silver, gold and pigments. As a climax, a huge globe of iridescent blown glass (containing the Smiths' young daughter, who represented a pearl) reflected Beauty's smile. In a final tableau the artist renewed his fealty to Beauty, surrounded by her handmaidens, Painting, Sculpture, Music and Architecture. Evidently the ballerina was able to transform her highly stylized dancing and gestures into the fury of uncontrolled Fire to Mr. Smith's satisfaction, but there were some rehearsal difficulties with Beauty, her beautiful figure draped in an enormous tiger skin. Dissatisfied, she threatened to walk out, but finally decided to play the part the way she was told. The masque was, according to Corinna Lindon Smith, "a stupendous triumph, cheered to the echo" and talked about for decades.

The guests at the birthday breakfast heard Tiffany's "few words" about art before adjourning to see the masque. "I never could make a speech," he said. "I remember when I was a boy and had a company of Zouaves (for it was in the time of the Civil War) we were presented with a banner—and when the time came for me to make the speech of thanks I commenced to tremble and not a word could I utter. The next time I wrote what I proposed to say on my cuff—but having used a lead pencil, my speech was utterly eliminated. Today I have written what I wanted to tell you in ink.

"Thank you for this visit to my Studio, on my birthday. I am not going to tell you how old I am; I reserve such secrets for my grandchildren—but I can claim to be one of the oldest active Academicians—and it was looking over the yearbook of the National Academy of Design that made me think of asking you here today—that I might say a few words about art, and then to ask you to adjourn to the hall above to see a masque called 'The Quest of Beauty.'

"What is the Quest of Beauty? What else is the goal that an artist sets before him but that same spirit of beauty! Who can give the formula for it? Are there not as many different paths to it as there are workmen, and are there not as many different definitions of beauty as there are artists—and yet I wish to express what I found in art. How can I say in a few words what I have been striving to express in art during my life!

"Literature and the drama express the sensations of tragedy and romance—but not with continuity and lasting effect. Art interprets the beauty of ideas and of visible things, making them concrete and lasting. When the savage searches for the gems from the earth—or pearls from the sea—to decorate his person—or when he decorates the utensils of war or peace in design and colors—he becomes an artist in embryo, for he has turned his face to the quest of beauty.

"Art starts from an instinct in all—stronger in one than another—and that instinct leads to the fixing of beauty in one of a hundred ways. But, if we look closer, we find some artists are drawn aside from the pursuit of beauty to worship the idol of technique, though only a small part of the effectiveness of a work in art can be credited to technique. The thirteenth-century stained-glass makers were great because they saw and reproduced beauty from the skies and stars—the gems and rugs; they translated the beauty into the speech of stained glass. In later days, ignoring the beauty of the glass by using paint, they destroyed, by this technique, the beauty for which they were striving.

"If I may be forgiven a word about my own work, I would merely say that I have always striven to fix beauty in wood or stone, or glass or pottery, in oil or water-color, by using whatever seemed fittest for the expression of beauty; that has been my creed, and I see no reason to change it. It seems as if the artists who place all their energies on technique have nothing left over for the more important matter—the pursuit of beauty. The 'Modernists'—as they are called for want of a better term—I mean Cubists, Futurists, etc.—wander after curiosities of technique, vaguely hoping they may light on some invention which will make them famous. They do not belong to art; they are not artists; they are untrained inventors of processes of the arts.

"One thing more—it seems to me that the majority of critics miss the chance of doing good by failing to understand the situation; too many of them waste their time in disapproval of what they dislike, instead of looking for what they can honestly admire. The public thinks that a critic is a person who attacks and condemns; a critic should be one who discriminates. The critic who can do good is one who does not neglect the highlights for the shadows but strives to find the best points in each work of art and to show his discrimination by setting them clearly before the public."

His oft-time preceptor Oscar Wilde had expounded on the creative role of the critic in his essay, "The Critic as Artist." Tiffany believed he himself understood precisely the ideal relationship between artist and sensitive mentor. Wilde had commented, "Some resemblance, no doubt, the creative work of the critic will have to the work that has stirred him to creation, but it will be such resemblance as exists, not between Nature and the mirror that the painter of landscapes or figures may be supposed to hold up to her, but between Nature and the work of the decorative artist. Just as on the flowerless carpets of Persia, tulip and rose blossom indeed and are lovely to look on, though they are not reproduced in visible shape or line; just as the pearl and purple of the seashell is echoed in the church of St. Mark at Venice; just as the vaulted ceiling of the wondrous chapel at Ravenna is made gorgeous by the gold and green and sapphire of the peacock's tail, though the birds of Juno fly not across it; so the critics reproduces the work that he criticises in a mode that is never imitative, and part of whose charm may really consist in the rejection of resemblance, and shows us in this way not merely the meaning but also the mystery of Beauty and, by transforming each art into literature, solves once for all the problem of Art's unity."

Tiffany ended his birthday-masque prologue by quoting an English poet and lawyer, Philip James Bailey, the author of *Festus*, "Art is man's nature; nature is God's art," and "The worst way to improve the world is to condemn it." He thanked his friends for their good wishes and concluded, "Forgive me for this delay; I wanted to protest that beauty can be found in any material, through the proper channel."

As part of his birthday celebration a retrospective exhibition of Tiffany's work was held at the Tiffany Studios. Ezra Tharp's commentary in *The New Republic* was devastating. "Tear-bottles, vases, lamps and brooches, each had been more precious in his eyes, and dearer to his heart, because nothing else in the world was precisely like it. And with Mr. Tiffany's aversion from the duplicate we must put his aversion from the copy. He has taken this model and blurred its sharp outlines, that model and smeared its distinct pattern. A singular result of his effort to make his things look rare is that nearly all of them look expensive. . . . Woman, had Mr. Tiffany created her, instead of having two only, would have had many breasts, and each breast, instead of having one only, would, if Mr. Tiffany had created woman, have been all encrusted with nipples." Mr. Tharp did, however, acknowledge Tiffany's sincerity of purpose: "His own human kindness, his desire to give by his art as much pleasure as art and nature have given him, is both real and obvious."

Tiffany expressed his creed once again in a speech to the Rembrandt Club of Brooklyn. In this lecture, entitled "Color and Its Kinship to Sound," he declared, "Styles are merely the copying of what others have done, perhaps done better than we. God has given us our talents, not to copy the talents of others, but rather to use our brains and our imagination in order to obtain the revelation of True Beauty." By the time he discussed "The Quest of Beauty" in *Harper's Bazaar* in an interview in

December, 1917, he conceded he was not as certain as he had been in his youth of its true meaning.

In the summer of 1916 Tiffany chartered a yacht to take a party of relatives and friends to Alaska. During the First World War Tiffany enjoyed contemplating at Laurelton Hall the beauty he had created, firmly convinced that if the world had followed his example there would be no more war. Soon he began to work out a plan by which he could share with the deserving and discerning the objects of beauty he had acquired and created over the years. He discussed with his friend Robert W. de Forest, who was now the director of the Metropolitan Museum of Art, a scheme he had mulled over for some years, one which had been originally suggested by Oscar Wilde: "Now, what America wants today is a school of rational art. Bad art is a great deal worse than no art at all. You must show your workmen specimens of good work so that they come to know what is simple and true and beautiful. To that end I would have you have a museum attached to these schools—not one of those dreadful modern institutions where there is a stuffed and very dusty giraffe and a case or two of fossils, but a place where there are gathered examples of art decoration from various periods and countries." The idea for such a special museum-school did not become a reality, however, until July 30, 1918, when the way was cleared to set up the Louis Comfort Tiffany Foundation, which was established to operate Laurelton Hall as a retreat for artists. A gift of more than 62 acres and the several structures on it, together with the personal property they contained, was made to the Foundation. The trustees, in addition to Louis C. Tiffany, included his son Charles L. Tiffany, Robert W. de Forest, who served as chairman and first president, Henry W. de Forest, the sculptor Daniel C. French, the painter Francis C. Jones, and George F. Kunz, jewelry expert for Tiffany & Company. When Charles W. Gould politely declined to serve as a trustee, he was replaced by George Frederick Heydt, of Tiffany & Company, who was secretary to the board. In addition to French and Jones, an art advisory committee included Cass Gilbert, Robert Vonnah, Harry Watrous and Frances de Forest Stewart, the daughter of Robert W. de Forest. Stanley Lothrop was appointed as resident director of the Foundation.

The board met on September 12, 1918. As recorded in the minutes of this meeting of the Foundation, Robert W. de Forest remarked, in part, "All of you who were present at the luncheon meeting recently held at Laurelton heard Mr. Tiffany's statement of his intention to devote his present Laurelton Home, and a substantial endowment to the cause of art education . . . Mr. Tiffany's plan . . . is an old one. It antedates the present war and the new conditions which the war has brought about. He is putting that plan into operation at a time when the future is filled with uncertainties . . ." A constitution was presented to the trustees, setting forth the lines along

[*152*]

which the Foundation would be organized: "The nature of the institution is an art institute, the object and purpose of which are art education directed toward both art appreciation and production, within the scope of industrial as well as the fine arts, and as one means toward those . . . the establishment and maintenance of a museum to contain objects of art."

Across the Atlantic the reorganized Weimar Art School, headed by Walter Gropius, was opened in a building designed by Van de Velde in 1919. Gropius, who sought to bridge the arbitrary divisions between "intellectual and manual worker, artist and craftsman," declared that its curriculum was an effort to merge the best of craft training with all that was valid in the academy. Some 500 students were trained in the Staatliches Bauhaus, and its influence was apparent in many fields of design. To Gropius art was "not a branch of science which can be learned step by step, from a book," and his purpose was to create an organic unity in all phases of design.

On May 1, 1920 the first nineteen students approved by the Louis Comfort Tiffany Foundation began their unique nonacademic session, lasting from May through the summer, their curriculum based on Tiffany's *laissez-faire* principles of art-by-absorption. The students were the guests of the Foundation and had access to Laurelton Hall's bowling alleys and tennis courts whenever they wished. The stables had been converted into a studio-dormitory and the gatehouse into an art gallery.

The favored guests were, of course, screened by the Foundation. Applicants had to be American citizens, between 25 and 35 years of age. They were to be selected on the basis of ability, previous technical training and upon the recommendation of three or more recognized artists in their field. Candidates were chosen from annual judgings held by the National Academy of Design in New York, the Yale School of Fine Arts in New Haven and the Vesper George Art School in Boston. The Foundation was described in a brochure, which assured prospective guests that it was not Mr. Tiffany's intention "to establish an Art School in the ordinary sense of the word." There was to be there no "Head Master, with hard and fast methods of teaching. His desire is rather by stimulating love of beauty and imagination to give free play to development without the trammels of schools or conventions. . . . The Galleries and Art Library of Laurelton Hall will also be open to the students, although Mr. Tiffany will continue to reside there during the summer months."

A review of the first year of operation was published in *Arts and Decoration*, concluding with the statement: "It is one of the interesting developments of the first year's experience that the lesson which seems to have fixed itself in the minds of all alike is that decoration is the inevitable objective of all creative effort, whether it

[153]

professes that purpose or not." Out of the fifty-two young men and women selected as "resident members" between 1920 and 1922, a large percentage continued in careers as artists, designers and craftsmen. Prominent "graduates" included Hugh McKean, a student in residence at Laurelton Hall about 1930, now president of Rollins College, Winter Park, Florida; Joseph Margulies, and Bradley Walker Tomlin, who became the leader of a group of abstract Expressionist painters. As there was no formal instruction at Laurelton Hall there was, of course, no appreciable uniformity of academic influence of those artists awarded fellowships by the Foundation. Its role was, and has continued to be, one of providing assistance and encouragement to serious young artists in many media.

The last major commission carried out by Tiffany Studios, executed about the time the Foundation was beginning its operations, was the decoration of the Presidential Palace in Havana, Cuba. The furnishings consisted largely of period reproductions but also included 23 Tiffany rugs and 15 Tiffany lamps. Tiffany, then in semi-retirement, had little to do with this project. While the palace was under construction in 1917 Hugh White, general manager, submitted to President Mario G. Menocal a cost estimate of $998,600. His prompt reply was "You can proceed . . . to the preparation of said specifications and of large-scale drawings." The cost of these preliminary preparations was $15,000. A formal contract was signed with Tiffany Studios for $1,167,392 on June 3, 1918, and the work was completed by the end of the year, when a memorandum of extras (an additional $199,123) was submitted.

Tiffany was still overseeing, at least, the production of special projects. The Metropolitan Museum of Art acquired a Tiffany landscape window in 1925, probably at the suggestion of Robert W. de Forest, who was still serving as its director. A drawing for this window, preserved in the museum's collection, is dated October, 1920, and approved by Louis C. Tiffany in his handwriting, but it is not signed by him. It was originally intended for a Mr. L. D. Towle of Boston. Tiffany found time to attend various gallery openings and visited every important exhibit, accompanied by Stanley Lothrop and his erstwhile housekeeper, Sarah Hanley. They made a strange trio, Tiffany with his gray hair and full gray beard, commenting softly about the paintings, his reddish-blonde companion occasionally asking a question in a thick Irish brogue, and the silent Lothrop, stooped by a back deformity, peering sharply at each work. All three were as indifferent to the fads of the "roaring twenties" as they had been to the war. Tiffany may have yearned for a return to days of prosperity, when there would again be time for people to enjoy the refinements of gracious living. Although his popularity was on the wane by the twenties, several articles by René de Quelin extolling his work appeared in magazines devoted to decoration. De Quelin had been associated with Tiffany since 1895, when he had been introduced by Augustus Saint-Gaudens and taken on as a draftsman, eventually becoming manager of the decorating department. He was responsible for the glowing review in *Arts and Decoration* of an exhibit of paintings by Tiffany displayed in his private gallery at Laurelton Hall in 1922.

Tiffany was frequently interviewed and asked his opinion on a variety of topics. He was against the United States' becoming a member of the League of Nations; he felt international problems could be better solved by strengthening the World Court. In 1925 he was interviewed by Hugh Weir for *Collier's* on the use of glass for making imitations of precious gems. His comments were consistent with what he had always believed: "The possibilities of glass for duplicating the most precious creations of nature are almost uncanny, and history proves that these possibilities have been known to the artist for thousands of years. . . . Perhaps it is because we place too much emphasis on the *cost* of art and not enough on the *appreciation* of art. Real art cannot be measured in dollars and cents. That is why the trickster and the knave flourish. They capitalize on our commercialism." But had he not also been accused of commercialism?

Everywhere commercialism was rampant. Collectors were buying spurious Renaissance paintings on the advice of "experts," and the market was being flooded with quantities of "carnival glass," mass-produced by being pressed or molded and then dipped to give it a thin coating of pale iridescence. Tiffany, whose name at one time had been almost synonymous with iridescent glass, could not compete. He turned over the management of the Tiffany Furnaces to A. Douglas Nash in 1919. But the son of the man who had started the fires at Corona could not keep them going—Arthur J. Nash also retired in 1919. Production was soon curtailed. In 1928 Tiffany withdrew his financial support. Within a few months the production of Favrile glass ceased forever.

World War I virtually marked the end of the production of collectors' items by Tiffany Studios. Although the plant continued in operation until 1928 there were few new designs, the output was curtailed and the items lacked the colorfulness and effectiveness of earlier examples. About the time the Foundation began its operation, the building which housed the Tiffany Studios at 345 Madison Avenue was sold, the various departments were separated and all operations reduced. The main office and the ecclesiastical department were set up first at 361 Madison Avenue, then at 391 Madison Avenue. The last location was at 46 West 23rd Street, in a building erected originally for Stern Brothers. When the entire stock of Tiffany Studios was offered at a clearance sale in 1920, many items were on hand which had remained unsold for more than two decades. From the time the Tiffany Studios moved out of their large Madison Avenue showrooms they ceased to be a major factor in the field of decoration. However, a large green Aubusson rug with the state seal in the center was ordered from the Tiffany Studios for the White House in 1927 and was used for some time on the floor of the Green Room.

The last quarter-century of operation was devoted to the making of gift items, stained-glass windows and funerary monuments, none of which reflected the vigor and exuberance of the true Art Nouveau. The artistic importance of Tiffany Studios indubitably declined. However, a large stock of glass was kept on hand and the business continued in operation six years after a petition of bankruptcy was filed in 1932. This listed liabilities of $81,595 and assets of $315,907, consisting largely of accounts receivable. The firm was not liquidated for a few more years, however, until the death of Joseph Briggs, who had continued as manager by Tiffany's express provision.

Louis C. Tiffany remained active even in his eighties. One of the Foundation's art students recalled Laurelton Hall's benevolent patron and genial host as he appeared some three years before his death. Hugh McKean recalled the central court with its fountain. "Water flowed quietly out of the top of a tall glass vase of the simplest and most arresting possible shape . . . which changed colors very slowly, from dark red to dark purple to dark green. There were plants around its base and throughout the house. The total effect of the music [from a pipe organ] and the fountains and the light, airy architecture was one of fascinating unreality. I did not quite understand it then [in 1930] but I know now that, even though it was built in the first years of the 1900's, Laurelton Hall was actually a modern house . . .

"We had nothing to do all day except to work where and how we wished at our art, and at night we sat down to dinner to be served by two rather elegant butlers. Every Saturday morning at eleven o'clock we assembled in the gallery, along with our latest work. A magnificent old car [a 1911 Crane] would come whirling into the courtyard, a little dog with fantastic jumping ability would hop out—and then Mr. Tiffany, frail and benign. His face was always radiant with smiles and kindness and he seemed to be pleased at the happiness he was giving all of us.

"Mr. Tiffany would walk around the gallery, sitting down abruptly anywhere at all, because he knew Mr. Lothrop, the director of the Foundation, would always have a chair behind him. He would study very carefully any pictures which attracted his attention. After he had made his rounds he would discuss the importance of beauty and sharing it with others. He usually gave us gentle words of encouragement, but his real thoughts were revealed, I thought, when he would say often at the end of his visit that paintings should not 'hurt the eye.' Mr. Tiffany was a gentleman."

part three
ILLUSTRATIONS

Louis C. Tiffany
AS THE CREATOR OF FAVRILE GLASS,
TIFFANY STUDIOS AND LAURELTON HALL

S. Bing's shop, "L'Art Nouveau" (*top left*) was advertised in *Dekorative Kunst* in 1898. Eugène Colonna's display, "Art Nouveau Bing," in Paris, 1900 (*center*) featured Tiffany glass. The typical swirling lines of Art Nouveau were also evident in Beardsley's 1893 illustration, "The Peacock Skirt," for *Salomé* (*top right*), Horta's Brussels vestibule of 1894 (*bottom left*) and Gaudi's Casa Milá in Barcelona 1905-07 (*bottom right*).

TIFFANY FAVRILE GLASS
considered in its chronological
relationship to other glass, as
well as its usefulness in the
decorative arts, and appropriateness when
blown into vases and other objects for
collectors' cabinets, Holiday and Wedding
presents. ❦ ❦ ❦ ❦ ❦

TIFFANY GLASS & DECORATING COMPANY
333 TO 341 FOURTH AVENUE
NEW YORK

From the Tiffany Furnaces in Corona,
L. I. (*below*) came the first examples of
Favrile glass, "a composition of various
colored glasses worked together while
hot," in 1894. This was not introduced
on the market in New York until 1896.
Three of Tiffany's trademarks are shown
(*below*). The mark used by the Tiffany
Glass and Decorating Company was registered in 1894. The other two were used
by Tiffany Studios after 1900. The title
page of *Tiffany Favrile Glass*, a brochure
of 1896, is reproduced (*top left*), a brochure announcing the curtailment of production in 1920 (*right*).

TIFFANY *Favrile Glass*

Tiffany, while drawing on traditional European and Oriental prototypes for some shapes, evolved many striking new forms. Ancient glass excavated from the Middle East is shown (*top*), an 18th-Dynasty Egyptian vase of core-wound glass (*bottom right*) and a mold-blown cup of about 150 A.D., probably from Gaul (*bottom left*).

In Tiffany's personal collection were two iridescent Roman cinerary urns (*top*). A footless blown beaker from the Rhineland of the 5th-6th century is shown (*center left*), a 16th-century German *waldglas* vessel with prunts, or hand holds (*center right*) and an Islamic bowl of glass simulating turquoise and ornamented with gold, presented by a Shah of Persia to a Doge of Venice in the 9th century (*bottom*).

A near Eastern perfume dropper or sprinkler in the form of a bird (7th-10th century) is shown (*top left*), a long-necked Persian rosewater sprinkler (17th-18th century) (*bottom left*) and a Persian vase of the same period (*bottom center*). An Islamic rock crystal bowl (9th-century) with relief decoration is shown (*bottom right*).

The rosewater sprinkler of blue and green bubbly glass (*top left*) is from eastern Spain of the 18th century. The Sandwich glass epergne (*top right*) was made in the third quarter of the 19th century. Two Peachblow vases, an Amberina decanter and cordial glass are examples of Victorian art glass of about 1885 (*bottom left*). The flower-form, bronze-based and five-spouted Favrile glass vases (*bottom right*) were designed by Tiffany.

The 1901 decanter, with applied lily-pad decoration, (*top left*) is in The Victoria and Albert Museum. Two vases (*top right* and *bottom right*) were purchased by The Musée des Arts Décoratifs (The Louvre) through Tiffany's agent, S. Bing, in 1895. One is yellow, veined with white and gray, the other opaque brown, veined with blue. The 1897 vase (*bottom left*), orange-red with a bluish surface, is in the Landesmuseum, Darmstadt.

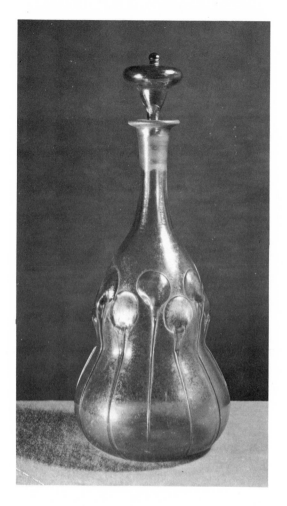

[164]

An iridescent blue vase with gold decoration of 1897 (*top left*) another iridescent vase in gold tones (1898-1900) (*top right*) and a 1910 compote, gold with blue iridescence, engraved with a floral vine motif (*bottom*) are in the Landesmuseum, Darmstadt, the site of an artists' colony, "Mathildenhohe."

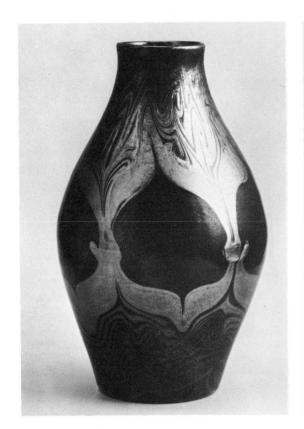

The Smithsonian Institution in Washington, D. C. acquired some 38 items of Favrile Glass made by the Tiffany Glass and Decorating Company in 1894, the first year of operation for the Tiffany Furnaces. Including a piece presented by Charles C. Tiffany in 1896, they have been catalogued and described in detail by Paul Gardner, curator.

PLATE I. (*above*) *From left to right:* Vase, h. 12"; d. 7⅝. Body, of common amber bottle glass, is of double gourd shape, has large opening and no neck. Decorated with striped leaf designs in blue, gray and red with an iridescent surface. Vase, h. 10⅝", with cover, 19½"; d. 11¼". Body, of light green

bottle glass, is shortened ovoid with a short large concave neck and flaring lip. For cover, see Plate IV. (The jar served as an illustration for the booklet, *Tiffany Favrile Glass*, published in 1896). Vase, h. 13⅜", d. 6¾". Body of nearly white bottle glass clouded with a bluish yellow with an iridescent effect. Lower part has shape of bowl, shoulder contracts slightly into high, large neck, upper part expanding outward. Lip, body, neck and shoulder have 21 narrow flat sides. Jardiniere, h. 8¼"; d. 10¼". Body of common green glass over which or upon which iridescent colors are placed. Lower part has a deep bowl shape, above which is a large waist and a flaring lip bent into a waved form.

PLATE II. (*opposite page, below*) *From left to right:* Vase, h. 13", d. 4⅞". Body, of common bottle glass, flattened, bulbous, with a large, high tapering cylindrical neck wound with a spiral thread of glass. Decorated with a glass coating which changes, according to the light, from a deep blue-green to a red-purple. Vase, h. 18", d. 8". Body of common bottle glass splashed with reddish-brown and shades of blue. A bulbous top and bottom connected by a concave waist with a large opening in the top but no neck. Decorated with reddish-brown seaweed-shaped leaves from top to bottom and shades of blue painted leaves, all covered with an iridescent covering. Vase or bottle, h. 19⅝", d. 8⅞". Body of brown bottle glass covered with black. Double gourd shape, lower part much larger, neck slender and cylindrical. Vase, h. 17", d. 9". Body of green bottle glass covered with a deep blue and green, with an iridescent effect. An inverted, elongated balloon shape.

PLATE III. (*below*) *From left to right:* Bowl, h. 3½", d. 6¼". Body of common amber bottle glass covered outside with a mirror-like coating of blue, clouded with a smoky yellow which has iridescent changes. Lower part outside has a concave flare with a sloping shoulder and a short large cylindrical neck. Vase, h. 6", d. 6⅝". Body of amber bottle glass. Form a jar or bowl with double body, ring sides, no neck and a large opening. While the glass was hot the lip was bent in a triangle with the sides slightly curving in. Decorated with broad leaves in metallic blue, the surface made iridescent. Vase, h. 6¼", d. 7". Body, of amber bottle glass, pear-shaped, largest end up, sides slightly concave. From the shoulder, clouded with a greenish-yellow, and extending to center of vase are five branches of striated coarse leaves. Whole surface has iridescent effect. Vase, iridescent blue-green glass with irregularly applied decoration of metallic glass shaded from silver to purple-violet. Trefoil top. Vase or Jar, h. 6⅞", d. 7⅜". Body of common yellow or amber bottle glass, the outer surface somewhat deadened. Over this transparent waved lines pass around body. The decorations, like brown seaweeds, made before surface was deadened. Bowl, h. 4½", d. 6⅝". Made of mixed opaque brown shades of red- and cream-colored glasses, something like banded agate. Rather deep flaring body.

PLATE IV. (above) *From left to right, top row:* Cover for jar shown on Plate I. Shouldered on its lower side, the top has a conical center, trumpet-shaped, terminating in a tapering rod, its end looped back and bent partly around the shaft. Bowl, h. 3¾", d. 5⅜". Body of common amber bottle glass streaked with a yellowish gray; over all are streakings of an opaque lava brown glass. Lower part of body is flaring, with a conoidal shoulder and neck. Vase and Gilt Wire Stand, h. 5", on stand 5¾"; d. 2⅝"; h. of stand, 3¾", d. 2⅞". Common amber bottle glass, the outside covered with a silvered coating, at top shading to a fiery purple toward bottom. Lower part is of an inverted bell shape. Above this body expands to the sloping rounded shoulder on short large cylindrical neck. Vase, h. 4⅛", d. 3⅛". Made of a dark brown opaque glass streaked with a brick red. An ovoid body with a slightly shrunken shoulder, a short cylindrical neck with a wide flanged lip. (Condemned and destroyed 3/31/53.) Vase, h. 2⅛", d. 3¼". Made of a dark opaque glass, covered with a red glass streaked with a brighter red and black. Base and body of different markings and appear to be cemented together. Lower part of body is flaring, shoulder sloping and convex, the neck concave, short and large with a flaring lip. *Bottom row: From left to right:* Bottle, h. 4¾", d. 4½". Body is of an opaque

smoky yellow, streaked with gray; over this are drawn green leaves, etc. in bright changeable iridescent colors. Flattened globular body with an almost flat shoulder and a short cylindrical neck. The sides have been pressed in, forming five large depressions or dimples around its greatest diameter. Bottle, h. 4", d. 4⅛". Made of a dark opaque glass. A globular body, the shoulder deeply indented in four places, the top depressed, a short cylindrical neck. Decorated with designs formed of yellow and silver lines, something like the leaves of the wild turnip, on a ground of dark metallic lustre. Vase and Bronze Stand, h. 8¼" on stand; h. 10½", d. 6⅜". Made of a mixed translucent and opaque glass, veined with a creamy white and red brown. An ovoid body with pointed bottom, a short large neck and flaring rim on a three-branched and footed bronze stand. (The vase and stand were illustrated in *Tiffany Favrile Glass*, 1896.) Vase, h. 4⅝", d. 5⅜". Made of green glass almost covered with clouds of bluish purple and drab. A nearly spherical body without a neck. Vase, h. 5", d. 5⅜". The body is of common white glass over which is spread a dark brown and a bluish gray streaked with a smoky yellow, with splashes of opaque lava-like glass from lip down on the shoulder. In form like an inverted fire balloon with a large neck.

PLATE V. (*opposite page, below*) *Top row: From left to right:* Vase, h. 5¼", d. 2⅜". Body of common greenish glass, upper part colored with a creamy gray. Two conoidal bodies united by three tubular necks and a middle one of triangular shape. Upper part of body has 16 sides with a circular, slightly flaring lip. Vase, h. 5", d. 4". Made of brown glass in an inverted fire balloon shape. Decorated with spiral bands of smoky drab, yellow and bluish gray and vertical double bands of yellow, changing to brown and green spots between the latter. Vase, h. 7¼", d. 4⅛". Made of a brown glass covered with a yellow and smoky gray. Lower part of body is of a shallow, flaring cup shape; above this is a high sloping shoulder and neck. Six knobs are formed on shoulder by pressing the glass out from the inside. Decorated with black and gray lines, forming something like the leaves of the wild turnip. Bottle, h. 7⅜", d. 3⅞". Made of a yellowish-green glass covered with an iridescent film. A spindle-shaped body with a short cylindrical neck, the shoulder indented in five places. *Bottom row: From left to right:* Vase, h. 7", d. 4¼". Made of a green tinted glass, the upper part covered with a thin metallic blue. An ovoid body, except a bulbous swelling near the base, a short large concave neck and a cup-shaped lip. Decorated from top to bottom with five groups of yellow lines, and over all a changeable iridescent coating. Bottle, h. 5⅝", d. 3". Made of clouded amber glass, shading through yellow to a smoky agate at the bottom. A spindle-shaped body, no neck. Bottle, h. 9½", d. 6¼". Made of an opaque pearly gray glass, over which are splashings of smoky yellow with changeable iridescent colors. An ovoid body with a cylindrical neck. Vase, h. 10¾", d. 4⅛". Body of blue glass. Lower half is trumpet-shaped, expanding above the waist to a slightly bulbous top, with a short, large cylindrical neck. Decorated with vertical stripes like grass leaves, surface iridescent. Vase, h. 8", d. 3⅞". Made of a common glass. A bulbous bottom, the shoulder contracting into a tapering neck of 18 sides, near the mouth in a greater degree. On every alternate side

gives the appearance of streams of liquid running and spreading out in a puddle near base, surface iridescent.

PLATE VI. *From left to right:* Bottle, h. 3¼", d. 3". Body of white crystal glass, the outside ground or etched. Spherical body with a small cylindrical neck. Decorated with three tear-like patches of thick yellow glass; between these are three plant-like designs, made up of narrow spreading lines of yellow, colored brown at their converging point. Vase, h. 5½", d. 4½". Body composed of three layers of opaque glass, a green, yellow and dark lava brown. Lower part of body is of a flaring bowl shape, the shoulder bell-shaped, with a short cylindrical neck, flaring lip. Decorated by cutting designs through the outer or lower coating, showing mostly the yellow; in some cases, particularly below the greatest diameter, the yellow has been cut through, showing the green. Bowl, h. 2⅞", d. 5⅝". Lower part flares like a deep plate; above this the sides are almost vertical. Vertical part of sides has a yellowish tint; below this the glass has a blue tint. Sides have mushroom-shaped figures in green shaded with brown. Vase, presented as a gift to the Smithsonian by Charles L. Tiffany, h. 7⅛", d. 6¾". Made of green bottle glass, short ovoid body with the pointed end up, no neck but a large opening. Decorated with fish in colors and water lines, scrollwork, etc., cut by the lapidary's wheel, as are outlines of fish, scales and fins. Bowl on Low Foot, h. 4⅜", d. 6⅞". Made of an opaque black and dark brown glass veined with blue, purple and yellowish gray. Low foot, of a different mixture, is fastened to the body. Decorated near the lip with threads of aventurine glass (mixed with brass filings). Nearly hemispherical on low molded base. Vase, h. 5½", d. 4". Made of opaque glass. An ovoid body, the pointed end up, no neck, 1¼" opening. Glass shades from a dark brown at top through a green, reddish-brown and yellow to a green at the base. Bottle, h. 4⅞", d. 2⅛". Made of a striated dark amber glass.

The long-necked vase (*top left*) and tulip vase (*top right*) by Tiffany are both dated 1895. They are in the collection of the Metropolitan Museum of Art. The flared vase with peacock markings (*opposite page, bottom right*) is also from The Metropolitan Museum of Art. The vase with peacock-feather decoration shown (*opposite page, top right*) is from The Cooper Union Museum. The vase (*opposite page, left*) is in the collection of The Museum of Modern Art.

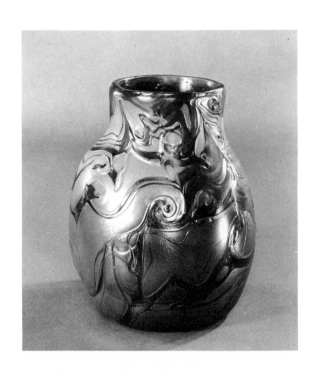

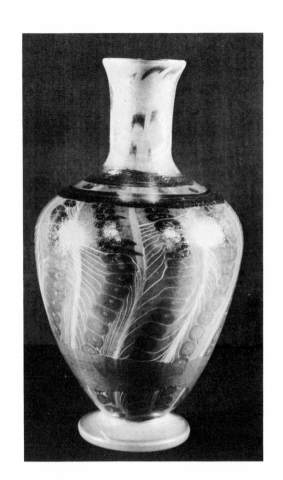

[172]

The slender silver-plated bronze vase (*opposite page, left*), 15⅞" high, the one (*opposite page, center*) 4⅝" high (both c. 1900) and the vases (*right*) are Tiffany vases in the collection of The Museum of Modern Art. The vase (*opposite page, right*) 16⅜" high, with calla-lily decoration encased in clear glass, is from the Joseph Heil collection. The vases (*bottom*) are from the collection of The Carnegie Institute, Pittsburgh. *From left to right:* A vase, h. 7⅝", d. 4⅞", an exhibition piece, purple iridescent with a green vine motif; a vase, h. 6", d. 4¾", purple to blue iridescent, with bosses around center; a vase, h. 9½", d. 3⅞"; and a vase, h. 6½", d. 5", with morning-glory design, exhibited in 1914.

The laminated iridescent bottle (*opposite page, top left*) is an early unmarked piece owned by the author, h. 7⅛". The paperweight vase (*opposite page, top right*), privately owned, has a design of blue and gray morning-glories with mustard-colored leaves. The group (*opposite page, bottom left*), owned by the author, include a peacock glass vase, h. 10¾", a transparent gourd-shaped vase, h. 8⅜", a vase on a bronze stand, turquoise overlay on white with gold flecks, h. 9¼", and a vase of aquamarine iridescent glass, h. 3¾", with a design of orange and green-gold embedded in the body. The paperweight vase (*opposite page, bottom right*), stands 15" high. Privately owned, it has a design of white narcissus. Five of the miniature vases (*above*), privately owned, are signed by Tiffany, excluding the "pinch" bottle. These include a vase, h. 2", silvery iridescent with gold and green feather design; a vase, h. 3¼", gold iridescent with violet and green flowing stripes; a vase, h. 2½", white opalescent with a vivid green and silver-green leaf design; a flat melon-shaped orange iridescent bottle, h. 1¼"; a vase, h. 1¾", gold iridescent with ochre shadings, a green and silver design; and a bottle, h. 2½", with amber to green shading. The vase (*bottom right*), privately owned, is 7¾" high, carved with an intaglio design of lilies-of-the-valley.

[*175*]

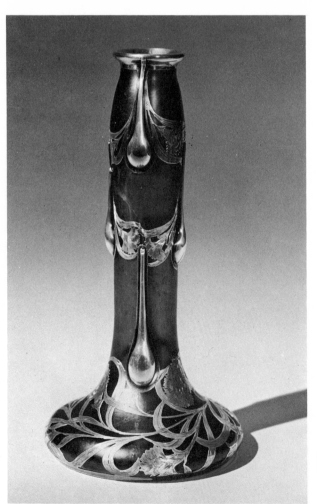

[176]

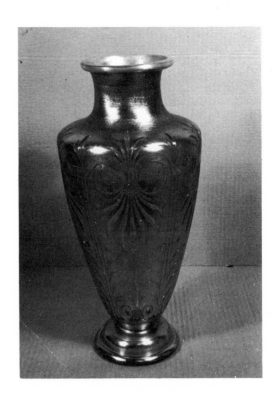

The three vases (*opposite page, top left*) and the vase (*opposite page, bottom right*) are owned privately. Those in the top group have iridescent gold, green and dark blue surfaces. The piece at the far right is known as "lava glass." The gray vase (*opposite page, bottom right*) is 10″ high, with black stripes and green dots. The opalescent green teardrop vase (*opposite page, bottom left*), 13″ high, has a silver mounting and is privately owned. The amber urn-form vase with silvered foot (*top right*), 18½″ high, once at Laurelton Hall, is now privately owned. The gold iridescent diatreta, or latticework, vase (*below*), 5½″ tall, is owned privately, as is the amphora-form vase (*bottom right*), 17¼″ high, made of deep wine-red glass, set in a floriform bronze doré-stand. The flaring neck of this vase, which was once at Laurelton Hall, has a ring of peacock blue medallions on an iridescent green ground.

[177]

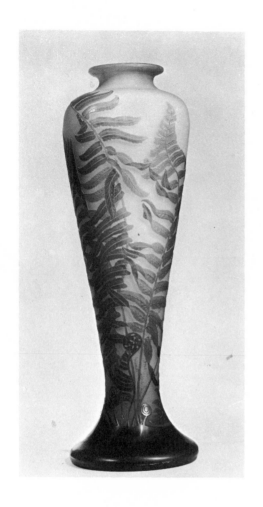

Tiffany had seen, on a trip to Europe in 1889, vases by Emile Gallé of Nancy, two of whose "cameo" vases are shown (*top left* and *top right*). The one at right (c. 1900) is in the collection of The Museum of Modern Art. The green iridescent vase in the bronze and marble stand (*bottom left*) and the striped and dotted vase (*bottom right*) are by Loetz Witwe of Austria.

The vase having the thread decoration (*top left*) was made by Victor Durand, while the fluted vase (*top right*) is an example of Quezal ware. The molded vase (*center left*) is by the French designer René Lalique, famous also for his jewelry. The group of Tiffany-type vases in the author's collection, (*bottom left*) includes a compote and small vase by Frederick Carder. The tallest vase is signed Kew Blas and the two other vases are marked Durand.

The Tiffany Glass Company
Memorial Windows & Colored Glass
for Churches and Dwellings
Stained Glass Mosaic Glass Wrought Glass
333-335 Fourth Avenue,
New York, ____ 18

you gave up & did not keep to your
plan you would despise yourself
afterwards & it would be harder any
time after. You also ought to
think of Hilda, I wanted to have
you not leave her any longer alone
as I am sure that you can look
out for her & that was one of
the reasons that we wanted you
to stay. Make the best of it and
busy yourself making others happy
& then time will pass & you will be
happier. It is very lonely without
you. Give much love & all & tell Charles
& Hilda that I feel really hurt that they
have not written. Your loving Papa

[180]

POTTERY AND GLASS DEPARTMENT

Among Tiffany & Co.'s important additions to their stock of pottery, porcelain, rock-crystal and art glassware are comprehensive displays of Rookwood, Marblehead, Ruskin and Moorcroft Pottery, Doulton's Sang-de-bœuf, choice specimens of Solon's Pâte-sur-pâte Vases, the new Lancastrian Lustre Pottery, and Bernard Moore's Rouge Flambé

Tiffany & Co.'s exhibit of Favrile Glass has been augmented this season by many new color and decorative studies which reveal effects of rare beauty, in bowls, vases, and other objects

This unique glass is made under the personal supervision of Mr. Louis C. Tiffany. It was awarded the Grand Prix at Paris in 1900, and at St. Petersburg in 1901, and received the highest awards at Buffalo in 1901, at Turin in 1902, and St. Louis in 1905. Examples of the glass have been purchased by the principal art museums of the world, as it marks a new epoch in glass-making

As Tiffany Favrile Glass is being imitated, patrons are cautioned to look for the distinguishing mark. Large and medium size pieces bear the name "Louis C. Tiffany" or "L. C. Tiffany-Favrile," and small pieces the initials "L. C. T."

673

706 TIFFANY BLUE BOOK—1911 EDITION

Tiffany Favrile Glass

Grand Prix, Paris, 1900; St. Petersburg, 1901
Also Highest Awards, Buffalo, 1901; Turin, 1902

Made under the supervision of Mr. Louis C. Tiffany

As this unique glass is being imitated, and inferior products represented as "Favrile Glass" or "Tiffany Glass," patrons are cautioned to look for the distinguishing mark on every piece of Tiffany Favrile Glass, the large and medium size pieces being signed with the full name, "Louis C. Tiffany" or "L. C. Tiffany-Favrile," the smaller with the initials "L. C. T."

In New York the genuine "Tiffany Favrile Glass" is sold only by Tiffany & Co., and at the Tiffany Studios, Madison Ave., corner of 45th Street

Examples of this unique glass have been purchased by the principal art museums of the world, as marking an epoch in glass-making

Tiffany & Co.'s collection includes a large variety of vases, bowls, table glass and small cabinet pieces

Almond dishes	each	$1.	and	$1.50
Berry bowls	"	8.	to	18.
Bonbon dishes	"	1.	and	1.50
Bouillon cups, no saucers	dozen	60.	upward	
Brandy and soda tumblers	each			10.
Butter plates, individual	"			1.50

POTTERY AND GLASS DEPARTMENT 707

Tiffany Favrile Glass—*Continued*

Candle shades and globes	each	$5.	to	$8.
Candlesticks	"	6.	to	10.
" electric	"	10.,	12.,	14.
Champagne glasses	dozen	60.	to	120.
Choice cabinet pieces	each	5.	to	400.
Cigar jars	"	35.	upward	
Claret glasses	dozen	45.	to	100.
Cocktail glasses	"	48.	upward	
Cologne bottles	each	5.	to	25.
Compotiers	"	8.	to	15.
Cordial glasses	"	1.	upward	
Cracker jars	"			30.
Decanters	"	10.	upward	
Desk lamps, shade extra	"			18.
Épergnes	"	15.	and	18.
Finger bowls and plates	dozen	75.	upward	
Flower holders for automobile	each	9.	and	12.
Flower vases	"	5.	to	250.
Fruit bowls	"	8.	to	18.
" dishes	"	10.	to	15.
" " individual	"			3.50
Goblets	dozen	100.	upward	
Hock glasses	"	45.	"	
Ice-cream plates	"	37.50	"	
Jardinières, with wire mesh	each	10.	to	50.
Liqueur bottles	"	10.	upward	

708 TIFFANY BLUE BOOK—1911 EDITION

Tiffany Favrile Glass—*Continued*

Liqueur glasses	dozen	$12.	upward	
Loving cups	each	10.	to	$50.
Nut bowls	"	8.,	$10.,	12.
Olive dishes	"			6.
Peach Melba glasses	dozen	60.	upward	
Plaques	each	10.	"	
Port-wine glasses	dozen	30.	to	85.
Pottery lamps, oil and electric	each	18.	upward	
Powder boxes	"	18.	and	25.
Punch bowls	"	75.	upward	
Punch cups	dozen	60.,	72.,	84.
Rhine-wine glasses	"	45.	upward	
Salad bowls	each	18.	"	
Salt cellars	"	1.50	"	
Seals, desk, with Old English initial				1.50
Shades, oil and electric	each	15.	to	60.
Sherry glasses	dozen	30.	to	85.
Sorbet glasses	"	72.	and	84.
Syrup pitchers	each	8.	to	22.
Tankards	"	8.	to	22.
Tumblers	"	4.	upward	
Wine glasses	dozen	30.	to	85.

POTTERY AND GLASS DEPARTMENT 709

Tiffany Favrile Glass—*Continued*

Vases

Gold and Blue Lustre

4 inches	each	$6.	and	$7.
3½ to 9 inches	"	6.	to	10.
4½ " 12 "	"	12.	to	15.
6 " 22 "	"	16.	to	25.
10 " 24 "	"	30.	to	35.

Blue and Gold Lustre, Leaf and Vine Decoration

3 to 6 inches	each	$15.	to	25.
6 " 12 "	"	30.	to	40.
8 " 20 "	"	45.	to	75.
22 " 24 "	"	100.	to	150.

Carved Cameo and Rock-crystal Effects

4 to 6 inches	each	20.	to	45.
6 " 8 "	"	50.	to	70.
10 " 12 "	"	75.	to	100.
12 " 14 "	"	120.	to	135.
16 " 18 "	"	150.	to	175.

[181] Tiffany's oldest daughter Mary, to whom he penned an affectionate letter about 1890, advising her to "busy herself making others happy" (*opposite page, top left*) married Graham Lusk. For one of his grandsons Tiffany designed the child's silver and copper dinner set. Tiffany's son Charles was graduated from Yale in 1900 and became an executive of Tiffany & Company, which moved to 37th Street and Fifth Avenue (*right*) in 1905. Tiffany, who had designed the decorations for the Yale Bicentennial, received an honorary master of arts degree from the University in 1903.

Tiffany spent many of his summers at The Briars (*opposite page*). Some interiors designed and decorated by Louis C. Tiffany were photographed for *Dekorative Kunst* in 1900. The furniture for these surprisingly modern interiors, including the library (*top right*), parlor (*top left*), dining-room (*bottom left*) and billiard room (*bottom right*), was produced by a firm under Tiffany's supervision.

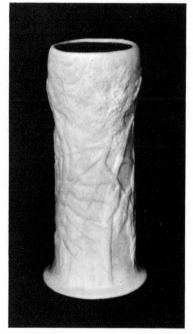

After the death of his father in 1902 Louis C. Tiffany became a vice-president of Tiffany & Company and moved the Tiffany Studios uptown to Madison Avenue and 45th Street to a building which had been designed for the Manhattan Athletic Club. (*opposite page, bottom*)

Lamps and lampshades were being produced in great quantity. After 1905 the ceramics department designed a variety of original lamp bases as well as vases and bowls, some molded, some thrown, in a variety of shapes and glazes (*opposite page, top*).

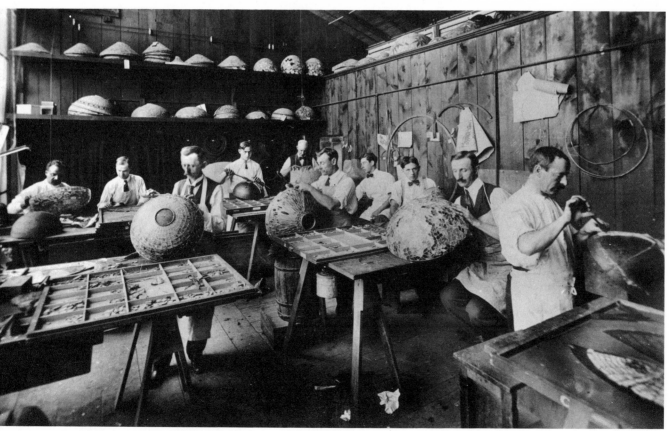

Although Tiffany did not originate models of hanging lamps with leaded glass shades those made in his studios achieved great popularity. Showroom samples such as these, "October Night" (*center left*), "Chestnut," (*bottom left*) and "Tyler" (*bottom right*), were widely copied. A design for a fluted lampshade (*center right*) was submitted to the Patent Office in 1914.

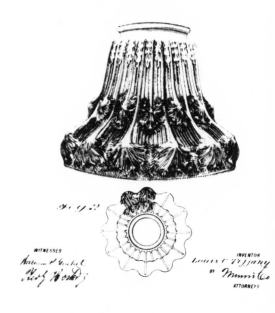

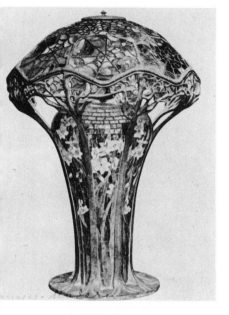

Tiffany constantly introduced new patterns, many of them designed by his employees. Many of the lamps, like the vases of the period, were bulbous in shape such as the kerosene lamp with mother-of-pearl shade (*top center*). Floral patterns (*top left* and *bottom left*) were very popular. The nymph and butterfly lamp pendant (*bottom right*) was designed by Alphonse Mucha.

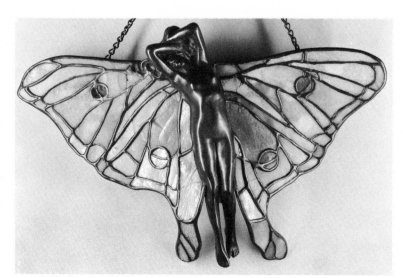

Among the popular bronze and metalwork items made by Tiffany Studios were a clock (*top right*), a bronze and glass inkwell, (*center right*), designed by Tiffany about 1900, a variety of candelabra and candlesticks (*below*) and an enamel-on-silver box (*bottom right*), designed and made by Julia Munson Sherman. The bronze box (*opposite page, center right*) is from Tiffany Studios. Desk sets were made in a number of designs (*opposite page, top right*). The enameled bronze ovoid jars, pear-shaped dish and petaled repoussé silver tea service and hammered copper tea tray (*opposite page*) were pieces from Laurelton Hall.

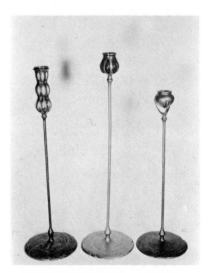

[188]

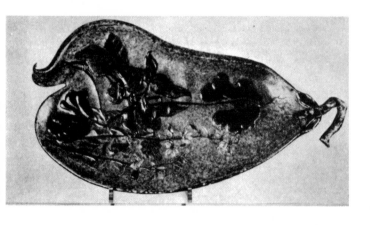

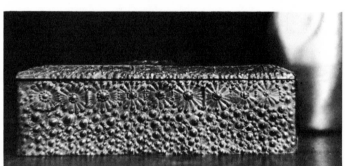

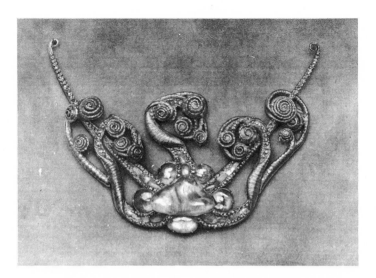

The brooch (*top left*) was made from a design by Tiffany, and exhibited in Paris. The two necklaces (*left*), one of gilded silver set with garnets and baroque pearls, the other of gold and enamel with a pendant, were among the items auctioned from Laurelton Hall. The necklace (*top right*) is in the collection of the Metropolitan Museum of Art. The gold brooch (*bottom right*), marked Tiffany & Company, is set with demantoids and sapphires. The figured velvet cushions (*opposite page, top left*), as well as the medallion carpet with birds (*opposite page, top right*) are also from Laurelton Hall. Shown also (*opposite page*) are a jeweled antependium designed by Tiffany and a copy of *The Art Work of Louis C. Tiffany*.

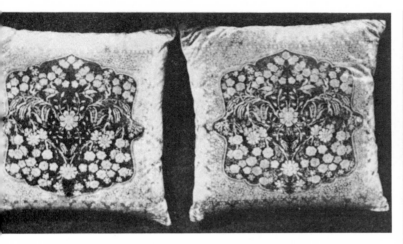

The last major job of interior decoration undertaken by Tiffany Studios was the furnishing and decorating of the newly-constructed Presidential Palace in Havana, Cuba, for President Menocal in 1918. This included 23 Tiffany rugs and 15 Tiffany lamps, reproductions of period furniture. In 1927 an Aubusson rug with the United States Seal in the center, 21' x 15' 3", was purchased for the White House from Tiffany Studios and used for many years in the Green Room (*right*). The punch set (*bottom left*) was one of the many tableware items in Favrile glass available from Tiffany Studios or Tiffany & Company.

[*193*]

The New York Times

Picture Section, Part 1 — Sunday, February 16, 1913

MOST LAVISH COSTUME FÊTE EVER SEEN IN NEW YORK.

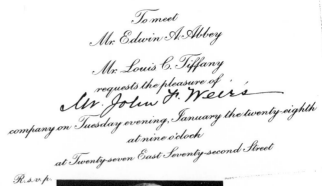

Invitation

To meet
Mr. Edwin A. Abbey

Mr. Louis C. Tiffany

requests the pleasure of

Mr. John F. Weir's

company on Tuesday evening, January the twenty-eighth

at nine o'clock

at Twenty-seven East Seventy-second Street

R.s.v.p.

Louis C. Tiffany played host at many gala gatherings at his New York home, where a lavish costume fête and reception was given in 1913, even dressing up himself as an Egyptian potentate. He also entertained often at his new estate near Oyster Bay, Laurelton Hall, designed and decorated by him, from its poppy-columned portico (*below*) to its indoor fountain. The Armory Show of 1913 (*right*) was a great shock to him; he thought it "all ugly" and spoke out against "those modernists."

[195]

Tiffany made Laurelton Hall one of the showplaces of the century. When fully decorated and landscaped the estate was valued in 1910 at nearly $2,000,000. A rock crystal was set in a pool on a terrace overlooking Cold Spring Harbor (*above*). The large cavelike fireplace in the dimly lit living-room (*left*) was complete with bearskin rug. The lighting fixtures, containing turtle-back tiles, were suspended from iron yokes (*below*).

The dining-room was well lit by long panels of clear glass, with wisteria borders of stained glass. The green marble fireplace had clocks· for the day of the week, hours of the day and days of the month.

In a sheltered alcove of the living room of Laurelton Hall (*opposite page, top, left and center right*) Tiffany displayed several of his stained glass windows, including "Eggplants," "Flowers, Fish and Fruit," "Feeding the Flamingoes," "The Four Seasons," (cut into separate panels) and "The Bathers." Also on this level of the house was a Chinese octagonal room, (*opposite page, bottom*) in which he displayed his fine Oriental antiques. Through the central court with a domed skylight of blue iridescent glass, ran a small stream. A bubbling fountain rose from a pool (*top right, center right*). Tiffany's prized vases and bowls were arranged in niches along the sides. A portrait of him among his flowers, painted by Sorolla, was prominently displayed. A later addition to Laurelton Hall was the art gallery (*below*).

The balcony of the court, entrance and bell-tower of Laurelton Hall are shown (*opposite page*). Sarah Hanley, for whom Tiffany built a house on the estate, is shown on a tigerskin (*top left*). The tiled fireplace (*right*) is from her house. Stanley Lothrop, resident director of the Louis Comfort Tiffany Foundation, is shown (*above*) in the Art Gallery. These two were the lone companions of Tiffany's old age.

While Stanley Lothrop and the student-guests of the Foundation dined at Laurelton Hall, served by two butlers, *(top left)* Joseph Briggs *(center)* was supervising Tiffany's business affairs. His home was in Jersey City. The living room, like that of Laurelton Hall, featured works of art and foliaged plants.

Tiffany lived to be almost 85, enjoying his flowers, painting them occasionally, and thanking Julia Munson Sherman in 1928 for her "lovely enamels."

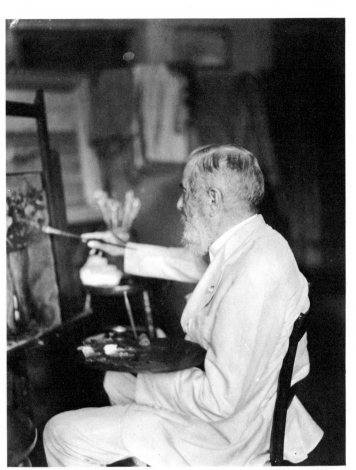

Feb 24"

COMFORT LODGE
1865 BRICKELL AVENUE
MIAMI, FLORIDA

My dear Mrs Sherman
Many thanks for
your lovely piece of
enamel. It was so
good of you to think
of me & I hope to see
you as soon as I return
I had a wonderful day-
So many lovely flowers
&c Yours as ever
Louis C. Tiffany

[203]

After Tiffany's death in 1933 the Foundation continued to erate Laurelton Hall as an art institute until 1946 but could afford to maintain it in its former opulent state. It was l used for marine research, the 60-acre property subdivided the house, with a 4-acre plot, sold for $10,000. The new ow acquired 84 rooms, 25 bathrooms, a yacht basin, a pipe or and a bell tower with a replica of the Westminster chimes.

In 1957 a fire razed Laurelton Hall, destroying the stately home once guarded by a pair of fierce K'ang Hsi lions, glazed a brilliant fluctuating blue. These, along with the treasures of a life-time, had been sold to the highest bidder at the Parke-Bernet Galleries auction of 1946.

part four

"*Afterword*"

DECADES OF DERISION

On January 17, 1933, Louis C. Tiffany died in his 72nd Street home, one month short of reaching his 85th birthday. He was, by now, almost forgotten. Very few mourned his passing. In his later years his only companions had been Stanley Lothrop and Sarah Hanley, his only "guests" the student members of the Louis Comfort Tiffany Foundation. Only Tiffany's children and grandchildren had found it possible to overlook his eccentricities and there were few admirers left. Many of the young artists who had enjoyed the gracious hospitality of Laurelton Hall and its landscaped grounds had little respect for their aged host and only a few of his former employees remembered his past benevolence.

One loyal ex-employee, however, rose indignantly to Tiffany's defense after reading a newspaper item about an exhibit of "Machine Art" at the Museum of Modern Art. Emily Genauer had commented in the New York *World Telegram* on March 10, 1934, "Even if you haven't clasped modernism to your bosom and used

[207]

all your period pieces for firewood this winter, every last one of you has unconsciously adopted its most important principle, namely, simplicity, and the discarding of things superfluous or trivial. Else where are the gimcracks of yesterday, the antimacassars and Tiffany glass lamps and the bronze ladies whose billowing skirts were spread to receive calling cards? Long since they vanished from the current scene as being silly and fussy and always in the way." Miss Agnes F. Northrop, who had designed some stained glass windows for Tiffany, sought to compose a proper reply. "In glancing at the article on 'Utility Is Stressed in Objects for Home'" she wrote, "the writer has shown her ignorance in classing as 'fussy and silly' Tiffany glass lamps, etc. As one who has worked for years with Mr. Tiffany, I protest the criticism. One thing that he always advocated in design was "simplicity." To prove that my statement is true one can easily take the 5th Ave. bus to 23rd Street and at 46 West 23rd St. (the Studios) he can find many articles of value—simple, useful and beautiful."

Tiffany's death occasioned, among many obituaries, an item in *Art News:* "Mr. Tiffany was generally regarded as one of the earliest exponents of the modern art movement in the United States, and, at one time, his painting, glass and architectural designs aroused considerable controversy." The controversy as to his place in art has continued to this day.

Tiffany was always concerned with basic principles of aesthetics. He rejected wholly imitative historical forms, yet did not hesitate to draw upon aspects of the past in evolving shapes or in planning large-scale decorative schemes which he managed to mark by his own originality.

With his delight in the richly varied aspects of nature, he needed no urging to take advantage of "the endless wealth of precept and suggestion in air and water and earth, in all the vast, teeming bosom of nature." Flowers and marine forms suggested myriads of lines and masses, hues and shades to his vivid imagination. His plea for a return to forms derived from nature as the greatest source of aesthetic pleasure was revealing of a major tenet of his philosophy. Forms of growth have long served as a major source of inspiration and probably will continue to do so, however much some artists may deliberately "offend the eye" in order to provoke a strong emotional reaction. Perhaps as long as there are those who respond to subtle refinements of shape and color there will be an interest in the unique objects produced by Tiffany or influenced by his concept of beauty. His dream that America could become an important center of the arts has been realized and his unswerving devotion to the cause of creating beauty in objects in everyday life can be acknowledged even by those who do not share his predilections.

Louis Comfort Tiffany was essentially a romantic, a flamboyant late-Victorian individualist and nonconformist. He felt keenly the surge of an expanding economy, when the new millionaires spent fortunes to build and decorate their red-plush mansions, yachts and private railway carriages. He reveled in beauty and he was free to find it in exotic climes. He passionately wanted to open the eyes of the public to the delights of color and form. He let it be known that he, for one, as a leader of the arts, would gladly educate by helping the public to distinguish between deep, strong coloration and gaudiness, by making it more familiar with works of powerful color and accustoming it to something "richer and more virile than the drabs and greys and anemic color schemes of the past."

Throughout his life he did not shun the limelight and he freely cultivated the sensual side of nature, refining his tastes with the widest variety of experience. Yet James McNeill Whistler and Oscar Wilde both attracted far more attention in the daily press for their exploits and peculiarities. Sarah Bernhardt, the "Divine Eccentric," was another iconoclast of the "red plush" generation. The spirit of some of the artists of this era was characterized by Holbrook Jackson in *The Eighteen-Nineties:* "If luxury had its art and its traffic, so had a saner and more balanced social consciousness. If one demanded freedom for an individual expression tending towards degeneration and perversion, the other demanded a freedom which would give the common man opportunities for the redemption of himself and his kind. . . . But again, it must not be assumed that these characteristics were always separate. To a very considerable extent they overlapped, even where they were necessarily interdependent. Oscar Wilde, for example, bridged the chasm between the self-contained individualism of the decadents and the communal aspirations of the more advanced social revolutionaries."

The objects of art garnered from his travels, the luxuries with which the pleasure-loving Tiffany surrounded himself, he wanted to share with others. He did exert a powerful influence on the taste of his times. He was a tireless worker and a prolific innovator. In glass he found a media in which he could fully express the rebel side of his nature. It was also a product which could be widely distributed. If one could not afford a large Tiffany glass window, one could at the very least possess a richly glowing vase or lampshade. Even today glass has an element of luxury which cannot be duplicated in a synthetic substance.

Tiffany revolutionized the techniques of working with glass, first for the making of artistic tiles and stained-glass windows and then in applying these methods to a wide variety of objects. His experience first as a painter and then as a decorator gave him a richly varied background, and he applied his developed sensitivity to the design and quality of all that was produced under his supervision. One of the most versatile and prolific artists who worked in glass, Tiffany remained keenly aware of his tradition and responsibility as an American artist.

[*209*]

Tiffany himself had a definite opinion of his own niche in American art and set forth his views clearly in the "Afterword" of his testament, *The Art Work of Louis C. Tiffany*, couched in the respectful language of Charles de Kay. In it they collaborated to set the public straight on what Tiffany considered to be his "uncommon endowment" and far-flung influence. It fixed his image, as he saw it, on the eve of a world war, after which a change in taste would relegate his wares to attics, only to retrieve them after a second holocaust in order to provide notes of rich color in austere interiors.

Tiffany, by means of the "introductory" text, called attention to his own life-long emphasis on color. "The value attributed to color has been denied by theorists who have started from an untenable assumption that there is a purity, a moral worth attached to the absence of color, in opposition to sensuousness and luxury in a bad sense attached to its presence. This is a convenient theory for a vast majority of artists who are born without the peculiar eyes and senses that distinguish values and respond with sympathy to the vibrations of light.

"Persian textiles, Japanese water colors, Chinese porcelain, Venetian paintings, the works of Rembrandt and Velasquez can be forced into appeals to sensuousness and luxuriousness only by a twist in the meaning of words which may satisfy the narrow-minded and the bigot. Some painters do not make their mark without having this characteristic to any great extent, although it would appear from the nature of things that it ought to be the painter's strongest trait."

Tiffany categorized himself primarily as a colorist, placing himself in the illustrious company of such American artists as Gilbert Stuart, Malbone, Henry Peters Gray, George Inness, George Fuller, James McNeill Whistler, John La Farge, Homer D. Martin, Albert P. Ryder and John Singer Sargent. If the relationship was not always recognized, Charles de Kay pointed out, the reason lay in the fact that Tiffany had made so great a name in the arts and crafts that his achievements in this field threw his work as a painter in the shade. De Kay pointedly recalled a time when Tiffany's works had been recognized when they were exhibited as the work of a colorist by those "who knew enough to value the rare gifts of an eye for color and a hand capable of making color sing from the canvas." The claim was put forth adroitly that other forms of art demanded more color-feeling in an artist than oil painting and offered no avenues for getting 'round the issue, as oil painting could be made to do, as Tiffany saw it, for the near-colorist. "Mosaics that admit of no shadows and confused lines, glass through which the light shines revealingly, textiles that are moved about in this or that light, these are things that test an artist on the color-side and permit of no evasion."

The knuckles of those who were too obtuse to appreciate Tiffany's unique qualities were rapped still further. "In the queer, half-conscious art faith of the artist, such works rank far below the painted canvas; in their unwritten book of nobility the workmen in the arts and crafts are mere *bons bourgeois*, while they are the upper crust. Without reasoning on the matter, they take opinions ready-made like the generality of people and learn from their school days that the painters of easel pictures form the aristocracy of the profession. Without going farther into the matter and showing historically and sociologically how this odd situation among painters has come about, let us merely note that Tiffany was too intelligent an artist to be thus deceived, and being naturally of an inventive turn of mind, proceeded to devote himself to other lines of work which called upon his talent with even greater force. . . . Indeed, as time went on, the number of different art-works to which he gave attention became so great that it seemed marvelous that one man, however well supported by capable assistants, could find the waking hours to keep track of them all. No one could have done it all except a person who could double his existence as a creative artist with the life of a business man."

There was a grandiloquent summing-up. "In one sense his life may be said to have been uneventful, if we speak from the traveler's point of view, but not so if we put ourselves in place of the artist and inventor. It can never be said of him that a rolling stone gathers no moss. When we think of the silent effect produced in a thousand families, and in more museums than could easily be named, by the inspiring art-works he has produced, we can say sincerely that he has deserved well of the republic."

For several decades, however, silence descended, Tiffany's name faded into obscurity and many of the articles he had created were tossed into discard heaps and rummage sales. Tiffany's will decreed an end to his own firm, and his only son was primarily occupied with the affairs of Tiffany & Company. The 72nd Street mansion was sold and razed in 1938 to make way for a modern apartment house. The remaining stock of Tiffany Studios, comprising some 1,100 items, was auctioned in Washington, D. C. from March 14 to March 19,1938. These included paintings, tapestries, rugs, fabrics, furniture, bronze chandeliers, pottery, antique stained-glass windows and some twenty Tiffany windows. Two paintings by Tiffany were included. One was lunette-shaped, 88" x 51", showing a woman with a baby on her lap extending a wreath to a boy and two girls. It was said that members of Tiffany's family had posed for this painting, entitled "Devotion." Also included in the articles auctioned was the original design for a stained-glass window entitled "The Entombment," 94" x 64". This was dated 1893 and was signed by Louis C. Tiffany.

Laurelton Hall was maintained by the Louis Comfort Tiffany Foundation after Tiffany's death, but during World War II the upkeep became prohibitive. When the Foundation gave up the estate the number of rooms totaled 84, and there were 25 baths. In 1946 the courts granted the trustees' request to modify the original plan of operation. A decision dated July 17, 1946 stated: "The proposal of the Trustees that the available income from the trust funds be applied to the creation of fellowships for creative work in the fine arts is entirely consistent with the purposes for which the trust was created, will afford a wider range of selection and would permit the extension of assistance by the Foundation in accordance with the artists' financial need, without burdensome restrictions as to age, sex, race or marital status." Through the ensuing years the Foundation has continued to encourage young American artists.

The contents of Laurelton Hall, from Mazarin-blue rugs to Indian baskets, were sold at an auction held at the Parke-Bernet Galleries in New York in 1946. At this sale many treasures Tiffany had saved for his personal enjoyment went to bidders for only a fraction of their original value. From 1942 and during the war years the house was used as the headquarters of a marine research organization, the National Defense Research Committee. The land and buildings were sold in 1949. The entire property, comprising some sixty acres, was disposed of in parcels ranging from four to twelve acres, for approximately $65,000. The main residential building, along with a four-acre plot, went for $10,000, but a few years later it was destroyed by fire.

Tiffany's name was cloaked with derision during the thirties and forties, which witnessed the spread to America of the austere functional aesthetic emanating from the German *Bauhaus*. Glass, in order to be effective, was thought then to be necessarily transparent, and structure, to be valid, had to be rectilinear. Applied ornament was considered anathema and a profusion of colors was condemned as gaudy. The functionalists and purists, who advocated the extensive use of glass curtain-walls and the unadorned use of natural materials, held up the work of Tiffany and all he stood for as the ultimate in vulgarity. In a volume on American glass compiled by George and Helen McKearin in 1941, the work of Tiffany was dismissed in a single brief paragraph under the heading of "Fancy Glass." In 1950, however, in their volume *Two Hundred Years of Blown Glass*, the McKearins, in referring to Tiffany's wares, conceded "even the purist must acknowledge that they represent the triumph of the glassmaker over his materials and his equipment."

THE REVIVAL OF ART NOUVEAU

After several decades of neglect, during which great quantities of Tiffany ware were destroyed as worth little or nothing, a renewed interest began to develop simultaneously in several areas. In 1949 the Museum of Modern Art published *Pioneers of Modern Design* by Nikolaus Pevsner, which made reference to Tiffany and his

[*212*]

Favrile glass as an expression of Art Nouveau. A few collectors, among them the painter Theodore Stamos and the art historian Milton W. Brown, began to acquire unusual examples of the products of Tiffany Studios, and by 1952 a definite interest in Tiffany glass was dawning among museum curators and antique dealers. That year an exhibition, *Um 1900, Art Nouveau Jugendstil*, at the Kunstgewerbe Museum in Zurich gave Tiffany a prominent place and for the first time pinpointed the unique quality of his designs.

In the decade following, interest in Tiffany and his work swelled. In October, 1956, there was a revival of interest in iridescence, which *House Beautiful* that fall called "the new dimension" in decorating. In 1960, an exhibition, "The Sources of the Twentieth Century," was organized in Paris by Jean Cassou, Emil Langui and Nikolaus Pevsner, authors of *Gateway to the Twentieth Century*, published in 1962.

An exhibition of Tiffany's work was held at the Morse Gallery at Rollins College, Winter Park, Florida, in 1955, followed by a display of various Tiffany windows. The Museum of Contemporary Crafts in New York held a retrospective exhibit in 1958, to which Tiffany's protégée Sarah Hanley lent several items and his grandson Louis Tiffany Lusk a child's silver and copper dinner set, which had been designed for him by Tiffany. Ten pieces of jewelry were shown. Maurice Grosser, recalling this exhibit in *Critic's Eye*, found content lacking in "a window like a grape arbor, vases like flower calices, ten bronze lilies intertwined into an electric table lamp, a lamp which is a bronze tree trunk with a leaded glass shade—a Tree of Knowledge for some library table . . . The colors and textures are rich and intricate; the shapes often more decorative and exotic than useful or beautiful. Their spindly flower forms, their butterfly-wing colors and their Byzantine shapes and encrustations irresistibly call to mind some elaborate setting for Strauss' *Salomé*." But Stuart Preston, art critic of *The New York Times*, commented that, "It will be an insensitive eye that fails to respond to the artistry of his hand-fabricated Favrile glass." An observation in *Time* magazine in the same year characterized Tiffany's distinctive style: "In an age when man's vision seems increasingly hemmed in by a machine-made environment, there is an urge to draw new strength from adventuresome craftsmen who knew how to combine richness with beauty."

Within a few years the number of private collectors increased enormously and many designers such as Edward Wormley and interior decorators began to incorporate Tiffany glass tiles and other items in furniture and in interiors. Tiffany glass and metal ware today are well on their way to becoming valued antiques. Good early examples of Tiffany's work have become collectors' items because they possess the inherent style and quality that characterize the finest decorative arts of the past. There is no reason to believe Tiffany ware will again be condemned to the junk heap.

The revival has received the support of many art historians who consider Tiffany a gifted artist. Although he only rarely achieved the sublimity which is the mark of true greatness, he was nevertheless responsible for the production of many objects of real beauty of an enduring quality. Scholars and curators have begun the task of sorting the characteristic and significant objects from the ordinary and commercial products. A major step toward re-evaluating Tiffany's role as a pioneer in modern design has been taken by the proposal to re-establish, in Winter Park, Florida, the Tiffany chapel of 1893. This would form, along with examples of his important windows, the core of a museum of turn-of-the-century art. When the process of cataloguing and selecting outstanding pieces has advanced sufficiently for the finest of Tiffany's creations to be assembled in a definite exhibition, his reputation as one of America's great artists will undoubtedly be assured.

It has been said that we often deride the arts of our parents and revive those of our grandparents, an aphorism certainly true in the case of Louis C. Tiffany. It has taken the test of time to recognize the value of his contribution for his time and our own. In the history of art there are many examples of the rediscovery of obscure and neglected artists but perhaps none as timely as the reappearance in the limelight of Louis C. Tiffany. Today America has developed a new self-confidence in the visual arts. New public buildings have been enhanced by ornament, sculptural and mosaic. More artists have begun to work in glass, and as a highly versatile art medium it is more generally understood and appreciated than ever before. Architects have worked out striking new ways to embellish modern structures, in some cases even incorporating pieces of old Tiffany glass. Tiffany's dream of a fusion of art and everyday life has become a reality, and with it has come a belated understanding and appreciation of his far-sighted aims and ambitions.

part four
ILLUSTRATIONS

Louis C. Tiffany
IN RETROSPECT

With the revival of interest in Art Nouveau came the use by designers such as Edward Wormley of Tiffany tiles, lamps and vases (*top right, bottom left, bottom right*). An Art Nouveau table-setting featuring Favrile glass, from nut dishes to goblets and flower-like finger bowls, with Tiffany vermeil flatware and accessories, was designed by Van Day Truex (*right*).

Tiffany's experimental tiles of 1880 were mounted in a table-top for his own living room by the designer Edward Wormley in 1956 (*above* and *left*).

Tiffany and Tiffany-type windows were also used in contemporary interiors, such as in an alcove behind a marble-topped bar (*bottom left*). Pieces of old stained glass were also incorporated in designs for modern windows, such as those by Robert Sowers installed in Temple Beth Emeth, Albany, N. Y. (*top*).

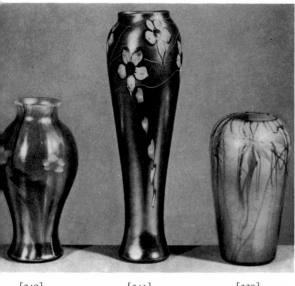

[240]   [241]   [239]

TIFFANY VASE WITH FLORAL DECORATION
ter-shaped, decorated with milky semi-opaque white blossoms and green   25.0
;e, on an amber iridescent ground. Signed. (*McGinnis*)
                                              Height 11 inches
              [See illustration]

TIFFANY VASE WITH FLORAL DECORATION
ated baluster-shaped vase painted and etched with a collar of clematis   40 0
ms and scrolling vines, in iridescent tones of blue. Signed. (*McGinnis*)
                                              Height 17½ inches
              [See illustration]
                        43

Tiffany-designed art glass has now become a sought-
after collector's item, commanding prices such as
those noted in right margins of the Parke-Bernet
Galleries auction catalogues reproduced here. The
auctions were held in 1963 and 1964.

[62]   [63]   [61]

63. TIFFANY FLORIFORM VASE
Slender vase, the ruffled wide rim resembling a flower, in brilliant amber iridescent
tones. Signed. (*McGinnis*)   *Height 16½ inches*   175
              [See illustration]

64. TWO WHITE SATIN ROSE VASES
Plain opaque white spherical vase with ruffled rim. [Lot.] (*McGinnis*)
                                              Height 6¾ inches   40

65. TWO TIFFANY GLASS AND GILDED METAL BOWLS
One with swirled petal molding in amber iridescent tones, the other shallow with a
granulated texture. Signed. [Lot.] (*McGinnis*)   *Diameters 7 and 9 inches*   60

9

"The Bathers."

Louis C. Tiffany

Bibliography

ARTICLES BY LOUIS C. TIFFANY

"American Art Supreme in Colored Glass," *The Forum*, Vol. XV, 1893, pp. 621–28.

"The Gospel of Good Taste," *Country Life in America*, Vol. XIX, No. 2, November, 1910, p. 105.

"The Tasteful Use of Light and Color in Artificial Illumination," *Scientific American*, Vol. 104, 1911, p. 373.

"What Is The Quest of Beauty?" *The International Studio*, Vol. 58, 1916, p. lxiii.

"Color and Its Kinship to Sound," *The Art World*, Vol. 2, 1917, pp. 142–43.

"The Quest of Beauty," *Harper's Bazaar*, December, 1917, pp. 43–44.

"The Dream Garden," Curtis Publishing Company, Philadelphia, Pa.

BROCHURES AND PUBLICATIONS
ISSUED BY LOUIS C. TIFFANY'S
TIFFANY GLASS AND DECORATING COMPANY

A Synopsis of the Exhibit at the World's Fair, Chicago, 1893.
Memorial Windows, 1896.
Tiffany Glass Mosaics, 1896.
Tiffany Favrile Glass, 1896.
Memorial Tablets, 1896.
A List of Windows and Extracts from Letters and Newspapers, 1897.

ISSUED BY LOUIS C. TIFFANY'S
TIFFANY STUDIOS

(Not Dated)

Tiffany Favrile Glass
Tiffany Domestic Windows
A Partial List of Windows
Antique Textiles

[*221*]

Bibliography

(Dated)

Portfolio of Work of the Tiffany Studios, 1901.
Esposizione d'Arte Decorativa Moderna, Turin, 1902.
Bronze Lamps, 1904.
God's Acre by James Burrell, 1906.
Collection of Notable Oriental Rugs by Mrs. J. C. Ripley, 1st ed., 1906; 2nd ed., 1907.
A Collection of English Furniture by Luke V. Lockwood, 1907.
Collection of Antique Chinese Rugs, 1908.
The Art of American Indians, 1909.
Examples of Recent Work from the Studio of Louis C. Tiffany by Ethel Syford, 1911.
The Mosaic Curtain for the National Theater of Mexico, 1911.
Memorials in Glass and Stone, 1913.
Character and Individuality in Decorations and Furnishings, 1913.
Mausoleums, 1914.

ARTICLES IN NEWSPAPERS AND PERIODICALS
PUBLISHED DURING LOUIS C. TIFFANY'S
LIFETIME*

ANONYMOUS ARTICLES

American Architect and Building News, "On the Exhibit of Stained Glass at the Fair," November 11, 1893, pp. 74–75.
American Art Annual, "Mural Paintings in Public Buildings in the United States," Vol. 19, 1922, pp. 407–38.
American Magazine of Art, "Watercolors by Louis C. Tiffany," Vol. 13, 1922, pp. 258–59.
Architectural Record, The, "How The Rich Are Buried," Vol. 10, 1900, pp. 23–51.
Art Digest, "Tiffany Studios Bankrupt," May 1, 1932.
Bulletin of the Stained Glass Association of America, The, "A Tribute to Mr. Louis Comfort Tiffany," December, 1928, pp. 8–12.
Century Magazine, The, "Some of the Union League Decorations," Vol. 23, 1882, pp. 745–52.
Dekorative Kunst, "L. C. Tiffany," Vol. 3, 1899, pp. 108–20.
Harper's Magazine, "A Piece of Glass," Vol. 79, 1889, pp. 245–64.
International Studio, The, "Louis C. Tiffany and His Work in Artistic Jewelry," Vol. 30, 1906, pp. 33–42.

* "planted" promotion (RK)

[222]

Bibliography

Scribner's Monthly, "Dr. Schliemann at Mycenae," January, 1878, pp. 307–20.
Scribner's Monthly, "The Society of Decorative Art," Vol. 22, 1881, pp. 697–709.
Scribner's Monthly, "American Progress in the Manufacture of Stained Glass," January, 1881, pp. 485–86.
Town and Country, "Modern Art in Glassware," (A.T.A.), December 2, 1905, pp. 15–16.

SIGNED ARTICLES

AVERY, MARY L., "The Opening of the New Library Building," *Pratt Institute Monthly*, Vol. IV, No. 10, June, 1896.
BEBARBIERI, ISABELLA, "Mosaics as an Independent Art," *The Architectural Record*, Vol. 2, 1893, pp. 291–302.
BING, S., (ed.) *Artistic Japan*, 36 issues, Paris, 1888–1891.
———, "Die Kunstgläser von Louis C. Tiffany,", *Kunst und Kunsthandwerk*, Vol 1, 1898, pp. 105–11.
———, "L'Art Nouveau," *The Architectural Record*, Vol. 12, 1902, pp. 281–85.
———, "L'Art Nouveau," *The Craftsman*, October, 1903, pp. 1–15.
BOUILHET, ANDRÉ, "L'Exposition de Chicago," *Revue des Arts Décoratifs*, Vol. 14, 1893, pp. 65–79.
BRECK, JOSEPH, "Louis C. Tiffany's Window," *Metropolitan Museum of Art Bulletin*, Vol. 20, 1925, pp. 287–88.
BROWNELL, WILLIAM C., "The Younger Painters of America," *Scribner's Monthly*, July, 1881, pp. 321–34.
COLE, CHARLES, "Painted Glass in Household Decoration," *Harper's Monthly*, October, 1879, pp. 655–64.
COLEMAN, CARYL, "A Sea of Glass," *The Architectural Record*, Vol. 2, 1893, pp. 264–85.*
———, "The Second Spring," *The Architectural Record*, Vol. 2, 1893, pp. 473–92.*
———, "A Comparative Study of European and American Church Glass," *House Beautiful*, April, 1898, pp. 143–48.*
COOK, CLARENCE, "Recent Church Decoration," *Scribner's Monthly*, February, 1878, pp. 569–77.
CONWAY, EDWARD HAROLD, "Mr. Louis C. Tiffany's Laurelton Hall at Cold Spring, Long Island," *The Spur*, August 15, 1914, pp. 25–29.*
DAY, LEWIS F., "Modern Mosaic in England," *The Architectural Record*, Vol. 2, 1892, pp. 65–88.
———, "Favrile Glass," *Magazine of Art*, Vol. 24, 1900, pp. 541–44.

[223]

Bibliography

DE CUERS, RENÉ, "Domestic Stained Glass in France," *The Architectural Record*, Vol. 9, 1899, pp. 115–41.

DE KAY, CHARLES, "A Western Setting for the Beauty of the Orient," *Arts and Decoration*, October, 1911, pp. 468–71.*

DE QUELIN, RENÉ, "A Many-Sided Creator of the Beautiful," *Arts and Decoration*, Vol 17, 1922, pp. 176–77.*

————, "This Te Deum Is Sung in Glass," *The International Studio*, Vol. 76, 1923, pp. 360–61.*

DREISER, THEODORE, "The Making of Stained Glass Windows," *Cosmopolitan*, Vol. 26, 1899, pp. 243–52.

FRANTZ, HENRI, "The Art Movement: Stained Glass in France," *The Magazine of Art*, Vol. 20, Part 2, 1897, pp. 270–71.

FRED, A. W., "Interieurs von L. C. Tiffany," *Dekorative Kunst*, Vol. 9, 1901, pp. 110–16.

FUCHS, GEORG, "Eindrüke aus der Amerikanischen Abteilung," *Deutsche Kunst und Dekoration*, Vol. 11, 1902, pp. 182–92.

GENSEL, WALTHER, "Tiffany-Gläser auf der Pariser Welt-Ausstetlung 1900," *Deutsche Kunst und Dekoration*, Vol. 7, 1900–01, pp. 44–45, 86–93, 95–97.

GOODHUE, H. E., "Stained Glass in Private Houses," *The Architectural Record*, Vol. 18, 1905, pp. 347–54.

GUIMARD, HECTOR, "An Architect's Opinion of 'L'Art Nouveau,' " *The Architectural Record*, Vol. 12, 1902, pp. 126–33.

HAMLIN, A. D. F., "L'Art Nouveau," *The Craftsman*, December, 1904, pp. 129–43.

HARRISON, CONSTANCE CARY, "Some Work of the Associated Artists," *Harper's Magazine*, Vol. 69, 1884, pp. 343–51.

HARVEY, JAMES L., "Source of Beauty in Favrile Glass," *Brush and Pencil*, Vol. 9, 1901, pp. 167–76.

HEINIGKE, OTTO, "Random Thoughts of a Glassman," *The Craftsman*, December, 1902.

HENDERSON, W. J., "Some New York Theatres," *Magazine of Art*, Vol. 9, 1886, pp. 401–7.

HOWE, SAMUEL, "The Use of Ornament in the House," *The Craftsman*, Vol. 3, 1902, p. 91–.*

————, "Enamel as a Decorative Agent," *The Craftsman*, Vol. 2, 1902, pp. 61–68.*

————, "The Making of Glass," *The Craftsman*, Vol. 3, 1903, pp. 367–.*

————, "One Source of Color Values," *House and Garden*, September, 1906, pp. 104–13.*

————, "The Dwelling Place as an Expression of Individuality," *Appleton's Magazine*, February, 1907, pp. 156–65.*

————, "An American Country House," *The International Studio*, Vol. 33, 1907–08, pp. 294–96.*

————, "The Long Island Home of Mr. Louis C. Tiffany," *Town and Country*, September 6, 1913, pp. 24–26, 42.*

————, "The Silent Fountains of Laurelton Hall," *Arts and Decoration,*" September, 1913.*

————, "A Country Home with a Human Appeal," *Long Island Home Journal*, March, 1914, pp. 4–6.*

————, "The Garden of Mr. Louis C. Tiffany," *House Beautiful*, January, 1914, pp. 40–42.*

KOBBÉ, GUSTAV, "Angel of Truth for the John G. Shedd Mausoleum," New York *Herald*, December 26, 1915.*

————, "Mr. Louis C. Tiffany, Famous Artist in Stained Glass," New York *Herald Magazine*, April 23, 1916, p. 6.

LAMB, CHARLES R., "How An American Stained Glass Window Is Made," *The Chautauquan*, Vol. 29, 1899, pp. 513–52.

LAMB, FREDERICK S., "Stained Glass in Relation to Church Ornamentation," *The Catholic World*, Vol. 74, 1902, pp. 661–77.

————, "The Painted Window," *The Craftsman*, Vol. 3, 1903, p. 348–; "Modern Use of Gothic," Vol. 8, 1905, pp. 150–70.

LATHROP, GEORGE PARSONS, "John La Farge," *Scribner's Monthly*, Vol. 21, 1881, pp. 503–16.

LOTHROP, STANLEY, "Louis Comfort Tiffany Foundation," *American Magazine of Art*, Vol. 14, 1923, pp. 615–17.

LOUNDSBERY, ELIZABETH, "Aquamarine Glass," *American Homes and Gardens*, December, 1913, pp. 418, 441.

LOW, WILL H., "Old Glass in New Windows," *Scribner's Magazine*, Vol. 4, 1888, pp. 675–86.

LYMAN, CLARA BROWN, "Recent Achievements in Decorative Lighting," *Country Life in America*, October, 1914, pp. 52–54.

MAGNE, LUCIEN, "Le Vitrail," *Art et Décoration*, Vol. 1, No. 1, 1897, pp. 1–10; No. 2, pp. 9–16.

MEIER-GRAAFE, J., "M. Louis C. Tiffany," *L'Art Decoratif*, Vol. 1, No. 3, 1898, pp. 105, 106, 116–28.

MILLET, FRANK D., "Some American Tiles," *The Century Magazine*, April, 1882, p. 896.

MOLINIER, ÉMILE, "Les Arts de Feu," *Art et Décoration*, Vol. 3, 1898, pp. 189–200.

MITCHELL, DONALD G., "In and About the Fair," *Scribner's Monthly*, Vol. 12, 1876, pp. 742, 889; Vol. 13, 1877, p. 115.

————, "Industrial and Architectural Designs," *Reports and Awards*, Vol. 7, Group 27, Washington, D. C., 1880, pp. 642–51.

————, "From Lobby to Peak," *Our Continent*, Vol. 1, Philadelphia, 1882, pp. 5, 21, 37, 69, 85, 101, 132, 148, 185, 217.*

————, "The Country House," *Scribner's Magazine*, Vol. 8, 1890, pp. 313–35.

MUMFORD, J. K., "A Year at the Tiffany Foundation," *Arts and Decoration*, Vol. 14, 1921, pp. 272–73.

RIORDAN, ROGER, "American Stained Glass," *The American Art Review*, Vol. 2, Division 1, pp. 229–34; Division 2, pp. 7–11, 59–64, Boston, 1881.

SAYLOR, HENRY H., "Indoor Fountains," *Country Life in America*, August, 1908, p. 366.*

————, "The Country Home of Mr. Louis C. Tiffany," *Country Life in America*, December, 1908, pp. 157–62.*

SCHEPFER, JEAN, "L'Art Nouveau," *The Craftsman*, July, 1903, pp. 229–38.

SCHUYLER, MONTGOMERY, "The Romanesque Revival in America," *The Architectural Record*, Vol. 1, 1891, pp. 151–98.

SINGLETON, ESTHER, "Glass and Glassmaking," *The Mentor*, Vol. 7, No. 5, April 15, 1919.

SMITH, MINNA CAROLINE, "Louis C. Tiffany—The Celestial Hierarchy," *The International Studio*, Vol. 33, 1908, pp. 96–99.

STONEHOUSE, AUGUSTUS, "A Glance at New York Theatres," *Art Review*, April, 1887, pp. 6–8.

SULLIVAN, LOUIS H., "Reply to Mr. Frederick S. Lamb on 'Modern Use of the Gothic,'" *The Craftsman*, Vol. 8, 1905, pp. 338–.

TEALL, GARDNER C., "The Art of Things," *Brush and Pencil*, Vol. 4, 1899, pp. 307–10.

THARP, EZRA, "Iridescent Art," *The New Republic*, April 1, 1916.

THOMAS, W. H., "Glass Mosaic: An Old Art with a New Distinction," *The International Studio*, Vol. 28, 1906, pp. 73–78.

TOWNSEND, HORACE, "American and French Applied Art at the Grafton Galleries," *The International Studio*, Vol. 8, 1899, pp. 39–46.

VIVIAN, H. L., "Pictures in Mosaic," *Harper's Bazaar*, May, 1914.

WAERN, CECILIA, "The Industrial Arts of America: The Tiffany Glass and Decorating Co." *The International Studio*, Vol. 2, 1897, pp. 156–65; Vol. 5, 1898, pp. 16–21.

WEIR, HUGH, "Through the Rooking Glass—An Interview with Louis C. Tiffany," *Collier's*, May 23, 1925.

WEST, MAX, "The Revival of Handicrafts in America," *Bulletin of the Bureau of Labor*, No. 55, November, 1904, Washington, D. C., pp. 1573–1622.

ZUEBLIN, RHO FISK, "The Production of Industrial Art in America," *The Chautauquan*, March, 1903, pp. 622–27.

ARTICLES IN NEWSPAPERS AND PERIODICALS
PUBLISHED AFTER TIFFANY'S DEATH
(JANUARY 17, 1933)

ANONYMOUS ARTICLES

Art and Archaeology, "Tiffany Studios Active," May, 1933.
Art Digest, "Louis C. Tiffany" (obituary), February 1, 1933.

Bibliography

Art Digest, "Tiffany's Great Curtain," October 15, 1934.

Art Digest, "Tiffany Foundation: Note on the Founder," October 15, 1949.

Harper's Magazine, (Mr. Harper), "Revival of the Fanciest: Tiffany Glass," September, 1956, p. 80.

House Beautiful, "Iridescence, the New Dimension in Decorating," October, 1956, pp. 176–81.

Time, "New Art Nouveau," March 10, 1958, pp. 74–77.

SIGNED ARTICLES

AYTES, BARBARA, "Iridescent Art Glass," *Treasure Chest*, May–June, 1961, pp. 10–15.

BUECHNER, THOMAS S., "The Glass of Frederick Carder," *Connoisseur Year-Book*, 1961, pp. 52–53.

————, "Art in Glass," *Art News Annual*, 1955, pp. 136–50, 172–74.

CLAY, LANCASTER, "Oriental Contributions to Art Nouveau," *The Art Bulletin*, Vol. 34, 1952, pp. 297–310.

————, "Indian Influence on the American Architecture of the XIX Century," *Marg*, Vol. 6, No. 2, 1953, pp. 6–21.

————, "Japanese Buildings in the United States Before 1900," *The Art Bulletin*, Vol. 35, 1953, pp. 217–25.

DAVIDSON, R. B., "Tiffany Glass and Bristol Glass at the Metropolitan Museum of Art," *Antiques*, December, 1956, p. 582.

DAVIS, FELICE, "Art Nouveau a Long Time Reviving," New York *World-Telegram and Sun*, September 6, 1963, p. 20.

FARRER, SAMUEL, "Durand Glass," *Antiques Journal*, August, 1960, pp. 12–16; May, 1961, pp. 8–12.

FELD, STUART P., "Nature in Her Most Seductive Aspects," *Bulletin of the Metropolitan Museum of Art*, November, 1962, pp. 100–112.

FOX, DOROTHEA M., "Tiffany Glass," *Antiques*, Vol. 44, 1943, pp. 240–41, 295–96.

JACKSON, WARD, "Art in Glass," *The Flamingo*, Rollins College, Winter Park, Fla., Winter, 1955, p. 5.

KAUFMANN, EDGAR, JR., "Tiffany, Then and Now," *Interiors*, February, 1955, pp. 82–85.

————, "At Home with Louis Comfort Tiffany," *Interiors*, December, 1957, pp. 118–85, 183.

KELLOGG, CYNTHIA, "Designs by Mr. Tiffany," *The New York Times Magazine*, January 26, 1958, pp. 50–51.

KOCH, ROBERT, "A Tiffany-Byzantine Inkwell," *The Brooklyn Museum Bulletin*, Spring, 1960, pp. 5–8.

————, "Art Nouveau Bing," *Gazette des Beaux Arts*, March, 1959, pp. 179–90.

LA COSSITT, HENRY, "Treasure-House on Fifth Avenue," *The Saturday Evening Post*, January 24, 1953, pp. 30–31, 102–6; January 31, 1953, pp. 30, 108–10.

MC KEAN, HUGH F., "A Study of Louis Comfort Tiffany," *The Flamingo*, Rollins College, Winter Park, Fla., Winter, 1955, pp. 3–4.

MESSANELLE, RAY, "Art Glass Signed Nash," *Spinning Wheel*, February, 1962, pp. 12–13.

O'NEAL, WILLIAM B., "Three Art Nouveau Glass Makers," *Journal of Glass Studies*, Vol. 2, 1960, pp. 125–37.

PEPIS, BETTY, "Revival of Tiffany Lamps," *The New York Times*, July 9, 1956, p. 28.

PERROT, PAUL, "Frederick Carder's Legacy to Glass," *Craft Horizons*, May/June, 1961.

POLAK, ADA, "Tiffany 'Favrile' Glass," *Antique Dealer and Collector's Guide*, January, 1962, pp. 39–41.

———, "Gallé Glass," *Journal of Glass Studies*, Vol. V, 1963, pp. 105–15.

SAARINEN, ALINE B., "Famous, Derided and Revived," *The New York Times*, March 13, 1955, p. 9.

SCHAEFER, HERWIN, "Tiffany's Fame in Europe," *The Art Bulletin*, December, 1962, pp. 309–28.

SOTTSASS, ETTORE, JR., "Liberty: la Gibbio di Mezzo Secolo," *Domus*, March, 1953, pp. 43–46.

VAN TASSEL, VALENTINE, "Louis Comfort Tiffany," *The Antiques Journal*, Vol. 7, 1952, No. 7, pp. 19–21, 42; No. 8, pp. 13–15, 42.

WEISSBERGER, HERBERT, "After Many Years: Tiffany Glass," *Carnegie Magazine*, October, 1956, pp. 265–68, 279.

CATALOGUES

Art Nouveau, catalogue, Lyman Allyn Museum, Robert Koch and Jane Hayward, New London, Conn., 1963.

Auction Catalogue, The Louis C. Tiffany Studios of New York, Lester Dutt Associates, Washington, D. C., March 14–19, 1938.

Catalogue of Chinese and Japanese Objects of Art, Louis Comfort Tiffany Foundation, Dana H. Carroll, privately printed, Baltimore and New York, 1921.

Catalogue of the 23rd Annual Exhibition, The Architectural League of New York, Samuel Howe, 1907.

Exhibition of L'Art Nouveau, S. Bing, the Grafton Galleries, introduction by S. Bing, London, 1899.

Louis Comfort Tiffany, catalogue, Museum of Contemporary Crafts, Robert Koch, Thomas S. Tibbs and Robert Laurer, New York, 1958.

Bibliography

Salon de l'Art Nouveau, Catalogue Premier, S. Bing, Paris, 1895.
Catalogues, Parke-Bernet Galleries, #789, *Objects of Art of the Louis Comfort Tiffany Foundation*, September 24–28, 1946; December 14, 1963; February 14, 1964, New York.

BOOKS

ALEXANDER, JAMES W., *A History of the University Club of New York*, 1865–1915, Chas. Scribner's Sons, New York, 1915.

ANDREWS, WAYNE, *Architecture, Ambition and Americans*, Harper & Brothers, New York, 1955.

ARMITAGE, E. L., *Stained Glass*, Charles T. Branford Co., Newton, Mass., 1959.

ARMSTRONG, HAMILTON FISH, *Those Days*, Harper & Brothers, New York, 1963.

ARMSTRONG, D. MAITLAND, *Day Before Yesterday*, privately printed, New York, 1922.

BALDWIN, CHARLES C., *Stanford White*, Dodd, Mead & Co., New York, 1931.

BANCROFT, HUBERT HOWE, *The Book of the Fair*, Chicago, 1895.

BARKER, VIRGIL, *American Painting*, The Macmillan Company, New York, 1950.

BAUR, JOHN I. H., *Revolution and Tradition in Modern American Art*, Harvard University Press, Cambridge, 1951.

————, *American Painting in the Nineteenth Century: Main Trends and Movements*, Frederick H. Praeger, Inc., New York, 1953.

BEER, THOMAS, *The Mauve Decade*, Alfred A. Knopf, New York, 1926.

BING, S., *La Culture Artistique en Amérique*, privately printed, Paris, 1896.

BLASHFIELD, EDWIN HOWLAND, *Mural Painting in America*, Chas. Scribner's Sons, New York, 1913.

BOK, EDWARD, *The Americanization of Edward Bok*, Chas. Scribner's Sons, 1922.

BROWN, MILTON W., *Story of the Armory Show*, The Joseph H. Hirshhorn Foundation, New York, 1963.

BURNHAM, ALAN, *New York Landmarks*, Wesleyan University Press, Middletown, Conn., 1963.

CASSOU, JEAN, LANGUI, EMIL, and PEVSNER, NIKOLAUS, *Gateway to the Twentieth Century: Art and Culture in a Changing World*, McGraw-Hill Book Company, New York, 1962.

CLARK, COL. EMMONS, *History of the Seventh Regiment*, 2 vols. privately printed, New York, 1890.

Bibliography

COAD and MIMS, "The American Stage," *The Pageant of America*, Vol. 14, Yale University Press, New Haven, 1929.

CONNICK, CHARLES J., *Adventures in Light and Color*, Random House, New York, 1937.

COOK, CLARENCE, *Art and Artists of Our Time*, S. Hess, New York, 1888.

————, *The House Beautiful*, Scribner, Armstrong & Co., New York, 1878.

————, *What Shall We Do with Our Walls?*, Warren Fuller & Co., New York, 1880.

CORTISSOZ, ROYAL, *John La Farge, A Memoir and a Study*, Houghton, Mifflin Co., Boston, 1911.

GRAM, RALPH ADAMS, *The Gothic Quest*, The Baker & Taylor Co., New York, 1907.

————, *My Life in Architecture*, Little, Brown & Co., Boston, 1936.

DAY, LEWIS F., *Windows*, B. T. Batsford Ltd., London, 1909.

DE FOREST, LOCKWOOD, *Indian Domestic Architecture*, Heliotype Printing Co., Boston, 1885.

————, *Indian Architecture and Ornament*, G. H. Polley & Co., Boston, 1887.

DE KAY, CHARLES (anonymous author), *The Art Work of Louis C. Tiffany*, Doubleday, Page & Co., New York, 1914.

DESMOND, HARRY W. and CROLY, HERBERT, *Stately Homes in America*, D. Appleton, New York, 1903.

DIAMOND, FRIEDA, *The Story of Glass*, Harcourt, Brace & Co., New York, 1953.

DICKASON, DAVID HOWARD, *The Daring Young Men*, Indiana University Press, Bloomington, Ind., 1953.

DREXLER, ARTHUR and DANIEL, GRETA, *Introduction to Twentieth Century Design*, Museum of Modern Art, New York, 1959.

DUFFUS, ROBERT L., *The American Renaissance*, Alfred A. Knopf, New York, 1928.

DUNN, WALDO H., *The Life of Donald G. Mitchell*, Chas. Scribner's Sons, New York, 1922.

DUTTON, RALPH, *The Victorian Home*, B. T. Batsford Ltd., London, 1954.

ELLIOTT, CHARLES W., *The Book of American Interiors*, privately printed, Boston, 1876.

ERICSON, ERIC E., *A Guide to Colored Steuben Glass, 1903-1933*, The Lithographic Press, Denver, 1963.

FREEMAN, LARRY, *Iridescent Glass*, Century House, Watkins Glen, N. Y.

FROHMAN, DANIEL, *Memoirs of a Manager*, Doubleday, Page & Co., New York, 1911.

————, *Daniel Frohman Presents New York*, C. Kendall and W. Sharp, New York, 1935.

GARCZYNSKI, EDWARD R., Auditorium, privately printed, Chicago, 1890.

GROSSER, MAURICE, *Critic's Eye*, The Bobbs, Merrill Company, Inc., New York and Indianapolis, 1963.

HAMLIN, TALBOT, F., "The American Spirit in Architecture," *The Pageant of America*, Vol. 13, Yale University Press, New Haven, 1926.

HARRISON, CONSTANCE CARY, *Woman's Handiwork in Modern Homes*, Chas. Scribner's Sons, New York, 1881.

HITCHCOCK, HENRY-RUSSELL, *Architecture, Nineteenth and Twentieth Centuries*, Penguin Books, Baltimore, 1959?5?

HOFMANN, WEINER, *Das Iridisch Paradies*, Prestel & Verlag, Munich, 1963.

HOWE, WINIFRED E., *A History of the Metropolitan Museum of Art*, New York, 1913.

HUETHER, ANNE, *Glass and Man*, J. B. Lippincott, Philadelphia, 1963.

HUGHES, GRAHAM, *Modern Jewelry*, Crown Publishers, Inc., New York, 1963.

IRWIN, WILLIAM H., *A History of the Union League Club of New York City*, Dodd, Mead, 1952.

ITTEN, JOHANNES, *et al, Um 1900*, Kunstgewerbemuseum, Zurich, 1952.

JACKMAN, RILL E., *American Arts*, Rand, McNally & Co., Chicago, 1928.

JACKSON, HOLBROOK, *The Eighteen Nineties*, Penguin Books, London, 1913.

JENKINS, DOROTHY H., *A Fortune in the Junk Pile*, Crown Publishers, Inc., New York, 1963.

KAUFMANN, EDGAR, JR., *What Is Modern Design?*, Museum of Modern Art, New York, 1950.

KING, MOSES, *King's Handbook of New York City*, second edition, Boston, 1893.

————, *King's Photographic Views of New York*, Boston, 1895.

KOCH, ROBERT, *Stained Glass Decades* (unpublished doctoral dissertation), Yale University, New Haven, 1957.

LARKIN, OLIVER W., *Art and Life in America*, Rinehart & Co., New York, 1949.

LEE, RUTH WEBB, *Nineteenth Century Art Glass*, M. Barrows & Co., New York, 1952.

LENNING, HENRY F., *The Art Nouveau*, M. Nijhoff, The Hague, 1951.

Life, EDITORS OF, *America's Arts and Skills*, Time, Inc., New York, 1957.

LLOYD, JOHN GILBERT, *Stained Glass in America*, Foundation Books, Jenkintown, Pa., 1963.

LOURGES-LAPOUGE, C., *The Old Masters*, Crown Publishers, Inc., 1963.

LUCAS, E. V., *Edwin Austin Abbey*, Chas. Scribner's Sons, New York, 1921.

LYNES, RUSSELL, *The Tastemakers*, Harper & Brothers, New York, 1954.

MAC KAYE, PERCY, *Epoch: The Life of Steele MacKaye*, Boni & Liveright, New York, 1927.

MC CABE, JAMES D., *The Illustrated History of the Centennial Exhibition*, The National Publishing Co., Philadelphia, 1876.

MC CONNELL, JANE AND BURT, *The White House*, Studio Publications, New York, 1954.

MC KEARIN, GEORGE S. AND HELEN, *American Glass*, Crown Publishers, Inc., New York, 1941.

————, *Two Hundred Years of American Blown Glass*, Crown Publishers, Inc., 1950.

MADSDEN, STEPHAN TSCHUDI, *Sources of Art Nouveau*, Wittenborn & Co., New York, 1955.

MAYER, GRACE, *Once Upon a City*, The Macmillan Company, New York.

MEEKS, CARROLL L. V., *The Railroad Station*, Yale University Press, New Haven, 1956.

MENDELOWITZ, DANIEL M., *A History of American Art*, Holt, Rinehart & Winston, New York, 1960.

MITCHELL, DONALD G., *My Farm at Edgewood*, Chas. Scribner's Sons, New York, 1863.

MITCHELL, LOUIS, *The Woodbridge Record*, Tuttle,. Morehouse & Taylor, New Haven, 1883.

MORRIS, WILLIAM, *The Decorative Arts*, Roberts Brothers, Boston, 1878.

OPPENHEIMER, HERBERT, *Louis C. Tiffany: His Legacy*, unpublished thesis, Columbia University, New York, 1954.

PENNELL, E. R. and J., *The Life of James McNeill Whistler*, J. B. Lippincott Co., Philadelphia, 1908.

PERKINS, MARY E., *Chronicles of a Connecticut Farm, 1769–1905*, privately printed, Boston, 1905.

PEVSNER, NIKOLAUS, *Pioneers of Modern Design*, Museum of Modern Art, New York, 1949.

REVI, ALBERT CHRISTIAN, *Nineteenth Century Glass*, Thomas Nelson & Sons, New York, 1959.

ROSENTHAL, R. and RATZKA, A., *The Story of Modern Applied Arts* Harper & Brothers, New York, 1948.

SAARINEN, ALINE, *The Proud Possessors*, Random House, Inc., New York, 1958.

SAINT-GAUDENS, HOMER, *The Reminiscences of Augustus Saint-Gaudens*, The Century Co., New York, 1913.

SCULLY, VINCENT J., JR., *The Shingle Style: Architectural Theory and Design from Richardson to the Origins of Wright* (doctoral dissertation) Yale University Press, New Haven, 1955.

SELING, HELMUT, *et al, Jugendstil,* Keyser, Munich, 1959.

SELZ, PETER, *et al, Art Nouveau,* Museum of Modern Art, New York, 1960.

SHELDON, GEORGE W., *American Painters,* D. Appleton & Co., New York, 1881.

————, *Artistic Houses,* D. Appleton & Co., New York, 1882–84.

SIZER, THEODORE, *The Recollections of John Ferguson Weir,* Yale University Press, New Haven, 1957.

SMITH, CORINNA LINDON, *Interesting People: Eighty Years with the Great and Near-Great,* University of Oklahoma Press, Norman, Okla., 1962.

SMITH, WALTER, "Industrial Art," *Masterpieces of the Centennial,* Vol. 2, Gebbie & Barrie, Philadelphia, 1876.

SOWERS, ROBERT, *The Lost Art,* Wittenborn & Co., 1954.

SPEENBURGH, GERTRUDE, *The Arts of the Tiffanys,* Lightner Publishing Corp., Chicago, Ill., 1956.

STERN, MADELINE B., *We The Women,* Schulte Publishing Co., New York, 1962.

STODDARD, WILLIAM O., "Charles L. Tiffany," *Men of Business, Men of Achievement,* Chas. Scribner's Sons, New York, 1893.

TIFFANY, NELSON OTIS, *The Tiffanys of America,* privately printed, Buffalo, New York, 1903.

VEDDER, ELIHU, *The Digressions of Elihu Vedder,* Houghton, Mifflin Co., Boston, 1910.

Veterans' Room of the Seventh Regiment Armory, The, privately printed, New York, 1881.

WAERN, CECILIA, *John La Farge, Artist and Writer,* The Macmillan Company, London, 1896.

WATKINS, LURA WOODSIDE, *American Glass and Glassmaking,* Chanticleer Press, New York, 1950.

WELD, RALPH FOSTER, *A Tower on the Heights,* Columbia University Press, New York, 1946.

WERFEL, ALMA MAHLER, *And Love Is The Bridge,* Harcourt, Brace & World, New York, 1958.

WHALL, CHRISTOPHER W., *Stained Glass Work,* J. Hogg, London, 1905.

WHEELER, CANDACE, *Principles of Home Decoration,* Doubleday, Page & Co., New York, 1903.

————, *Yesterdays in a Busy Life,* Harper & Brothers, New York, 1918.

————, *The Development of Embroidery in America,* Harper & Brothers, New York, 1921.

WILDE, OSCAR, *The Complete Works of Oscar Wilde,* Vol. 6, National Library Company, New York, 1909.

WINCHESTER, ALICE, *The Antiques Treasury,* E. P. Dutton & Co., New York, 1959.

YOUNG, MAY, *Singing Windows,* Abingdon Press, New York, 1962.

Picture Credits *

Picture Credits* t-top; b-bottom; r-right; l-left; c-center

Picture Credits

36 tl, R. Koch photo; bl, *Grammar of Ornament* by Owen Jones; br, *Scribner's Monthly*.

37 Albert L. Waks photos.

38 tl, *Artistic Houses*, Vol. II, Part 2; tr, courtesy of The Mark Twain Memorial Commission, Hartford.

39 t, courtesy of the New-York Historical Society; b, *A History of the Union League Club of New York City* by William H. Irwin.

40 tl, b, *Artistic Houses*, Vol. I, Part 1; tr, *The Art Work of Louis C. Tiffany*.

41 t, *The Art Work of Louis C. Tiffany;* c, b, *Artistic Houses*, Vol. I, Part 1.

42 t, courtesy of The New-York Historical Society; bl, reproduced from the original in the Yale University Library; br, *Stately Homes in America* by Harry W. Desmond and Herbert Croly.

43 t, courtesy of the Library of Congress; b, *Artistic Houses*, Vol. II, Part 1.

44 t, courtesy of The Library of Congress; b, National Archives.

45 t, National Archives, b, courtesy of The Library of Congress.

46 tl, courtesy of The Library of Congress; tr, bl, National Archives. *Monthly*.

47 tr, courtesy of The Library of Congress; tl, b, National Archives.

PART II

Page
88 t, reproduced from the original in The Yale University Library; cr, courtesy of The Metropolitan Museum of Art; b, courtesy of The New-York Historical Society.

89 tl, R. Koch photo; tr, courtesy of Hugh F. McKean, Winter Park, Fla.; bl, courtesy of David R. Russell, Dallas, Tex.; from *Brush and Pencil*, Vol. 4, 1899, courtesy of David R. Russell.

90 tl, courtesy of Leland A. Cook, Leland A. Cook photo; tr, from *The Art Work of Louis C. Tiffany;* cl, cr, br, R. Koch photos; bl, courtesy of Dr. Gerhard Woeckel, Munich.

[*235*]

Picture Credits

91 tl, courtesy of The Yale Art Gallery; cl, from *Architect and Building News*, 1890; bl, courtesy of The Church of the Ascension; br, courtesy of The Paulist Fathers.

92 t, courtesy of The New-York Historical Society; b, courtesy of The Metropolitan Museum of Art.

93 t, from *The Magazine of Art*, 1884; b, courtesy of Aaron Siskind, Aaron Siskind photo.

94 t, bl, br, from *The Art Work of Louis C. Tiffany;* cr, courtesy of The New-York Historical Society.

95 tr, courtesy of The Metropolitan Museum of Art; l, courtesy of the Yale Art Gallery, De Cusati photo; bl, br, from *Stately Homes in America* by Harry W. Desmond and Herbert Croly.

96 l, courtesy of The Museum of the City of New York; tr, from *The Art Work of Louis C. Tiffany;* br, author's collection, De Cusati.

97 t, courtesy of The Landesmuseum, Darmstadt, Germany; b, from *Memorials in Glass and Stone.*

98 t, br, courtesy of St. Paul's Church, Troy, N. Y.; bl, courtesy of Christ Church, Rye, N. Y., J. Walworth photo.

99 tl, tc, tr, courtesy of the First Presbyterian Church, Bath, N. Y.; cr, Tiffany Studios brochure; bl, Pratt Institute, Brooklyn, N. Y.; br, courtesy of the Chicago Public Library, Burke & Dean photo.

100 t, Wayne Andrews photo; b, from *The Architectural Record.*

101 t, b, courtesy of Edgar Kaufmann, Jr. and Aline B. Saarinen, from *Interiors*, December, 1957.

102 tl, tr, courtesy The University of Michigan News Service; b, from New York County Clerk's office.

103 t, David Aronow photo, c, bl, br, R. Koch photos.

104 t, b, R. Koch photos.

Picture Credits

105   tl, from *The Art Work of Louis C. Tiffany;* tr, bl, br, from *The Magazine of Art,* 1898.

106   t, David Aronow photo, b, photo by Chicago Architectural Photographing Co.

107   t, David Aronow photo; b, from *A Synopsis of the Exhibit of the Tiffany Glass and Decorating Company.*

108   tl, tr, R. Koch photos, bl, from *The Art Work of Louis C. Tiffany;* br, author's collection, De Cusati photo.

109   t, c, courtesy of Hugh F. McKean, De Cusati photos; b, from *The Mentor,* 1912.

110   t, Martin Linsey photo; bl, from *Memorials in Glass and Stone;* br, courtesy of The Metropolitan Museum of Art.

111   tl, cl, courtesy of *The Progress-Index,* Petersburg, Va.; b, courtesy of the American Red Cross.

112   tl, bl, R. Koch photos; r, courtesy of Hugh F. McKean.

113   t, b, courtesy of The Mission Inn.

114   tl, br, courtesy of Christ Church, Brooklyn, N. Y.; bl, R. Koch photo.

115   tl, tr, R. Koch photos; br, courtesy of The Metropolitan Museum of Art.

116   t, Marcolor photo; b, courtesy of Leland A. Cook.

117   t, courtesy J. and F. Van Brink; b, courtesy of Curtis Publishing Company.

118   U. S. Patent Office.

PART III

158   tl, *Dekorative Kunst,* 1898; tr, illustration from Wilde's *Salomé,* cr, *Deutsche Kunst und Dekoration,* 1900; bl, courtesy of The Yale University Art Gallery; br, courtesy of The Museum of Modern Art, New York.

159   tl, courtesy of The Yale University Library; cr, courtesy of The New-York Historical Society; bl, U. S. Patent Office; br, Tiffany Studios brochure.

[237]

Picture Credits

160   Corning Museum of Glass.

161   t, courtesy Parke-Bernet Galleries, Inc.; cl, Corning Museum of Glass; cr, The Metropolitan Museum of Art, bequest of Edward C. Moore, 1891; b, Fratelli Alinari.

162   t, br, Corning Museum of Glass; bl, bc, The Metropolitan Museum of Art, bequest of Edward C. Moore, 1891.

163   tl, Corning Museum of Glass; tr, Sandwich Museum; bl, courtesy of Helen McKearin, Corning Museum of Glass; br, courtesy of Lillian Nassau, The Museum of Contemporary Crafts.

164   tl, courtesy of The Victoria and Albert Museum; tr, br, Musée des Arts Décoratifs, the Louvre; bl, courtesy of the Landesmuseum, Darmstadt.

165   Courtesy of the Landesmuseum, Darmstadt.

166-169   Courtesy of The Smithsonian Institution.

170   Courtesy of The Metropoiitan Museum of Art.

171   b, courtesy of The Metropolitan Museum of Art; tr, courtesy of The Cooper Union Museum; tl, courtesy of The Museum of Modern Art, New York.

172   Courtesy of The Museum of Modern Art, New York.

173   tr, courtesy of The Museum of Modern Art, New York; b, courtesy of The Carnegie Institute.

174   tl, bl, author's collection, R. Koch photo; tr, courtesy of Helen Eisenberg; br, courtesy of Maude Feld.

175   t, Courtesy of Lillian Nassau; br, courtesy of Maude Feld.

176   t, br, courtesy of Helen Eisenberg; bl, courtesy of Rice Estes, Pratt Institute.

177   tr, courtesy of Elliot A. Wysor; bl, courtesy of Lillian Nassau; br, Chrysler Art Museum, Provincetown, Mass., by courtesy of Roland Hartman, Inc., Nathan Rabin photo.

178   tl, Lyman Allyn Museum, New London, De Cusati photo; tr, courtesy of The Museum of Modern Art, New York; bl, author's collection, R. Koch photo; br, courtesy of Minna Rosenblatt, George Love photo.

179 tl, courtesy of Lillian Nassau, George Love photo; tr, courtesy of Miriam Rosenblatt, George Love photo; cl, "L'Art de René Lalique," *L'Illustration;* b, author's collection, R. Koch photo.

180 tl, courtesy of Louis Platt; tr, author's collection; bl, br, *Blue Book,* 1911, Tiffany & Company.

181 tl, cl, courtesy of Museum of Contemporary Crafts, Louis T. Lusk; cr, courtesy of the New-York Historical Society; b, author's collection.

182 t, *The Art Work of Louis C. Tiffany* b, courtesy of Louis T. Lusk.

183 *Dekorative Kunst,* 1900.

184 tl, cl, author's collection, R. Koch photos; tr, courtesy of Mr. and Mrs. Harold Rooff, R. Koch; br, courtesy of The New-York Historical Society.

185 t, courtesy of Lillian Nassau; b, courtesy of J. and F. Van Brink.

186 tl, bl, Hugh McKean collection, R. Koch photos; br, author's collection, R. Koch photo; tr, U. S. Patent Office.

187 tl, author's collection, R. Koch photo; r, *The Art Work of Louis C. Tiffany;* bl, courtesy of Lillian Nassau; c, Hugh McKean collection, photo from *Bronze Lamps;* br, R. Koch, photo.

188 tr, Robert A. Laurer photo; cr, courtesy of The Brooklyn Museum; cl, author's collection, R. Koch photo; cr, bl, private collection, Robert A. Laurer photos; br, courtesy of Julia Munson Sherman.

189 tr, courtesy of The Victoria and Albert Museum; cr, courtesy of Martin Grossman, George Love photo; cl, b, courtesy of Parke-Bernet Galleries, Inc.

190 tl, *The Art Work of Louis C. Tiffany;* cl, courtesy of Parke-Bernet Galleries, Inc.; tr, courtesy of The Metropolitan Museum of Art; br, courtesy of Hugh McKean, R. Koch photo.

191 tl, tr, courtesy of Parke-Bernet Galleries, Inc.; cl, *The Art Work of Louis C. Tiffany;* br, collection of William T. Lusk, Robert A. Laurer photo.

192 Courtesy of Emanuel Shulman.

193 tr, courtesy of The White House; bl, courtesy of The Museum of Contemporary Crafts, Mrs. Gordon Fisher, Jr. Talbot County Historical Society.

Picture Credits

194 tl, *The New York Times;* tr, courtesy of Theodore Sizer; cr, David Aronow photo, br, R. Koch photo.

195 Courtesy of The Museum of Modern Art, New York.

196 t, c, *The Art Work of Louis C. Tiffany;* b, David Aronow photo.

197 t, *The Art Work of Louis C. Tiffany;* c, b, courtesy of Parke-Bernet Galleries, Inc.

198 tl, cr, David Aronow photo; courtesy of Parke-Bernet Galleries, Inc.

199 t, c, David Aronow photo; b, R. Koch photo.

200 David Aronow photos.

201 tl, b, David Aronow photos; tr, R. Koch photo.

202 t, David Aronow photo; cr, b, courtesy of Emanuel Shulman.

203 tl, Hugh McKean collection, De Cusati photo; tr, br, David Aronow photos; bl, courtesy of Julia Munson Sherman.

204 David Aronow photos.

205 David Aronow photos.

206 tl, David Aronow photo; c, *The New York Times;* b, courtesy of Parke-Bernet Galleries, Inc.

PART IV

216 tr, bl, br, courtesy of Edward Wormley, Dunbar Furniture Company; cr, Tiffany & Company.

217 Courtesy of Edward Wormley, Dunbar Furniture Company, American Carpet Institute.

218 b, courtesy of *Town and Country*, James Forney photo; tr, tl, courtesy of Percival Goodman, Alexandre Georges photos.

219 tl, br, courtesy The Parke-Bernet Galleries.

220 David Aronow photo.

Picture Credits

I   Hugh McKean collection, Winter Park, Fla. Photo supplied by Hugh McKean.

II   Hugh McKean collection, R. Koch photos.

III   tl, Hugh McKean collection, photo supplied by Hugh McKean, cl, R. Koch, photo; tr, Leland A. Cook photo, b, Hugh McLean collection, R. Koch, photos.

IV   tl, Pauline Kael collection, Berkeley, Calif., R. Koch photo; tr, R. Koch photo; bl, Leo Reves collection, Leland A. Cook photo, supplied by Lillian Nassau; br, J. Jonathan Joseph collection, Leland A. Cook photo, supplied by Lillian Nassau.

V   t, George Love photo, supplied by Walter P. Chrysler; bl, private collection, Robert A. Laurer photo; br, George Love photo.

VI   tl, Albertus Magnus College collection, New Haven, Conn., Robert A. Laurer photo; tr, Hugh McKean collection, Robert A. Laurer photo; cr, two pieces from the collection of Elizabeth Gordon, two from The Metropolitan Museum of Art, Robert A. Laurer photo; b, George Love photo.

VII   t, George Love photo, supplied by Helen Eisenberg; b, photo supplied by J. Jonathan Joseph.

VIII   tl, George Love photo, bl, R. Koch photo; tr, Corning Museum of Glass photo; br, Dr. Raymond Beldgreen collection, Leland A. Cook photo, supplied by Lillian Nassau.

IX   tl, W. S. Wellington collection, Berkeley, Calif., R. Koch photo; tr, bl, R. Koch photos; br, Corning Museum of Glass photo.

X   tl, Musée des Arts Décoratifs, the Louvre, Robert A. Laurer photo; tr, Lillian Nassau collection, Robert A. Laurer photo; bl, Corning Museum of Glass collection, R. Koch photo; cr, courtesy of The Metropolitan Museum of Art, Robert A. Laurer photo; br, courtesy of The Museum of Modern Art, Robert A. Laurer photo.

XI   tl, private collections, Robert A. Laurer photo; tr, R. Koch collection, Robert A. Laurer photo; bl, Lillian Nassau collection, Leland A. Cook photo; br, Ward Mount collection, Robert A. Laurer photo.

XII   R. Koch photos.

[241]

Index